Contents

Foreword

People who try to be cynical at the expense of Bernard Shaw as a dramatist commonly complain that the characters in his plays are mere mouthpieces for Shaw, and have no life of their own. If I believed this I might, I suppose, have declined the honour of contributing a foreword to Miss Hartnoll's carefully compiled volume, on the grounds that the only 'Who' that could matter in a book called *Who's Who in Shaw* would be Shaw himself; and he is not included in her list of characters.

Cynics, however, are not very impressive people; they can never be more than partially right in anything they say. Miss Hartnoll, on the other hand, aims at (and, humanly speaking, achieves) absolute accuracy within her prescribed limits. This I find genuinely impressive and I have settled to my foreword with real satisfaction.

The point at which Shaw's detractors of the kind mentioned above often seem to go utterly astray is when they forget, or ignore, or simply do not recognise his superb sense of the theatre.

When he came into the theatre, first as critic and then as playwright, he found it a temple of the emotions only. Full of reforming zeal, he set about breaking its images and altering, or at any rate adding to, its doctrine. But he was always at ease in the temple and knew his way about it, and gradually it became his spiritual home where he could teach and preach as he liked.

The proof of all this is that whatever he wrote for the theatre was always completely actable. Even when he was producing one of the 'discussion plays', in which, admittedly, many of the characters had been created merely for the opinions he wanted them to express, he never forgot his players. It would have been a waste of precious stage time to make individual studies of such 'mouthpieces'; but he would endow them with characteristics and sketched-in backgrounds which would help actors and actresses to make human beings of them.

As a result, you didn't (and don't) find actors and actresses refusing to play these parts; and you will find, when reading Miss Hartnoll's accounts of such characters in this book, that they often take up as much of her space as the more deeply-considered principals.

'Damn the man!' said one of Shaw's exasperated admirers after a discussion play: 'He could dramatise a telephone directory.' That perceptive flight of fancy stated a profound truth about Shaw. I wonder if I shall be thought too fanciful if I say that this book (a directory in which he dramatised every entrant) strikes me as a restatement in more prosaic terms of that same truth.

W. A. DARLINGTON

A

A : *see* Author

ACHILLAS: General in command of the Roman army of occupation in Egypt, as well as of the Egyptian forces of Ptolemy. 'A tall handsome man of thirty-five, with a fine black beard curled like the coat of a poodle . . . not a clever man, but distinguished and dignified.' He prepares to resist Julius Caesar when the latter comes to Alexandria, but is taken prisoner. Released with the rest of Ptolemy's entourage, he is finally defeated by Caesar in a battle near Memphis. *Caesar and Cleopatra*

ACIS: The temple youth who assists at the ceremony of the hatching of the Newly-Born, whom he names Amaryllis, from her egg. He is also present when Pygmalion brings in his automata, and supervises the removal of his body after he has been killed. After listening uncomprehendingly to the Ancients, whom he advises kindly not to think too much about the future or they will go mad, he picks up Amaryllis, who is falling asleep, and carries her into the temple. *Back to Methuselah, Part V: As Far as Thought Can Reach*

ADAM: Living with Eve in the Garden of Eden, he finds a dead fawn, and is torn between the terror of death and the terror of living for ever. Eve tells him that the Serpent has invented birth, which conquers death by bringing forth new serpents to take her place when she dies. She will teach Eve to bring forth new Adams and Eves so that they themselves can die, and yet life can continue. Adam is

I

afraid of the Serpent, and tries to drag Eve away, but when she says she has not yet learned the secret of giving birth, which is called conceiving, he leaves her with the Serpent. Centuries later, living in an oasis in Mesopotamia, he has become a dull, hard-working farmer, despised by his son Cain, the first murderer, and by his wife, who wants the men she has created to be something more than diggers or murderers. *Back to Methuselah, Part I: In the Beginning*

In the summer of A.D. 31,920 the ghost of Adam returns to earth, bewildered by the extraordinary way in which his descendants now behave. 'The fools have killed all the animals; and they are dissatisfied because they cannot be bothered with their bodies! Foolishness, I call it!' *Back to Methuselah, Part V: As Far as Thought Can Reach*

ADDY: *see* Utterwood, Lady Ariadne

ADELAIDE: *see* Gisborne, Adelaide

ADMIRABLE BASHVILLE: *see* Bashville

ADOLPHUS: *see* Bastable, Adolphus; Cusins, Adolphus

ADRIAN: *see* Blenderbland, Adrian

AIRE, JEAN D': One of the burghers of Calais sent with the keys of the city to Edward III after its surrender. He has nothing to say and is one of those whose life is spared after the queen, Philippa of Hainault, has begged her husband not to hang them. *The Six of Calais*

ALASTAIR, ALLY: *see* Fitzfassen, Alastair

ALFRED: *see* Lenkheim, Alfred; Mangan, Alfred

ALICE: The Princess Royal, eldest daughter of King Magnus. She comes in while her father is talking to Boanerges, the new President of the Board of Trade, and flatters him outrageously, much to the amusement of her father and his private secretaries. When she has gone out with the King, Boanerges remarks that he is glad to see she hasn't been spoilt. *The Apple Cart*

See also Bridgenorth, Alice

ALOYSIA: *see* Brollikins, Alderwoman Aloysia

AMANDA: *see* Postlethwaite, Amanda

AMARYLLIS: The Newly-Born in A.D. 31,920. She is hatched out of a large egg which is broken open by the She-Ancient, and is already seventeen. She grows up rapidly, but will have four years of music, dancing, love-making, and pretty clothes before she is ready to start on the process of thinking and reasoning which will eventually turn her into an Ancient, living for hundreds, or even thousands, of years. In the meantime she is rather a nuisance, always asking questions, bubbling over with enthusiasm, falling in love with the wrong people, and finally falling asleep and being carried off into the temple by Acis. *Back to Methuselah, Part V: As Far as Thought Can Reach*

AMBROSE, AMBY: *see* Bluebin, Ambrose Badger

AMELIA: *see* Knox, Amelia

AMERICAN AMBASSADOR: *see* Vanhattan, Mr.

AMERICAN BLUEJACKETS: members of the crew of the U.S. cruiser *Santiago* under Captain Kearney. One comes to the house of Rankin to announce the arrival of the Captain to preside at the trial of Captain Brassbound, and also announces the arrival of the prisoner. A petty officer and several men bring in the prisoners, stand on guard over them, and leave with their captain and his officers when the trial is over. *Captain Brassbound's Conversion*

AMERICAN JOURNALIST: While working in Geneva he makes friends with Begonia Brown, the Secretary of the International Committee for Intellectual Co-operation, and is in her office when the Bishop dies of shock on being confronted with Commissar Posky, thus securing a nice

3

little scoop for his newspaper. Later, when Begonia, who has rather neglected him since becoming a D.B.E., is awarded £4,000 damages against a number of newspapers which have referred to her as Mongolia Muggins, he regrets that he did not pursue their acquaintance more ardently. *Geneva*

AMERICAN NAVAL OFFICERS: from the cruiser *Santiago*. They come with their captain, Kearney, to attend the trial of Captain Brassbound, and leave when he is acquitted, without having spoken. *Captain Brassbound's Conversion*

ANA DE ULLOA, DOÑA: When John Tanner dreams that he is Don Juan in Hell, he meets there the newly arrived Doña Ana, one of Juan's many conquests, whose father, Don Gonzales, Juan killed in a duel. She looks remarkably like Ann Whitefield, whom Tanner is running away from. While he is explaining to her why she is in Hell, and how boring it is, her father comes on a visit from Heaven, which he finds equally boring. When he and Don Juan agree to change places, Doña Ana wants to go with Juan, but he manages to elude her, and she is left with her father and the Devil, who are discussing the philosophy of Nietsche. Hearing that Nietsche's Superman is not yet born, she exclaims: 'My work is not yet done!' and disappears in search of 'a father for the Superman!' *Man and Superman* (*Don Juan in Hell*)

ANARCHIST: One of the brigands with Mendoza, a mild, polite, respectable-looking elderly man, with reddish whiskers, weak eyes, and 'the anxious look of a small tradesman in difficulties'. He wears a tall hat, much the worse for wear, celluloid collar and cuffs, and a brown chesterfield overcoat with a velvet collar. He argues quietly and persistently with anyone who will listen to him, and is the only brigand to realise that the shot heard by Mendoza was not fired by a brigand but by one of the soldiers who had come to arrest them. *Man and Superman*

4

ANCIENTS: *see* He-Ancient and She-Ancient

ANDERSON, REV. ANTHONY: The minister resident in Websterbridge, New Hampshire, during the American War of Independence. Recently married to a pretty young wife, he is a shrewd, genial man of about fifty, an excellent parson, but 'still a man capable of making the most of this world'. He comes to tell Mrs. Timothy Dudgeon of her husband's sudden death, and of a new will which leaves the farm she had expected to inherit to her profligate son Richard. When the British arrest Richard in mistake for Anderson, the latter rides to the next town, Springtown, enrols as a captain in the militia, drives out the enemy, and arrives back in Websterbridge just in time to save Richard from the gallows. *The Devil's Disciple*

ANDERSON, JUDITH: The wife of the Rev. Anthony Anderson, twenty years younger than her husband, pretty and ladylike, with 'a spoilt child's self-assurance which serves her instead of strength'. Like almost everyone in Websterbridge, she disapproves of Richard Dudgeon, but is not proof against his charm, and when he has been arrested in mistake for her husband and condemned to be hanged as a rebel, she confesses that she loves him and tries to save his life. But when her husband returns from what she thought of as an ignominious flight in time to save Richard and the town, she is ashamed of herself, and begs Richard never to let her husband know what she has said to him. *The Devil's Disciple*.

ANDREW: *see* Undershaft, Andrew

ANDROCLES: A small, wiry, poverty-stricken Greek tailor, who is thought by some to be a sorcerer because he has such power over animals. He has become a Christian, and with his nagging wife Megaera is escaping from persecution. In the jungle they come face to face with a lion which is suffering from a thorn in its paw. Androcles pulls it out, and the lion fawns on him gratefully. Later, captured by the Romans, Androcles finds himself alone in the arena of the Colosseum in Rome, waiting to be eaten by a lion. But the animal turns out to be the one he befriended, and it will not harm him. Caesar, amazed at what he considers a miracle, allows himself to pet and tickle the lion, under Androcles' protection, and announces proudly that he has 'tamed' it. Asked by the menagerie keeper if he may have Androcles as a slave to work with his animals, Caesar says anyone can have him who can lay hands on him. But the lion keeps everyone away, and they walk off together unmolested. *Androcles and the Lion*

ANGEL: A feathered being who lands on a small tropical island to the sound of a trumpet to tell the assembled inhabitants that the Day of Judgement has arrived. The English are being judged first out of compliment to Dean Inge. Those who are worth their salt will be spared, the rest will disappear. He then goes up to a flat roof for his take-off back to Heaven, as, like an albatross, he cannot rise from the ground without great difficulty. *The Simpleton of the Unexpected Isles*

ANGELS: A choir of invisible angelic beings who sing while Lady Magnesia Fitztollemache is getting ready for bed, and again to wake her up when her husband comes to murder her; also when her lover Adolphus Bastable is poisoned, when he goes to sleep after swallowing an antidote, and finally when, as a plaster statue, he is raised to his feet in an attitude of benediction. *Passion, Poison, and Petrifaction*

ANN: *see* Whitefield, Ann

ANNAJANSKA: The Grand Duchess of Boetia, daughter of the deposed Panjandrum. She has become a revolutionary, and is brought by two soldiers to the office of General Strammfest, also a revolutionary, though an unwilling one. He accuses her of having eloped with a young officer, and refuses her request to speak with him alone, whereupon she

6

snatches his pistol, and drives everyone else out of the room. She then tells Strammfest that it is no use trying to restore the dynasty of the Panjandrum, as he secretly hopes to do, that she herself has no desire to go back to the stifling life of royal etiquette from which she once escaped to join a circus, and that she is all in favour of the Revolution. She intends to become the Bolshevik Empress and rally the revolutionaries to her standard, and to prove her point she throws off her cloak and reveals herself in the uniform of the Panderobajensky Hussars. She is, in fact, the young officer she was accused of eloping with. *Annajanska*

ANNIE: A parlourmaid in the service of Mr. Sartorius. A meek, affectionate creature, she is shamefully abused and ill-treated by her employer's daughter Blanche, whom she adores. In the text of the play she has no name, but is always called Annie on the playbills. *Widower's Houses*

See also Dudgeon, Mrs. Timothy; Whitefield, Ann

ANTHONY: *see* Soames, Rev. Oliver Cromwell

APJOHN, HENRY: A beautiful and unworldly young poet, always referred to as He, who has fallen in love with Aurora Bompas (She), and written a number of poems to her. When he discovers that these have fallen into the hands of her husband Edward, he begs Aurora to elope with him to escape the consequences; but she is shocked, and not only refuses to consider an elopement, but makes Apjohn promise to say that the poems were written not to her but to the goddess Aurora. He does so, but this only infuriates Edward, who thinks Apjohn is belittling his wife, and the two men come to blows. When Aurora has separated and calmed them down, Apjohn tells Edward the truth. He is so delighted to think his wife is properly appreciated that he offers to publish the poems at his own expense. *How He Lied to Her Husband*

APOLLODORUS: A Sicilian merchant, 'a dashing young

man, handsome and debonair, dressed in delicate purples and dove-greys', with beautiful jewellery and a fine sword 'in an open-work scabbard of purple leather and filagree'. He brings a selection of carpets to the palace of Cleopatra, and takes one by boat as a present to Julius Caesar, guessing that Cleopatra is hidden inside it. When they are all besieged on the island of Pharos he dives into the sea to fetch a boat to the rescue. His wit and elegance amuse Caesar, who invites him to the banquet at which Pothinus is murdered, and he later appears on the quayside to watch Caesar embark for Rome. *Caesar and Cleopatra*

ARCHBISHOP OF RHEIMS: *see* Rheims, Archbishop of

ARCHBISHOP OF YORK: *see* Haslam, Rev. William

ARCHDEADON: *see* Donkin, Archdeacon Daffodil

ARIADNE: *see* Utterwood, Lady Ariadne (*see* Addy)

ARJILLAX: A bearded sculptor who, in the year A.D. 31,920, upsets his contemporaries by exhibiting at a festival of the arts not the figures of graceful youths they had expected, but busts of the Ancients, who have no claims to beauty. He defends himself by pointing out that in the old legend the Archangel Michael painted the beautiful newly-born Adam on the ceiling of his temple, but surrounded him with the prophets and sybils who were the Ancients of his own time. This, though he knows the story is not true, has inspired him. He is shocked when his master, Martellus, says he too once made busts of the Ancients, but destroyed them because he realised they were false and life alone is true, and even more shocked when Pygmalion brings in his automata, made in the likeness of human beings. He is the first to notice that the female figure intends to kill the male figure, and when Pygmalion is himself killed by her, he says it serves him right for making such a pair of horrors. But he cannot believe the Ancients when they tell him that one day his own works of

8

art will seem to him only horrors, though he has already got past the stage of admiring the beauty of women, and can only appreciate his companion Ecrasia 'at arm's length'. *Back to Methuselah, Part V: As Far as Thought Can Reach*

ARTHUR: *see* Chavender, Sir Arthur

ARUNDEL, LORD: A nobleman in attendance on Edward III when he accepts the surrender of Calais after a year-long siege. He has nothing to say. *The Six of Calais*

ASSESSORS: A group of Dominican monks, under de Courcelles and de Stogumber, who attend the trial of Joan of Arc. They whisper among themselves, occasionally raising their voices in horror when Joan says something particularly heretical, and rush out in disorder at the end to watch her being burnt. *Saint Joan*

AUBREY: *see* Bagot, The Hon. Aubrey

AUFSTEIG, GENERAL: *see* Napoleon, Cain Adamson Charles

AUGUSTUS: *see* Highcastle, Lord Augustus

AURORA: *see* Bompas, Aurora

AUSTRALIAN CHALLENGER: *see* Byron, Cashel

AUTHOR: A literary-looking gentleman, known as A, who is trying to write a guide-book during a pleasure cruise on the *Empress of Patagonia*. He is constantly interrupted by one of the passengers, referred to as Z, who tells him that the money for her cruise was won in a newspaper competition, and that she is really an assistant and telephone operator in a village shop. Some months later, on a walking tour, he enters her shop to buy provisions. He does not recognise her, but eventually she reminds him that they have met before, and suggests that he shall buy the shop, settle down, and marry her. At first he refuses, but before

9

long he is in effect the owner of the shop, wearing pepper-and-salt trousers and an apron, having, he says, learned more in three months in his new job than in three years at Oxford. After an interminable conversation on the pros and cons of marriage, he is at last driven into agreeing that Z shall put up the banns. *Village Wooing*

AUTHORITATIVE NYMPH: *see* Ecrasia

AVIATOR: *see* Percival, Joseph

B

BABSY: *see* Women in the Barn

BABZY: *see* Buoyant, Clementina

BADGER BLUEBIN: *see* Bluebin

BAGOT, THE HON. AUBREY: The son of an atheist, brought up by a militant Christian mother. He discovers that his only gift is for preaching, so becomes a clergyman, but while in hospital he becomes infatuated with a petty criminal, Susan Simpkins, and together they plan to steal the pearl necklace belonging to Miss Mopply. After she has knocked them both down, Bagot, who is sorry for her, suggests that she should steal and sell it herself and come travelling with them on the proceeds. They soon run through the money they get for it, and write to Mrs. Mopply to say her daughter is being held for ransom by brigands. While waiting for the ransom money to arrive, Bagot comes across his father, who is horrified to learn his son has been ordained. But when he has heard the story of his latest adventures he decides that it is better for him to be a preacher than a thief, and Aubrey takes advantage of the occasion to embark on a long sermon, during which the rest of the company steal away, leaving him finally enveloped in thick fog. *Too True to be Good*

BAGOT, MR.: The father of Aubrey Bagot, always referred to as The Elder; a tall, gaunt man, suffering from despondency. An atheist, he complains that 'the universe of Isaac Newton . . . has crumbled . . . before the criticism of Einstein', and determinism is dead. He is further distressed by the discovery that his prodigal son has become a clergyman with a genius for preaching, and it is only after learning that he has also tried unsuccessfully to become a criminal that he urges him to preach rather than steal, and to stop making military crimes an excuse for civil ones. He then takes refuge in a convenient grotto while Aubrey continues his long sermon until finally enveloped in thick fog. *Too True to be Good*

BAINES, MRS.: A Commissioner in the Salvation Army; 'a woman of about forty, with a caressing, urgent voice and an appealing manner'. When money is needed for the Army's shelter in West Ham she prays for it, and has never yet been disappointed. Her faith is again justified when Andrew Undershaft gives her a cheque for £1,000 just as the shelter is on the point of closing from lack of funds. *Major Barbara*

BAKER, JULIUS: The son of Lucinda (or Lucy) Titmus. He has found among his dead mother's possessions some letters signed Tarleton which have led him to believe that John Tarleton, before her marriage to his father, seduced and then deserted her. Crazed with boredom from his dull clerking job, and full of half-digested notions of socialism from random reading in free libraries, he comes to Tarleton's house, intending to shoot him. He is foiled by Lina Szczepanowska, who disarms him, and is bullied into signing a retraction of his statement that from his hiding-place in a Turkish bath he saw Hypatia Tarleton behaving improperly with Joseph Percival. She was, in fact, chasing him with the intention of getting him to propose to her. When Mrs. Tarleton learns that Baker is the son of her old friend—it was her letters Baker found—she insists on his staying to dinner. Made tipsy on sloe gin, which he believes to be a fruit beverage, Baker, who has been introduced to Mrs. Tarleton as Mr. Gunner because no one knows his real name, and had then said he was John Brown, becomes aggressive, reveals his true name, abuses the company generally, and is taken away by Mrs. Tarleton for a nice cup of tea and a good sleep. *Misalliance*

BALBUS, BERT: Home Secretary in the Government of Proteus, ill-mannered and outspoken, constantly provoking quarrels among his colleagues in the Cabinet. Like them, he has a poor opinion of democracy, saying it needs poverty and hardship to flourish, and that present wages are too high. When King Magnus says he intends to abdicate he is in favour of it, as he thinks Magnus's son will make an excellent figurehead and not meddle with government. But when he realises that Magnus's ambition is to become Prime Minister, he hints that he would be willing to serve under him as Home Secretary. As he is the last to leave after the decisive Cabinet meeting, Magnus asks him to remind the Prime Minister that they have forgotten to discuss America's offer to rejoin the British Commonwealth. Balbus thinks this a great joke, and goes off laughing. *The Apple Cart*

BALMY WALTERS: *see* Boon, Walter

BALSQUITH: Prime Minister in an England which has introduced conscription and is living in dread of the militant suffragettes. The only way he can visit the War Office in safety is by disguising himself as one, much to the momentary terror of General Mitchener. Once there, he agrees to see the leaders of the anti-suffragette movement, Mrs. Banger and Lady Corinthia Fanshawe, believing they can help him to maintain order. But he finds that by a combination of ferocity and feminine wiles they have so frightened Mitchener that he is now on the side of the suffragettes, as being the lesser of two evils. When Balsquith learns that the head of the army, General Sandstone, has also fallen victim to Mrs. Banger, and is to marry her, he gives up in despair, and rejecting the offer of marriage made to him by Lady Corinthia, but agreeing that she may be his Egeria, he persuades Mitchener to grant the army civil rights, and stop treating soldiers as schoolboys, just as he himself must stop treating women as if they were angels. (*Note*: Owing to the Censor's objection to the combination of Baldwin and Asquith in this character's name, he was rechristened Johnson in performance.) *Press Cuttings*

BANGER, MRS. ROSA CARMINA: A masculine woman of forty, with a powerful voice and great physical strength. As secretary of the anti-suffragette league she comes to offer General Mitchener her help against the militant women, being quite prepared to lead a cavalry charge against them, as she did against the Egyptians at Kassassin, where she served as a trooper. When Mitchener refuses, she throws his orderly downstairs, and goes off to interview the head of the army, General Sandstone, who is so terrified by her that he agrees to her proposal that they shall marry so that she can rule the army. She is of the opinion that every really great man, including Napoleon and Bismarck, was a woman in disguise, and that Queen Elizabeth, by her vanity and levity, proved herself a disguised man. *Press Cuttings*

BANNAL, FLAWNER: A young dramatic critic who is invited to see the play by Fanny O'Dowda which is being acted anonymously in her father's country house by a cast of professionals. He demands a fee of ten guineas, which the impresario, Cecil Savoyard, pays because he values Bannal's completely commonplace opinions: 'they represent those of the average English playgoer'. After the performance Bannal says he cannot pass any useful judgement on

13

the play until he knows who wrote it; but, annoyed by the other critics' insistence that it must be either by Granville-Barker or by Pinero, he insists that it is by Bernard Shaw. *Fanny's First Play*

BARBARA: *see* Cleveland, Duchess of; Undershaft, Barbara

BARDO: *see* Bombardone, Bardo

BARKING, VISCOUNT: A powerfully-built loud-voiced young man just down from Oxford, defying convention in corduroys, pullover, and unshaven black beard. He is one of a deputation from the Isle of Cats which comes to see the Prime Minister, Sir Arthur Chavender, and meets his daughter Flavia, with whom he falls in love. Invited to lunch by Lady Chavender, he returns, clean-shaven and conventionally dressed, and inclined to side with Chavender instead of the delegation when it returns to protest against compulsory labour and the abolition of the right to strike. But when Flavia, disillusioned by her first contact, during a demonstration by the unemployed, with the English working-man, is reluctant to become engaged to him, he treats her with the violence and bad language she expected from a poor man, and she gives in. *On the Rocks*

BARLOW, JOSEPH POPHAM BOLGE BLUEBIN, O.M.: an inhabitant of Baghdad, the capital of the British Commonwealth, who in the year A.D. 3000 comes with his son-in-law Ambrose Bluebin, Prime Minister of the British Islands, to consult the oracle at Galway about the outcome of the next election. Ireland is now inhabited by the products of Creative Evolution, who attain the age of 300 years, and is dangerous for short-livers such as Barlow (who is always referred to as the Elderly Gentleman), who are liable to die of discouragement. He is therefore put in the charge of the 94-year-old Zozim, but escapes from him and is found wandering about in tears by the 200-year-old Fusima. After a baffling conversation, during which they talk at cross-purposes, she is glad to hand him back to Zozim, who finds him so childish that he nicknames him Daddy, and confines him to the care of Zoo, who is only fifty. She also calls him Daddy, though he confesses that his mother called him Iddy Toodles, and his friends Joe or Joseph, and takes him to rejoin his party at the temple. The oracle's reply is, as usual, unsatisfactory, so the Prime Minister decides to use the inspiring message invented by his predecessor, which won him the election. Barlow feels he cannot support this deception, and begs the oracle to allow him to remain on the island. Reluctantly she does so, but he dies almost immediately. *Back to Methuselah, Part IV: Tragedy of an Elderly Gentleman*

BARMECIDE: *see* Bridgenorth, Alfred

BARNABAS: A descendant of Conrad Barnabas, and in A.D. 2170 Accountant-General of the British Islands under its President Burge-Lubin. He goes to a film show arranged by an American who has invented a method of underwater breathing designed to prevent the numerous deaths by drowning of eminent persons, which have been taking place with monotonous regularity over the last 150 years, and realises that four of the victims—Archbishop Haslam, Archbishop Stickit, President Dickenson, and General Bullyboy, are all in fact the same person, the present Archbishop of York. When Haslam confesses that he is indeed all five persons, and is now 283, Barnabas refuses to believe it; and when Haslam and Mrs. Lutestring, aged 274, decide to marry in order to breed a race of long-lived Englishmen, he threatens to bring in legislation to prevent it, or even to kill them. His objection to them is purely emotional: 'If I have to die when I am seventy-eight, I don't see why another man should be privileged to live to be two hundred and seventy-eight.' *Back to Methuselah, Part III: The Thing Happens*

BARNABAS, CONRAD: An elderly biologist, who has written a book on longevity, and with his brother Franklyn has evolved the 'gospel of the Brothers Barnabas', which postulates that Creative Evolution will soon lead to the emergence of human beings able to live to 300 years. When the politicians Burge and Lubin visit the brothers in the hope of enlisting their support in the forthcoming election— this is in the early 1920s—they try to interest them in their idea. For a moment Burge thinks it may be useful politically, but in the end rejects it, while Lubin never really gives it a thought. Even Conrad's niece, Cynthia, who believed for a time that it might be possible, finally says it is absurd, as does the Rev. Haslam, to whom she is engaged. Conrad and Franklyn then decide to hold their tongues, or they will be laughed at. But Conrad says, 'Creative Evolution doesn't stop while people are laughing . . . The first man to live three hundred years may not have the slightest notion that he is going to do it, and may be the loudest laugher of the lot.' *Back to Methuselah, Part II: The Gospel of the Brothers Barnabas*

BARNABAS, CYNTHIA: The daughter of Franklyn Barnabas, usually known as the Savage, or Savvy, because of her outspokenness and bad manners. She is engaged to the local parson, the Rev. William Haslam, and is present when the Liberal leaders Burge and Lubin come to ask her father and uncle for their support in the forthcoming election. She rather likes Lubin, who flirts with her, but thinks Burge is a flaming fraud, and has a very poor opinion of their outmoded political notions. She persuades her father to reveal to them 'the gospel of the Brothers Barnabas'—based on the fact that Creative Evolution will soon produce men and women able to live for 300 years. She even produces an election cry for the party: 'Back to Methuselah!' But when her uncle Conrad points out that no one knows who will be the first long-lived person—it may even be their own parlourmaid—she decides that the whole thing is absurd. *Back to Methuselah, Part II: The Gospel of the Brothers Barnabas*

BARNABAS, FRANKLYN: An elderly man who was for some years a clergyman, but left the Church when he realised his own ignorance and self-conceit. With his brother, the biologist Conrad Barnabas, who has written a book on longevity, he has formulated an hypothesis according to which Creative Evolution is about to produce a race of human beings who will live to 300 years. When the politicians Burge and Lubin come to ask him to support them in the next election, he tries to interest them in his ideas, but they laugh him to scorn. Even his daughter Cynthia becomes sceptical when he points out that no one knows who will be the first person to attain such an age, and it may even be their own parlourmaid, the future Mrs. Lutestring. *Back to Methuselah, Part II: The Gospel of the Brothers Barnabas*

BASHAM, MRS.: Isaac Newton's housekeeper. She is annoyed by the number of visitors who come and take up her master's valuable time, and extremely shocked at the irruption of Nell Gwynn, the Duchess of Cleveland, and the Duchess of Portsmouth into a respectable house. But she provides an excellent meal for them all, though when the Duke of York reminds her that it is Friday and he requires 'three or four different kinds of fish', she tells him plainly that all he will get is 'a nice piece of cod'. *In Good King Charles's Golden Days*

BASHAM, SIR BROADFOOT: Chief Commissioner of Police. A capable-looking man with pleasant, but not conciliatory manners. Having been a soldier, he is hampered by police regulations in dealing with demonstrators, but will not agree with the Prime Minister, Sir Arthur Chavender, that stronger measures are called for. He says it would be better to keep them occupied with speeches, and even suggests that Chavender should make a speech to them in Trafalgar Square. When, some months later, Chavender, having had his head turned by reading Karl Marx, makes what Basham calls a speech full of 'boiling socialism', he is rather wary of him. But when he discovers that it means an increase of 500 in the police force, as well as a substantial rise in wages for himself and his men, he begins to think it makes sense, and is half inclined to back Chavender against Rightside, who wants his job. However, he finally decides to go back to Scotland Yard and await events. *On the Rocks*

BASHVILLE: Footman to Lydia Carew, with whom he is in love. He is instrumental in revealing to her that Cashel Byron is a prizefighter, hoping that since she has stooped to love one so far beneath her, she might also love him. But when the Queen bestows Lydia's hand on Cashel and makes him, as the son of the former Overlord of Dorset, deputy lieutenant of the county, Bashville publicly forswears his love, and accepts Cashel's offer to make a prizefighter of him under the name of The Admirable Bashville, or Byron's Novice. *The Admirable Bashville*

BASTABLE, ADOLPHUS: 'A leader of fashion', and the lover of Lady Magnesia Fitztollemache. He comes to show her his new clothes—coat and trousers half yellow and half black, with a silver-spangled waistcoat and a crimson handkerchief—which he hopes will prevent his being mistaken for a waiter. Mad with jealousy, Lady Magnesia's husband poisons him, but on second thoughts tries to save him with plaster dissolved in water, which solidifies and turns him into a statue. *Passion, Poison, and Petrifaction*

BASTARD: *see* Dunois, Jack

BATTLER, ERNEST: One of the dictators (Hitler) summoned to appear before the Court of International Justice at The Hague. Accused by the Jew of trying to exterminate his race, Battler says the Jews have only to go somewhere else, and then he will not interfere with them. He considers his own countrymen best fitted to rule the world, under his guidance, and has already started a war to establish his supremacy, only to find that his allies have deserted him, and that the British, whom he counted on to keep quiet, are prepared to fight. Before he has had time to recover from the shock, it is announced that a new ice-age is about to begin, and Battler bursts into tears because his dog Blonda will be frozen to death. *Geneva*

BAUDRICOURT, ROBERT DE: A French captain, in command of the castle of Vaucouleurs. Against his better judgement, he allows Joan of Arc to talk him into giving her a horse, an escort, and some armour so that she can go to the Dauphin. *Saint Joan*

BAYEUX, CANON OF: *see* Estivet, Brother John d'

B.B.: *see* Bonington, Sir Ralph Bloomfield

BEADLE: An official in the town of Websterbridge, New Hampshire. He brings a ladder and places it against the gallows on which Richard Dudgeon is to be hanged, guarding it against unauthorised climbers. He has nothing to say. *The Devil's Disciple*

See also Wallaston, Joseph

BEAMISH, HORATIO FLOYD: An elderly man with white whiskers and beard and a red nose. He is the only clerk left in the Council offices of Little Pifflington—it is 1916—and in his resentment at being rejected for the army, and so losing his two-and-sevenpence a day, he has taken to drink. He is extremely unco-operative with Lord Augustus Highcastle, who has come to the town to make a recruiting speech, but softens when a beautiful Lady arrives, and shows her in politely. He then tries again to join the army and is successful, the recruiting sergeant saying that now that Highcastle is on the job they will need every man they can get. He returns to the office clean-shaven and in khaki, to bring Highcastle the secret list of gun emplacements which he left on his breakfast table, and is kicked downstairs for insubordination. *Augustus Does His Bit*

BEAUCHAMP: *see* Warwick, Earl of

BEAUVAIS, BISHOP OF: *see* Cauchon, Peter

BEEDLE-DEEDLE-DUMKINS: *see* Bonington, Sir Ralph Bloomfield

BEEFEATER: The Warden on duty at the Palace of White-hall on the night William Shakespear goes to meet Mary Fitton. They talk together, and the Beefeater utters several striking platitudes which Shakespear afterwards incorporates in his plays, particularly *Hamlet*. *The Dark Lady of the Sonnets*

BEGGAR: An old man who is sitting on a bench by one of the gates of Rome when a group of Christians on their way to the Colosseum stop for a breather. He snatches up the gold coin which Lentulus throws to Ferrovius. *Androcles and the Lion*

BEGONIA: *see* Brown, Begonia

BEL AFFRIS: A young Egyptian guard from the temple of Ra in Memphis who comes to warn Belzanor that Julius Caesar is advancing to sack the palace in which Cleopatra has taken refuge. *Caesar and Cleopatra*

BELZANOR: Egyptian captain in charge of the guard at Cleopatra's Syrian palace. Warned by Bel Affris that Julius Caesar is on his way to sack the palace, he leaves in search of Cleopatra, whom he hopes to betray either to Caesar or to her brother, and reappears briefly on the quayside at Alexandria to bid farewell to the victorious Caesar as he embarks for Rome. *Caesar and Cleopatra*

BEMROSE: *see* Hotspot, Admiral Sir Bemrose

BENI SIRAS: A band of Arab tribesmen in the Atlas Mountains who attack the party led by Captain Brassbound. *Captain Brassbound's Conversion*

BENJY: *see* Betrothed

BENTLEY: *see* Summerhays, Bentley

BERT: *see* Balbus, Bert

BERTRAND: *see* Poulengey, Bertrand de

BETROTHED: The nephew of Sir Orpheus Midlander. He is engaged to Begonia Brown (who calls him Billikins, whereas his uncle refers to him as Benjy) and gladly stands down as Conservative candidate for Camberwell so that she can take his place. He accompanies her to the Court of International Justice at The Hague and makes one useful contribution to the discussion when he points out that the 'notion of man on the battlefield and woman in the home wont wash nowadays'. The soldier is safe in the trenches while the woman at home is blown to pieces. *Geneva*

BIDDY: *see* Undershaft, Lady Britomart

BILL: *see* Boanerges, Bill; Buoyant, Bastable; Collins, Bill; Haslam, Rev. William; Walker, Bill

BILLIKINS: *see* Betrothed

BILLITER, MRS.: The elderly and discreet housekeeper in a block of small flats in Vienna, one of which is rented by Professor Bruno Haldenstedt for meetings with his mistress Jitta Lenkheim. She looks after Haldenstedt during the early stages of the heart attack from which he later dies. *Jitta's Atonement*

BILLY: *see* Cokane, William de Burgh; Dunn, Billy

BILTON: Foreman in one of the gun-cotton sheds in the armaments factory of Andrew Undershaft. When Charles Lomax is being shown round the factory, Bilton is quick to notice that he has lit a cigarette, and not only retrieves the match which Lomax has thrown away, but makes him leave the shed immediately. Later, he remembers that Undershaft has pocketed Lomax's matches, and takes them and drops them into the fire-bucket. *Major Barbara*

BISHOP: Old, soft, gentle, and rather infirm. He comes to the office of the International Committee for Intellectual Co-operation to complain to the secretary, Begonia Brown, that his footman has become a Communist. She promises to lay his complaint before the Court of International Justice at The Hague. Meanwhile, a gentleman has come in whom the Bishop recognises as a pleasant acquaintance from his Geneva hotel. He collapses with shock when he discovers that the man is really a Russian Commissar, Posky, has a heart attack when Posky asserts that the Komintern is the State Church in Russia just as the Church of England is the State Church in England, and dies when Posky says that the poor of Russia do not need the consolations of religion as there are no poor in Russia. *Geneva*

BISHOP OF BEAUVAIS: *see* Cauchon, Peter

BISHOP OF CHELSEA: *see* Bridgenorth, Alfred

BLACK PAQUITO: *see* Brassbound, Captain

BLACK PRINCE: The eldest son of Edward III, in attendance on his father when he receives the surrender of Calais. *The Six of Calais*

BLANCHE *see* Sartorius, Blanche

BLANCO: *see* Posnet, Blanco

BLEE, ALDERMAN: A member of the delegation from the Isle of Cats which comes to see the Prime Minister, Sir Arthur Chavender. He is a thin, undersized, lower-middle-class young man with a good opinion of himself, but leaves the talking to the other delegates until their second visit, when he expresses himself forcibly on the subject of compulsory labour and the outlawing of strikes. He is against both, and tells the Prime Minister that if he doesn't withdraw both items from his new programmes of reform he will lose every vote in the Isle of Cats. He is also very fluent on the subject of compensation to landowners for estates which have been nationalised. When Hotspot tells him he should be grateful to those who have kept England off the rocks, he retorts, 'You haven't kept us off the rocks. We're on the rocks, the whole lot of us.' *On the Rocks*

BLENDERBLAND, ADRIAN: An imposing, bearded man, handsome and well dressed. He is the tame lover of Epifania Fitzfassen, with the privilege of paying for meals, taxis, flowers, and theatre tickets when they go out together, since she, being a millionairess, never has any money. He goes to the solicitor, Julius Sagamore, for advice about Epifania's divorce, but finds her there already, together with her husband Alastair and his mistress Patricia Smith. The ensuing argument causes him to forget what he came for and he leaves, later lunching with Epifania at a dismal riverside inn called The Pig and Whistle. Upset by the poor food and dreary surroundings, he permits himself to criticise Epifania's dead father, whereupon she, an expert at Judo, throws him downstairs. Picked up by her chauffeur and taken to hospital, with injuries which he is still suffering from five months later, he decides to bring an action against her, but Epifania counters by saying she will bring an action against him first, and being rich, she will win. With the help of Alastair and Patricia, Sagamore succeeds in calming them both down, and Adrian contents himself by warning the Egyptian doctor whom Epifania intends to marry that nobody can live with her, and that he will regret the marriage to the end of his life. *The Millionairess*

BLENKINSOP, DR.: A shabby, flabby, poverty-stricken doctor, whose patients are mainly clerks, shopmen, and the members of working men's clubs. He can do little for them, in the absence of money and leisure, and is himself ill. He was a student with several medical men who have since become well known, including Sir Colenso Ridgeon, who, when he realises that Blenkinsop has tuberculosis, for which he himself has found a cure, takes him as a patient in the place of the artist Louis Dubedat. Blenkinsop is completely restored to health and becomes a Medical Officer of

23

Health, whereupon he rather ungratefully tells Jennifer Dubedat that 'private practice in medicine ought to be put down by law' because private doctors are ignorant licensed murderers. *The Doctor's Dilemma*

BLUEBEARD: *see* Rais, Gilles de

BLUEBIN, AMBROSE BADGER: Prime Minister of the British Commonwealth, which in A.D. 3000 has its capital in Baghdad. He has come with his wife, daughter and father-in-law to consult the oracle at Galway about the next election, and receives the same answer as his predecessor, Sir Fuller Eastwind, fifteen years before: 'Go home, poor fool!' But Eastwind had returned home with a grandiloquent speech, made up by himself, which won him the election, so Bluebin decides that he has only to say that he has received the same answer, which is true as far as it goes, and calls on his companions to back him up. Only his father-in-law, Joseph Barlow, feels unable to do so, and the Bluebins return to Baghdad without him. *Back to Methuselah, Part IV: Tragedy of an Elderly Gentleman*

BLUEBIN, ETHEL BADGER: Daughter of the Prime Minister, who in A.D. 3000 has come to Galway to consult the oracle there. She is very interested in the temple, and in the prospect of seeing a woman who is 300 years old. But Zoo tells her that she would drop dead if a tertiary so much as looked at her, and that the oracle is only 170. Even so, Ethel is badly frightened by her, and says she can see snakes curling in the vapour round the tripod. Afterwards she is able to remember the answer which the oracle is supposed to have given to her father's predecessor fifteen years before, as she learned it at school, and her father decides to use it instead of the true answer, which was 'Go home, poor fool!' *Back to Methuselah, Part IV: Tragedy of an Elderly Gentleman*

BLUEBIN, MOLLY BADGER: The wife of the Prime Minister of the British Commonwealth, who comes with her husband from the capital, Baghdad, to Galway in Ireland in the year A.D. 3000 to consult the oracle. She is affronted by the casual way in which the long-lived inhabitants of the island treat her, terrified of the oracle, and begs her husband to hurry up and ask his question. *Back to Methuselah, Part IV: Tragedy of an Elderly Gentleman*

BLUEJACKETS: *see* American Bluejackets

BLUNTSCHLI, CAPTAIN: A Swiss mercenary serving in the Austrian army in the war of 1885–6, of middling stature and undistinguished appearance, quick-witted and with a strong sense of humour. Routed in a Bulgarian cavalry charge led by Major Saranoff, he inadvertently takes refuge in the bedroom of Saranoff's fiancée, Raina Petkoff, who saves him from his pursuers. After the war he returns to the Petkoffs' house, ostensibly to return an overcoat lent him by Raina, but also because he is attracted by her. Hospitably entertained by Major Petkoff, who has already met him during the peace negotiations, he is present when Raina's engagement is broken off because Saranoff has been flirting with her maid Louka, and, having inherited the vast possessions of his hotelier father, he is accepted as a suitor for her hand. *Arms and the Man*

BOANERGES, BILL: A man of fifty, heavily built and aggressively self-assertive. Having just been appointed President of the Board of Trade by the Prime Minister Proteus, he comes to take his seat in the Cabinet for the first time wearing a Russian blouse and a peaked cap, much to the amusement of his colleagues. A foundling adopted by a policeman's wife, he is very proud of being a self-made man, and thinks himself a strong, hard-headed character, but is really very naïve, sentimental, and susceptible to flattery. When King Magnus threatens to abdicate rather than sign Proteus's ultimatum, Boanerges thinks it a good idea, as he envisages himself as Dictator of England. He is also quite content that Magnus should become a commoner and stand for Parliament, and can't understand why Proteus tears up the ultimatum. *The Apple Cart*

BOATMAN: On the quayside at Alexandria, 'a bullet-headed, vivacious grinning fellow, burnt almost black by the sun'. Apollodorus uses his small boat to smuggle Cleopatra to the island of Pharos as a surprise for Julius Caesar. The boat is wrecked when Caesar throws some heavy dispatches into it by mistake. *Caesar and Cleopatra*

BOBBY: *see* Gilbey, Bobby

BOETIA, GRAND DUCHESS OF: *see* Annajanska

BOETIAN SOLDIERS: *see* Soldiers

BOHUN, WALTER, Q.C.: The son of the head waiter at the Marine Hotel, Torbay (*see* Boon, Walter). 'A tall, stout man of between forty and fifty, clean-shaven . . . stiff black hair cropped short and oiled', he has made his way by scholarships and a tremendous personality to a lucrative practice at the Bar. Called in by Finch M'Comas to decide whether Fergus Crampton is entitled to demand custody of his 17-year-old twins, Dolly and Philip Clandon, he rules that going to law is absurd, as the children will be of age before the point can be decided. *You Never Can Tell*

BOLSHEVIK EMPRESS: *see* Annajanska

BOMBARDONE, BARDO: One of the dictators (Mussolini) brought before the Court of International Justice at The Hague to answer charges of crimes against humanity. He is the first to arrive, and is very surprised when Ernest Battler (Hitler), his deadly rival, also turns up. He says the third dictator, Flanco de Fortinbras (Franco), will not come because he, Bombardone, has not authorised him to do so, and is surprised to see him, and even more to be snubbed by one whom he thinks of as his 'valet'. He receives a further shock when he discovers Battler has declared war without consulting him. When the news of the new ice-age comes, he stoically predicts that his countrymen will be found 'erect at their posts like the Pompeian sentinel'. *Geneva*

BOMPAS, AURORA: The wife of Edward Bompas, who usually calls her Rory. She is 'a very ordinary South Kensington female of about thirty-seven', who has captured the imagination of a young poet, Henry Apjohn. When the poems Apjohn has written to her find their way into her husband's hands, she is terrified of his reaction, and begs Apjohn to save her. He suggests that they shall elope, but she refuses indignantly, as she has no real affection for him, 'being hopelessly inferior in physical and spiritual distinction to the beautiful youth' who loves her. She thinks everything will be settled when Apjohn tells Bompas that the poems were written to the goddess Aurora, and is very surprised when he accuses the poet of despising 'his Rory', and equally surprised when, after being told the truth, he offers to publish the poems at his own expense. *How He Lied to Her Husband*

BOMPAS, EDWARD: The husband of Aurora Bompas, whom he calls Rory. 'A robust, thick-necked, well-groomed city man, with a strong chin, but a blithering eye and credulous mouth,' he has been given by his mischief-making sister Georgina a sheaf of poems written to his wife by a young poet, Henry Apjohn. He is hurt and surprised when Apjohn tells him that they were really written to the goddess Aurora, and accuses him of despising Rory, who has been 'admired by better men than you, you soapy-headed little puppy'. After they have come to blows, Apjohn admits that the poems were written to Rory, and Teddy, as he is called, filled with pride at this further proof of his discrimination in choosing such an attractive wife, offers to publish them at his own expense. *How He Lied to Her Husband*

BONAPARTE, GENERAL NAPOLEON: A 27-year-old officer —later Emperor of France—who has just defeated the Austrians at Lodi and is waiting at an inn in Tavazzano for the arrival of a Lieutenant with important dispatches. When he learns that these have been stolen by the twin brother of a

Strange Lady who is also staying at the inn, he realises that they have been purloined by the lady herself, in disguise, and he succeeds in getting them from her. He is then given to understand that among them is a love-letter from his wife Josephine to a member of the Directoire, Barras, and that the scandal which must result if he reads and acts on it will ruin his career. He therefore reads the letter, pretends that he has not, and, at the instigation of the lady, burns it, consoling himself, one imagines, with the lady. When he discovers that the lady had an English grandfather and an Irish grandmother, he says prophetically: 'An English army led by an Irish general: that might be a match for a French army led by an Italian general.' He also gives her a long lecture on the English character: 'Every Englishman is born with a certain miraculous power that makes him master of the world . . . He does everything on principle.' *The Man of Destiny*

BONES: *see* Mitchener, General

BONINGTON, SIR RALPH BLOOMFIELD: A famous physician, whose principle in dealing with his patients is 'find the germ and kill it'. A tall, slender, handsome man, he has a beautifully modulated voice, and loves the sound of it, talking endlessly at every opportunity. He radiates enormous self-satisfaction, is cheery, reassuring, and a born healer, independent of mere treatment and skill. He takes over the young artist Louis Dubedat, who is suffering from advanced tuberculosis, when his colleague Sir Colenso Ridgeon refuses to treat him, and by his insistence on 'stimulating the phacocytes' (white corpuscles) kills him in about three days. For this he blames the anti-toxin produced by Ridgeon as part of *his* pet theory. B.B., as he is called (except by his wife, who calls him Beedle-Deedle-Dumkins in the privacy of the home), is immensely edified by Dubedat's calm and philosophical acceptance of death, and is moved by it to quote *Macbeth*. *The Doctor's Dilemma*

BOON, WALTER: Head waiter at the Marine Hotel, Torbay, known as Balmy Walters, or, by Dolly Clandon, as William, because he reminds her of Shakespeare. 'A silky old man, white-haired and delicate-looking, but so cheerful and contented that in his encouraging presence ambition stands rebuked', he is well-spoken, with a quiet voice that gives 'sympathetic interest to his most commonplace remark'. He waits at table during the luncheon party at which Fergus Crampton meets his wife and three children after a separation of eighteen years, and by his tact helps to mitigate the awkwardness of the situation. He is the father of Walter Bohun, Q.C. (who has reverted to the original spelling of the family name), and is very proud of him, though he sometimes wishes he had been a barman rather than at the Bar, as he 'had to support him till he was thirty-seven'. *You Never Can Tell*

BOOZY: *see* Daniels, Elder

BOSHINGTON, SIR CARDONIUS: The Lord Chancellor, who is visited, in his capacity as guardian of all wards in Chancery, by two foundlings, Horace Brabazon, who wants a wife, and Anastasia Vulliamy, who wants a husband. When Horace returns to the Lord Chancellor's office for his stick, they meet and agree to marry. *The Fascinating Foundling*

BOSS: *see* Mangan, Alfred

BOXER: *see* Bridgenorth, General Boxer

BRABAZON, HORACE: A nineteen-year-old foundling who wishes to go on the stage. He visits the Lord Chancellor, Sir Cardonius Boshington, and asks him, in his capacity as guardian of all wards in Chancery, to find him a wife and get him a job in the theatre. The Lord Chancellor, convinced he is mad, humours him and sends him away after promising to do what he can for him. He is then visited by Anastasia Vulliamy on a similar errand. She wants a husband; and when she sees Brabazon, who has returned to the office for the stick he left behind, she is convinced he is the husband of her dreams. He, however, will not agree to marry her until he learns that she too is a foundling. *The Fascinating Foundling*

BRANDYFACED JACK: *see* Drinkwater, Felix

BRASSBOUND, CAPTAIN: A smuggler and privateer, known as Black Paquito, master of the schooner *Thanksgiving*, based on the port of Mogador in Morocco. When Sir Howard Hallam sets off for an expedition into the Atlas Mountains, Brassbound and his crew provide his escort. But, unknown to Hallam, Brassbound is his nephew, brought up by his Portuguese mother to believe that his uncle has cheated him out of his father's West Indian estates, and left her to die in poverty. He has sworn revenge, and to achieve his purpose arranges for an Arab sheikh, Sidi el Assif, to capture Hallam and either kill or enslave him. He had not, however, foreseen the presence in the party of Lady Cicely Waynflete, Hallam's sister-in-law, who persuades Brassbound to forgive his uncle. He does so, but before he can get him safely home, he is himself arrested by the Cadi of Kintali, Muley Othman, who has been told of Brassbound's evil intentions by an American naval captain, Kearney. Fearing that the disappearance of two English travellers will lead to trouble with the authorities, the Cadi takes Brassbound back to Mogador to stand his trial. He is acquitted on the evidence of Lady Cicely, and is so overcome by her charm and common sense that he begs her to marry him. He is brought to his senses by the firing of a gun to recall him to his ship, and leaves after expressing his gratitude, firm in his intention to forget the past and start a new career. *Captain Brassbound's Conversion*

BRIDGENORTH, ALFRED: The Bishop of Chelsea, known to his family as the Barmecide. Slim and active, he exudes the confidence of 'a successful man who is always interested in himself and generally rather pleased with himself'. Happily married, he nevertheless sympathises with his young sister-in-law Leo when she says she really needs several husbands for different occasions, and ends by concluding that it is 'a mistake to get married, but a much bigger mistake not to get married'. When his daughter Edith suddenly decides on her wedding morning not to get married after all, he suggests that his chaplain shall draw up a civil contract which will meet her objections to the religious ceremony; but this proves impossible, and finally Edith and her fiancé go off to church and get married in the usual way, while the Bishop and his wife prepare to receive the guests at the belated wedding reception. *Getting Married*

BRIDGENORTH, ALICE: Wife of Alfred Bridgenorth, Bishop of Chelsea. 'A quiet, happy-looking woman of about fifty, placid, gentle and humorous, with delicate features and fine grey hair', she is supervising the arrangements for the wedding reception of her sixth and last daughter, Edith Bridgenorth, and is a little flustered by the arrival of her brother-in-law Reginald Bridgenorth at the same time as his divorced wife and her putative second husband. She soon recovers, however, and assists quietly at all the arguments between Edith and her fiancé as to whether they shall or shall not get married, and also at the fruitless efforts made to draw up a civil contract which shall take the place of the religious ceremony. She is rewarded for her patience by the marriage taking place, though somewhat later than arranged, and presides over the wedding reception. *Getting Married*

BRIDGENORTH, GENERAL BOXER: Brother of the Bishop of Chelsea, Alfred Bridgenorth, and in love with the Bishop's sister-in-law, Lesbia Grantham. He is a fine-looking man of about fifty, ignorant, stupid, and prejudiced, 'having been carefully trained to be so', but he has 'much natural simplicity and dignity of character'. He is constantly shocked by the conversation of those around him, particularly on the subject of marriage and English womanhood, and continues doggedly to pursue Lesbia in the hope that she will eventually marry him. But she does not, mainly because he is a heavy smoker, and she does not believe 'there is a man in England who really and truly loves his wife as much as he loves his pipe'. *Getting Married*

BRIDGENORTH, EDITH: The sixth and youngest daughter of the Bishop of Chelsea, Alfred Bridgenorth. She is about to be married to Cecil Sykes, but on her wedding morning reads a pamphlet from which she learns that even if her husband should turn out to be a murderer, a madman, a forger, or a thief, she cannot be released from her marriage vows. This upsets her so much that she refuses to go to church. When the Bishop discovers that Cecil also has been upset by reading an essay on man's wrongs, he suggests that his chaplain shall draw up a civil contract which will satisfy them both. But after much argument, this proves impossible, and while the rest of the family are still wrangling about it, the engaged couple slip away and get married in an empty church, the Beadle giving Edith away. They then return to a belated wedding reception, prepared to face whatever hazards matrimony may bring. *Getting Married*

BRIDGENORTH, LEO: The very young, pretty, restless, selfish wife of Reginald Bridgenorth, whom she has persuaded to give her grounds for divorce because she wishes to marry St. John Hotchkiss, who is nearer her own age, and amuses her. But when she meets Reginald again at the wedding of her niece Edith, she decides that she wants him as well as Hotchkiss—in fact, she could do with several husbands, she says; one for everyday, one for concerts and theatres, a great austere saint, and a blithering idiot of a boy. She is delighted at the idea of a civil contract to be drawn up for Edith and her fiancé instead of a church wedding, and says she is herself ready to enter into 'an honourable alliance' with both Reginald and Hotchkiss 'on terms favourable to herself'. But that is all forgotten when, during Edith's actual wedding ceremony, she goes to her husband's lodgings and finds how untidy and uncomfortable they are. She is already prepared to return to him, because he cannot do without her, when Hotchkiss tells her that he has fallen in love with the coal-merchant's wife, Mrs. George Collins, and she sends Reginald off to get 'that odious decree' of divorce 'demolished or annulled or whatever it is'. *Getting Married*

BRIDGENORTH, REGINALD: The eldest brother of the Bishop of Chelsea, Alfred Bridgenorth. 'Hardened and tough physically, hasty and boyish in manner and speech, he has not developed intellectually since his schooldays. A muddled, rebellious, hasty, untidy, forgetful, always late sort of man who needs the care of a capable woman, and has never been lucky or attractive enough to get it.' Late in life he has married Leo, a pretty, shallow girl thirty years younger than himself, and when she tells him she has fallen in love with a much younger man, he agrees to give her grounds for divorce. They meet again at the wedding of their niece Edith, where Hotchkiss, Leo's lover, tells her he has fallen in love with another woman, and husband and wife are reconciled. *Getting Married*

BRIGANDS: A band of about a dozen petty criminals operating in the mountains of the Sierra Nevada under their leader Mendoza. Among them are an Anarchist and three Social-Democrats. They have one gun between them, and are mostly dressed—being mainly Cockney or Americans—in seedy overcoats, woollen mufflers, hard hemispherical hats, and dirty brown gloves. They capture John Tanner and his chauffeur Straker, and are saved from arrest by a company of Spanish soldiers when Tanner claims them as his 'escort'. *Man and Superman*

BRITANNUS (BRITANNICUS): A slave from Britain who has

risen to be the confidential secretary of Julius Caesar. A man 'of about forty, tall, solemn, already slightly bald . . . with a heavy, drooping, hazel-coloured moustache, trained so as to lose its ends in a pair of trim whiskers', he is very conscious of the importance of his master's affairs, and utterly devoted to him. After Caesar has conquered Egypt he intends to give Britannus, whom he jokingly calls Britannicus—the conqueror of Britain—his freedom. But realising that he would rather stay as he is, he takes him back to Rome with him. *Caesar and Cleopatra*

BRITISH ENVOY: *see* Bluebin, Ambrose Badger

BRITISH SOLDIERS: *see* Soldiers

BROADBENT, TOM (THOMAS): A robust, full-blooded, energetic Englishman; a civil engineer in partnership with Larry Doyle. Being a simple, romantic creature, he is enraptured with everything Irish, and considers that England has a duty towards Ireland, at least until the establishment of Home Rule, which, he is sure, will be a great success—under English guidance. Meanwhile he intends to work on a development scheme, and goes to Ireland with his partner. Even more enchanted by the 'reality', as he thinks, of Ireland, he stays with the Doyle family, gets engaged to Larry's former sweetheart, Nora Reilly, and agrees to stand as Member of Parliament for Rosscullen. Even a ridiculous incident in which he is involved when he offers to drive a pig in his car, ending with the death of the pig and the wrecking of the car, fails to shake his faith in the Irish, whose defects he puts down to their whimsical Celtic heritage, and in spite of the solemn warning of Peter Keegan that he will kill the thing he loves, he goes ahead with his plans for a hotel and a golf club in Rosscullen. *John Bull's Other Island*

BROLLIKINS, ALDERWOMAN ALOYSIA: A member of the Labour deputation on unemployment which comes to visit the Prime Minister, Sir Arthur Chavender. She meets and falls in love with his son David, who has always said he wanted to marry a factory girl; but although she worked in a factory before becoming a trades union secretary, he hesitates to get engaged to her because he objects to her unusual surname. His father suggests that she should change it by deed poll. But David still vacillates, until Aloysia loses her temper and flounces out, whereupon he decides he must have her, and rushes out after her. *On the Rocks*

BROTHER JOHN: *see* Lemaître, Brother John

BROTHER MARTIN: *see* Ladvenu, Brother Martin

BROWN, BEGONIA: Secretary of the International Committee for Intellectual Co-operation. In her shabby office in Geneva she is visited by several people who wish to complain of injustice, and she promises to put their cases before the Court of International Justice at The Hague. This leads to a number of diplomatic incidents, which are investigated by the secretary of the League of Nations. He is surprised to find that Begonia acted entirely on her own initiative, but says that as warrants have been applied for, they must be issued and served. The matter is being discussed with the Senior Judge from The Hague when Begonia returns to say she has been asked to stand for Parliament. By the time the Court meets to try the cases she has referred to it, she is a D.B.E., and attends with her fiancé, Benjy, the nephew of the British Foreign Secretary, Sir Orpheus Midlander, whom she calls Billikins, but who is usually referred to as the Betrothed. During the trial, which is attended by the three dictators Battler, Bombadone, and Flanco, news comes that another ice-age is approaching rapidly. Begonia refuses to join her fiancé in one last spree 'before the icecaps nip us'; as a Dame of the British Empire, she must prepare to die like a Dame. *Geneva*

BROWN, JOHN: *see* Baker, Julius

BRUDENELL, REV. MR.: English chaplain to the troops under the command of General Burgoyne. He accompanies Richard Dudgeon to the gallows when he is to be hanged, 'in his surplice with his prayer book open in his hand', but is unable to make any impression on 'the Devil's Disciple' and retires to comfort Judith Anderson, who has insisted on watching the execution of the man she loves. After Richard's reprieve, Brudenell helps him down from the cart, and then returns to barracks with the escort. *The Devil's Disciple*

BRUNO: *see* Haldenstedt, Professor Bruno

BUCINATOR: A trumpeter in the army of Julius Caesar. His bucina is first heard when Caesar meets Cleopatra by the sphinx, and again as the troops approach the throne-room, which he enters 'with his instrument coiled round his body, its brazen bell shaped like the head of a howling wolf'. *Caesar and Cleopatra*

BULLYBOY, GENERAL: *see* Haslam, Rev. William

BUNNY: *see* Summerhays, Bentley

BUOYANT, BASTABLE: A millionaire, more familiarly known as Bill, or Old Bill, Buoyant. He sends for a solicitor, Sir Ferdinand Flopper, to explain to his numerous and somewhat eccentric offspring that on his death they will all be penniless, and meanwhile sits meditating in the Chinese temple arranged in his London drawing-room. When his eldest daughter, Clementina, the only child of his first wife, to whom he has already given an annuity, arrives from Panama, pursued by Junius Smith, who wants to marry her so that he can use her money for the betterment of humanity, he is in favour of the marriage and sends Smith to buy a marriage licence. *Buoyant Billions*

BUOYANT, CLARA: The wife of Harry, Old Bill Buoyant's third son, and usually referred to as Mrs. Thirdborn. She attends the meeting with Old Buoyant's solicitor without her husband, who leaves all business matters to his wife. She is beautiful, gentle, and extremely religious, and when told that they will all be left penniless when the old man dies, says: 'Why not? Our riches have not made us happy.' *Buoyant Billions*

BUOYANT, CLEMENTINA ALEXANDRA: The only child of Old Bill Buoyant by his first wife, usually called Clemmy, or by her father, Babzy. He has made her independent by giving her an annuity, on which she has gone to live in a hut near Panama, to get away from civilisation and 'the English gentleman'. When Junius Smith meets her there, and tries to arouse her interest in him, she sends him away. But she is in danger of falling in love with him, so goes back to London. He follows her there, and although he tells her plainly that he is really going to marry her so that he can use her money for 'world betterment'—though he is also strongly attracted to her physically—she eventually agrees to marry him by special licence, on the advice of her father. *Buoyant Billions*

BUOYANT, EUDOXIA EMILY: The youngest daughter of Old Bill Buoyant, usually known as Darkie. Because her mother was no good at housekeeping, preferring to paint, she has become most efficient at running her father's house. When the solicitor, Flopper, offers to adopt her as his daughter, she says it is not a role she feels drawn to, and after all the arguments over the wedding of her half-sister Clementina have ended in the departure of the bride and groom to be married by special licence, her only concern is with how many there will be for lunch. *Buoyant Billions*

BUOYANT, FREDERICK: The youngest child of Old Bill Buoyant, the millionaire, usually known as Fiffy, or the Youth. When told that his father's death will leave them all penniless, he says that they must make the most of him while he lasts. He objects to his half-sister's marriage to Junius Smith on the grounds that he is himself a world betterer, and so is Smith, and one in the family is enough. But when his brother Dick makes an impassioned speech praising mathematics and prophesying that one day scientists will discover a mathematical hormone so that all can profit by it, Fiffy says enthusiastically: 'World bettering be damned! I shall qualify as a doctor and look for that hormone.' *Buoyant Billions*

BUOYANT, JULIA: The wife of Bill Buoyant's second son, Richard or Dick, and usually known as Mrs. Secondborn. She is extremely aggressive, and during the conference arranged by her father-in-law so that the lawyer can tell his children there will be no money for them after his death, she and her husband do most of the talking. She dislikes her husband's half-sister, Clementina, whose mother was a working-class woman, because 'she knows things a lady ought not to know', and can cook, and clean, and sweep, and scrub. During the discussion over Clemmy's marriage to Junius Smith she says impatiently that 'it will just end in their getting married like other people'. She admits, after her husband has made an impassioned speech on the importance of mathematics, that he makes her feel a fool, but nevertheless she is very proud of him. *Buoyant Billions*

BUOYANT, RICHARD: Old Bill Buoyant's second son, usually known as Dick or Secondborn. He has a passion for mathematics, which he thinks will solve all problems if rightly applied, even those of love and marriage. He admits freely to his father's solicitor that he has no understanding of money, with which his father keeps him amply supplied, and that he does not believe the old man will ever die. 'He is a human calculating machine. Calculating machines don't die.' *Buoyant Billions*

BUOYANT, TOM: The eldest son of the millionaire Bill Buoyant. He has divorced his first wife and lost his second, and is usually called the Widower, or Firstborn. When told that his father's death will leave them all penniless, he says he knows nothing about money, and could not learn about it from his father, who 'makes money by instinct, as beavers build dams'. He tells his father, whom he calls by the nickname Ee Pee (meaning, not Esteemed Parent, as one might think, but Earthly Providence) that he and his brother Dick are going to act as witnesses at Clemmy's wedding, and that her fiancé has borrowed his late wife's wedding ring for the ceremony, the cost of the special licence having taken all his spare pocket money. *Buoyant Billions*

BURGE, JOYCE: A politician (in the 1920s) who was Prime Minister under a Coalition, and is now one of the half-dozen leaders of the Liberal Opposition. He visits Franklyn Barnabas, and his brother Conrad, hoping to enlist their support in the forthcoming election, but is rather taken aback by their advanced ideas, particularly their belief—'the gospel of the Brothers Barnabas'—that Creative Evolution is about to produce men and women who will live for 300 years. For a moment Burge thinks he can make political capital out of the idea, but when he realises that there is no elixir of life, or other formula for longevity, but that it depends on what Franklyn calls 'the tremendous miracle-working force of Will nerved to creation by a conviction of Necessity', he is not so sure. However, he decides to make it a stunt in his election programme, and promises Franklyn an O.M. if the Liberals get in. *Back to Methuselah, Part II: The Gospel of the Brothers Barnabas*

BURGE-LUBIN: The President of the British Islands in the year A.D. 2170. 'A stoutish middle-aged man, good-looking and breezily genial, dressed in a silk smock, stockings, handsomely ornamented sandals, and a gold fillet round his brows. He is like Joyce Burge, yet also like Lubin, as if Nature had made a composite photograph of the two men.' He is the nominal head of a country ruled by 'educated negresses and Chinese', and spends most of his time playing marine golf. When his Accountant-General, Barnabas, discovers from some old films that Archbishop Haslam, Archbishop Stickit, President Dickenson, General Bullyboy and the present Archbishop of York are all the same person, now aged 283, and that the Domestic Minister, Mrs. Lutestring, is only nine years younger, he is at first incredulous, and then inclined to believe that he too may be one of those destined to live for 300 years. He therefore refuses the invitation of the negress Minister of Health to join her on a cruise, although he is madly in love with her, because it means dropping by parachute into the sea, and this may give him rheumatism for the rest of his life. *Back to Methuselah, Part III: The Thing Happens*

BURGESS, MR.: The father of Candida Morell, a man of sixty, 'vulgar, ignorant, guzzling', offensive to his inferiors, respectful only to wealth and rank. Living on the proceeds of sweated labour, he thinks his commercial success is entirely due to his business acumen, and considers himself an easygoing, affectionate creature. But though outwardly sentimental, he is inwardly as hard as nails. Physically he is podgy, with a snoutish nose in a flat round face, a dust-coloured beard and small watery blue eyes—a most unexpected father for the wise and beautiful Candida. He despises his son-in-law, the Rev. James Morell, but after one of his lectures gives a small supper-party for the chairman (who, he thinks, may be useful to him in some of his business concerns) at which Morell's secretary, Proserpina Garnett, gets slightly tipsy. *Candida*

BURGLAR: *see* Bagot, The Hon. Aubrey; Dunn, Billy

BURGOYNE, GENERAL JOHN: Officer in charge of English and German troops in America during the War of Independence. Usually known as Gentlemanly Johnny, he is 'fifty-five, very well preserved, a man of fashion', gallant, an aristocrat, and a wit. He comes to Websterbridge just as Richard Dudgeon is about to be hanged in mistake for the Rev. Anderson, and is very much against it, saying that it only makes 'a martyr out of a rebel'. During the trial he learns that the neighbouring town of Springtown has been captured by the Americans, and that his own reinforcements have failed to arrive. He therefore signs a safe-conduct for the rebel leader, who turns out to be Anderson, now a captain in the militia, releases Richard, and agrees to evacuate Websterbridge. *The Devil's Disciple*

BYRON, CASHEL: A prizefighter, known as the Australian Challenger, who has fallen in love with the wealthy Lydia Carew, and she with him. He dare not tell her who he is, and when her footman Bashville, who is also in love with her, betrays his secret, he says there is worse to come: his mother, Adelaide Gisborne, is an actress. In spite of this Lydia is willing to marry him if he will give up his profession, but he refuses. He then goes to the Agricultural Hall, Islington, to fight Paradise in the presence of Cetewayo, who with his Zulu followers gets over-excited and joins in the fight. In the mêlée which ensues Cashel rescues Lydia single-handed and quells the Zulus. A second fight with Paradise is arranged in Lydia's own village of Wiltstoken, but, being illegal, is broken up by the police, who pursue Cashel into Lydia's castle, where she hides him in her own room. On hearing the voice of his mother, who has been brought to see the fight by Lord Worthington, Cashel emerges and gives himself up, preferring prison to life with mother. An incautious reference to himself as 'baseborn' causes her to reveal that he is the son of Bingley Bumpkin FitzAlgernon de Courcy Cashel Byron: whereupon the Queen pardons him, makes him deputy lieutenant of Dorset, and commands him to marry Lydia. *The Admirable Bashville*

BYRON'S NOVICE: *see* Bashville

BYSTANDERS: Several Cockneys who are present when Eliza Doolittle first meets Professor Higgins under the portico of St. Paul's, Covent Garden. One of them reassures her that Higgins's boots are those of a gentleman, not a copper's nark. Another, sarcastic, bystander dares Higgins to say where he comes from, and is amazed to be told correctly. In revenge he makes fun of Higgins's pronunciation; they all leave when the rain stops. *Pygmalion*

C

CADI OF KINTALI: *see* Muley Othman

CAESAR: Emperor of Rome when Androcles and his fellow-Christians are brought to the Colosseum to die. He offers Ferrovius a place in his Praetorian Guard, and when he refuses, says the Christians are to be given arms to fight against the gladiators. When the latter, intimidated by Ferrovius, are slow to attack, he sends for the Whip to drive them on, but when Ferrovius suddenly goes berserk and kills six men, he is delighted, and again offers him a place in his guard, which this time he accepts. Androcles, who has been put with the women for refusing to fight, finds that the lion who has come to eat him up is an old friend, and he persuades Caesar, not without difficulty, to come down from his box and pet him. Caesar then offers Androcles as a slave to 'the first man who lays hands on him', but as no one dares approach the lion, who stays beside him, Caesar lets them go off peaceably together. *Androcles and the Lion*

CAESAR, JULIUS: Marching through Syria, he finds Cleopatra hiding from the Roman soldiers. Having taken her back to her palace, and forced her to don her royal robes and receive him 'like a queen', he takes her on to Alexandria, hoping to arrange for her to rule jointly with her brother Ptolemy. Although he is not in love with her, he is quite willing to amuse her in his spare time, and to turn her into 'a woman with a Roman heart'. But his main object is to conquer Egypt, and having with difficulty captured the harbour and the lighthouse, from which he was forced to escape by swimming with Cleopatra on his back to the nearest Roman ship, he forgives Lucius Septimius the murder of Pompey, and joins with him to defeat the Egyptian army under Achillas, taking with him his chief officer Rufio and his secretary Britannus. On his return he decides to go back to Rome, but is delayed by Cleopatra, who comes to demand vengeance on Rufio for the murder of Ftatateeta, her head nurse. When Caesar learns that Ftatateeta had, on Cleopatra's orders, killed Pothinus, the governor of Ptolemy, because he tried to betray the queen to Caesar, he says Rufio was justified, makes him governor of Egypt, and consoles Cleopatra for his departure by promising to send her Mark Anthony, whom she fell in love with when she was twelve. *Caesar and Cleopatra*

CAIN: The firstborn son of Adam and Eve, who has murdered his brother Abel. He comes to the oasis in Mesopotamia where his parents are living centuries after they have left the Garden of Eden, and mocks his father, who is still nothing more than a hard-working farmer, while he, Cain, is a fighter and 'the master of woman, not her baby and her drudge'. But Eve reminds him that he is the slave of his sister-wife Lua, who can always bring him grovelling at her feet through his desire for her. Cain is proud of having invented fighting, and of his skill in living 'by the chase, by the killing, and by the fire'. He envisages a world full of men, with himself leading one half against the other half led by his dearest enemy. Eve says if he had the trouble of bearing children, he would not talk so glibly of murdering them. But Cain asks 'Who invented death?' and they cannot argue with him any more. *Back to Methuselah, Part I: In the Beginning*

In the summer of A.D. 31,920 the ghost of Cain returns to

earth to find that his invention of killing and conquest is outmoded, and there is no longer any place for him. But, he says, it was a splendid game while it lasted. *Back to Methuselah, Part V: As Far as Thought Can Reach*

CALL BOY: A youngster employed behind the scenes at the Colosseum in Rome. It is his duty to announce each item and see that the performers are ready to go into the arena. With three attendants he brings arms and armour for the Christian men who are to fight the gladiators; he is sent by Caesar to fetch the Whip when the gladiators are slow in attacking Ferrovius; he calls for ropes and hooks and a basket to remove the bodies of those Ferrovius eventually slays; and when Androcles is chosen to go into the arena after his fellow-Christians have been pardoned, he announces: 'Number twelve, the Christian for the new lion'. *Androcles and the Lion*

CANDIDA (CANDY): *see* Morell, Candida

CANON OF BAYEUX: *see* Estivet, Brother John d'

CANON OF PARIS: *see* Courcelles, de

CAPTAIN: A Roman officer, in charge of the men who are escorting a group of Christian prisoners to Rome. He falls in love with one of them, Lavinia, and asks her to marry him instead of dying in the arena, but she refuses. He says Christians are 'the proudest devils on earth'. He is on duty in the royal box when the Christians are brought to the Colosseum, and obtains a special pardon for Lavinia after Ferrovius has killed six gladiators, putting Caesar in a generous mood. Lavinia still will not give him a definite answer, but says 'yes' when he asks if he may visit and argue with her sometimes. *Androcles and the Lion*

See also Shotover, Captain

CARDONIUS: *see* Boshington, Sir Cardonius

CAREW, LYDIA: A wealthy young woman, owner of

Wiltstoken Park. Lonely and bored, she is walking in the park when she meets 'a sylvan god', Cashel Byron, and falls in love with him. He disappears before she can find out anything about him. Back in London, she is distressed to discover from her footman, Bashville, that Cashel is a prizefighter. When he comes to see her, she offers him £30,000 a week pocket money if he will give up his profession and marry her, but he refuses. She goes to watch him fight Paradise, and in the mêlée which ensues is thrilled to be rescued by him. But back in Wiltstoken she finds he is coming to the village to fight Paradise again, in spite of his promise to leave the ring. Nevertheless, when the police break up the fight and Cashel takes refuge in her castle, she hides him in her own room. Her cousin Lucian Webber then arrives, bringing the Queen's pardon for Cashel, and, in recognition of his noble birth, bestowing on him 'by an exercise of feudal right/Too long disused in this anarchic age' the hand of 'the wealthy heiress Miss Carew'. *The Admirable Bashville*

CARWELL, MADAM: *see* Portsmouth, Duchess of

CASHEL: *see* Byron, Cashel

CATHERINE: *see* Petkoff, Catherine

CATHERINE II: Empress of Russia, 1762–96. In 1776 she asks for some firsthand information about the American Revolution, and is sent as emissary a young Englishman, Captain Edstaston, who has been fighting against the rebels. He is brought to her bedroom by Prince Patiomkin, who impatiently carries him in when he protests that he is not properly dressed to meet the Empress. This amuses her, and as she also finds him attractive she intimates that she would not object to making him her next favourite. To her annoyance, he escapes from the palace; so she has him arrested and brought back, trussed to a pole. She then takes her revenge by tickling him spasmodically while reading a pamphlet by Voltaire, until his screams of laughter bring his fiancée Claire from the palace ballroom to rescue him. After a sudden spurt of jealousy from Claire, the two women discuss Edstaston until the news that the model of her new museum has come diverts the Empress's attention, and she allows the young couple to depart, summing up the situation by saying that she would have liked the young man not as a lover but as an exhibit for her museum. *Great Catherine*

CATHERINE OF BRAGANZA: The wife of Charles II. She finds him asleep on the sofa in her sitting-room, tidies away the clothes he has strewn about, and wakes him so that he will not be late for his Council meeting. She is upset because he talks of dying and tells her she must go back to her brother in Spain when he does, before the Protestants kill her. She knows she ought to allow herself to be divorced so that he can marry a Protestant who will give him an heir, but she loves him too much. She wishes she could rule England as her mother ruled Portugal, but Charles tells her that the English have an instinctive hatred of government, which she, being a fervent Catholic, interprets as a hatred of the true Church. Then she helps him on with his coat and wig, and sends him away, turning back to her prie-dieu to pray fervently for his salvation. *In Good King Charles's Golden Days*

CAUCHON, PETER: Bishop of Beauvais at the time of the trial of Joan of Arc. He acts as one of the judges, together with the Dominican, Brother John Lemaître, deputising for the Chief Inquisitor, and very reluctantly pronounces sentence of excommunication on her, after doing his best to get her to recant. In the Epilogue he complains that the rehabilitation of Joan has meant his own dishonouring, his dead body dug up and thrown into the common sewer, his name standing for the triumph of evil over good. Yet he protests that he was faithful and just, and could do no other than he did. *Saint Joan*

CECIL: *see* Sykes, Cecil

CENTURION: In charge of the soldiers guarding the Christian prisoners on their way to Rome. He carries a vinewood cudgel, and marches with the escort. He is horrified by Lavinia, who dares to argue with the Captain, and says of the prisoners that 'they are always laughing and joking something scandalous. They've no religion, that's what it is.' *Androcles and the Lion*

An officer in the army of Julius Caesar in Egypt. 'An unattractive man of fifty, short in his speech and manners, with a vinewood cudgel in his hand', he commands the troops who capture the palace in Alexandria, embarks the men for the assault on the lighthouse, gives the alarm when the Egyptians counter-attack, twice rescues a sentinel from the brutal attacks of Ftatateeta, and is present with his men when Caesar leaves for Rome. *Caesar and Cleopatra*

CETEWAYO: The Zulu chief, on a visit to London, is taken with his followers to see Cashel Byron fight William Paradise. Excited by Paradise's insistence on fighting with bare fists, Cetewayo plunges into the fight, and causes a riot; he gets the worst of it, being hit over the head with an umbrella by Lucian Webber and knocked down by Cashel, saying, as he rises from the floor: 'Have I been struck by lightning?' *The Admirable Bashville*

CHAMBERMAID: *see* Tinwell, Minnie

CHAPLAIN: *see* Brudenell, Rev. Mr.; Stogumber, John de

CHARLES: *see* Edstaston, Captain; Farwaters, Sir Charles; Lomax, Charles

CHARLES II: King of England, 1660–85. Five years before his death he goes incognito, as Mr. Rowley, to the house in Cambridge of Isaac Newton the philosopher, hoping to see his new telescope. There he meets Charles Fox the Quaker, and is joined by three of his mistresses, Nell Gwynn, the Duchess of Cleveland, and the Duchess of Portsmouth, and by his brother, James, Duke of York, who has returned unexpectedly from Holland. They all argue, quarrel, and drive Newton distracted with their demands on his time and energy, until they are summoned to a meal by Newton's housekeeper, Mrs. Basham, together with Geoffrey Kneller, who agrees to paint Newton's portrait. After lunch, Charles retires to his wife's boudoir for his siesta, because it is the only place where the women cannot follow him. He tells her that he is tired of all his mistresses, except Nelly, who amuses him, but that he keeps them because they are useful politically. He foresees the troubles that will fall on England after his death, and advises her to go back to Portugal. Then, refreshed and invigorated by his nap, he puts on his boots, hat, wig and coat, and goes off to a Council meeting. *In Good King Charles's Golden Days*

CHARLES VII: Third son of the mad king, Charles VI of France. He succeeded his father in 1422, but because of the Treaty of Troyes, which recognised Henry VI of England as King of France, and also because of the presence of English troops, he has not yet been crowned when Joan of Arc comes to persuade him to give her command of the army, and is therefore still addressed as the Dauphin. A poor creature physically, with small, close-set eyes, a long pendulous nose, and the expression of a young dog accustomed to be kicked, he is nevertheless not stupid, but has a rooted objection to any form of activity. After Joan has defeated the British and cleared the way for his coronation at Rheims, he shows no gratitude, and is only anxious that she should go home and leave him to make treaties instead of war, and when she has finally been betrayed to the English and condemned to be burnt at the stake as a heretic, he makes no effort to save her. Twenty-five years later he learns that she has been rehabilitated, and is pleased at the news only because it clears him of the imputation of owing his crown to a witch and a heretic. *Saint Joan*

48

CHARMIAN: One of Cleopatra's favourite slave-girls, 'a hatchet-faced, terracotta-coloured little goblin, swift in her movements and neatly finished at the hands and feet'. She arouses Cleopatra's anger when she calls Caesar 'old hook-nose', and longs for his departure, because he is making the queen 'prosy and serious and learned and philosophical'. It is 'worse than being religious, at our age'. *Caesar and Cleopatra*

CHARTERIS, LEONARD: A gentleman in his late thirties, first seen 'unconventionally but smartly dressed in a velvet jacket and cashmere trousers', blue shirt, blue socks, and leather sandals. 'The arrangement of his tawny hair, and of his moustache and short beard, is apparently left to Nature: but he has taken care that Nature shall do him the fullest justice.' A self-confessed philanderer—'I could love anybody: any pretty woman, that is'—he is a member of the newly-formed Ibsen Club in London, and approves of the concept of the 'New Woman', since it affords him plenty of scope for his philandering. Tiring of his free association with a fellow-member of the Club, Julia Craven, he tries to escape by proposing to marry a young widow, Grace Tranfield. But Julia refuses to give him up. In despair, Charteris encourages a young physician, Dr. Paramore, to propose to Julia, only to find, when they have got engaged, that Grace still will not marry him. Whereupon Charteris, who has shocked both Julia's father, Colonel Craven, and Grace's father, Mr. Cuthbertson, by his behaviour, announces that 'the doom of the philanderer' has come upon him. 'I shall have to go on philandering now all my life.' *The Philanderer*

CHAVENDER, SIR ARTHUR: Prime Minister, an engaging personality who considers himself grossly overworked, but does not doubt his own ability to deal with the situation. He is worried about the increasing rowdyism of street demonstrations by the unemployed, and wants the Chief Commissioner of Police, Sir Broadfoot Basham, to use stern methods. But Basham says the best thing is to keep them occupied with speeches. Chavender then receives a deputation on the subject of unemployment from the Isle of Cats, but with no result, except that one man, Mr. Hipney, advises him to read Karl Marx. This he does, with the result that he makes a fiery socialistic speech which horrifies his Foreign Secretary, Sir Dexter Rightside, but delights most of the others, who stand to gain from his suggested reforms. However, when Rightside threatens to resign, he carries the rest with him, rather reluctantly, and after another visit from the Isle of Cats deputation, who come to protest against the conscription of labour and the outlawing of strikes, Chavender decides to give up politics. He has discovered that the country needs a revolution, but he is not the man to lead one. So, as two members of the Isle of Cats deputation, Viscount Barking and Aloysia Brollikins, have decided to marry his daughter Flavia and his son David, he and his wife are free to live in a cottage on the golf links. *On the Rocks*

CHAVENDER, DAVID: Son of the Prime Minister, Sir Arthur Chavender. He has for some time been determined to marry a factory girl, but when Alderwoman Aloysia Brollikins, known as Brolly, falls in love with him, he resists her until she flares up and tells him everything is over between them, whereupon he immediately wants her and rushes out to fetch her back. *On the Rocks*

CHAVENDER, FLAVIA: Daughter of the Prime Minister, Sir Arthur Chavender. She and her brother David go with two members of the Isle of Cats delegation to a meeting of the unemployed, and invite their companions, Aloysia Brollikins and Viscount Barking, back to lunch. Flavia, who has sworn to marry a poor man, relents and allows herself to get engaged to Barking, because, being a socialist, he has assumed the rough manners, violence, brutality and filthy language which she thinks is characteristic of the working-man. *On the Rocks*

CHAVENDER, LADY: The wife of the Prime Minister, Sir Arthur Chavender. She is having a very difficult time with her children, Flavia, aged nineteen, and David, aged eighteen, and is really rather relieved when they get engaged, the girl to the socialist Viscount Barking, the boy to the trades union secretary Aloysia Brollikins. Though fond of her husband, she takes no interest in politics, and thinks he wears himself out doing nothing. To counteract this, she persuades him to see a lady doctor who has a sanatorium in Wales where he can go for a six weeks' rest. *On the Rocks*

CHELSEA, BISHOP OF: *see* Bridgenorth, Alfred

CHICKABIDDY: *see* Tarleton, Mrs.

CHINESE PRIEST: He officiates in a room in Belgrave Square which has been converted into a Chinese temple on a domestic scale, so that Old Bill Buoyant, the millionaire, can come every day and sit through an act of worship which he does not understand, but which refreshes his soul. When the family solicitor comes to talk to Buoyant's children about their father's intentions, he is made to conduct his interview in the Chinese room, in spite of his objections, and it is there that Old Buoyant greets his daughter Clementina when she returns from Panama. Talking to the priest, Bill says: 'I am repeating myself, and boring you'; but the priest replies: 'I repeat the service every day; yet it does not bore me. There is always something new in it. They tell me it is the same with your orchestral symphonies.' *Buoyant Billions*

CHINESE VOICE: An unseen operator on the television-telephone who announces to the President of the British Islands, Burge-Lubin, the arrival of his Chief Secretary, Confucius. *Back to Methuselah, Part III: The Thing Happens*

CHLOE: One of the Maidens dancing in a grove in the year A.D. 31,920. She is older than the others, and already beginning to turn away from childish pleasures towards those of pure intellect, much to the distress of her companion Strephon. When he tries to make love to her she repulses him, and says she wants to get away by herself to consider the properties of numbers. She has thousands of years to live, and cannot spend them eating and drinking, sleeping and listening to music. She then goes alone into the wood, to become eventually one of the Ancients. *Back to Methuselah, Part V: As Far as Thought Can Reach*

CHOLLY: *see* Lomax, Charles

CHRISTIAN PRISONERS: A group of both sexes and all ages, headed by the patrician Lavinia. On their way to die in the Colosseum at Rome they shock the Centurion in charge of them by their levity, singing hymns and keeping up their courage with laughter and jokes. Once in Rome they are joined by Androcles, Ferrovius, and Spintho. At the Colosseum the men are given arms and armour to defend themselves in single combat against the gladiators, and only the women are to be thrown to the lions. But after Ferrovius has lost his temper and hacked six gladiators to pieces, Caesar, thrilled by his exploit, pardons all the Christians except Androcles, who is sent into the arena to meet the lion so that the populace shall not be cheated of its entertainment. *Androcles and the Lion*

CHRISTY: *see* Dudgeon, Christopher

CLAIRE: The fiancée of Captain Edstaston, who tells her that they must leave St. Petersburg at once because the Empress has fallen in love with him. Before they can move, however, he is overpowered and taken to the palace, where Claire, who is attending a court ball, hears him screaming. Thinking that he is being tortured, she rushes to rescue him, but when Catherine tells her that he is only being tickled, and seems to be enjoying it, she is overcome with jealousy. However, she helps Catherine to undo the straps with which he is trussed up, and is persuaded to forgive him. The

Russians are very amused when he gives her one chaste kiss, and Catherine, losing interest in them both, hustles them away so that she can go and see the model of her new museum. *Great Catherine*

CLANDON, DOLLY: The twin sister of Philip Clandon, a spoilt, lively, high-spirited, unconventional, and impertinent youngster of seventeen, who has been brought up in Madeira by her mother, the celebrated authoress Mrs. Lanfrey Clandon, the estranged wife of Fergus Crampton. On a visit to England Dolly meets and captivates her father, who wishes to obtain custody of her. She is, however, far more interested in getting married, and in flirting with her mother's solicitor, Finch M'Comas. *You Never Can Tell*

CLANDON, GLORIA: The elder daughter of Mrs. Clandon, a 'celebrated authoress' of books on women's rights, who is separated from her husband, Fergus Crampton. Gloria is a firm believer in her mother's ideas, and 'the incarnation of haughty highhandedness', but she is also passionate by nature, and the 'conflict of her passion with her obstinate pride . . . results in a freezing coldness of manner'. On a visit to England she meets her father, but refuses to acknowledge his authority, and is, incidentally, furious to learn that she was christened Sophronia after his sister. She also rebuffs the young dentist Valentine when he makes love to her. But after he has kissed her she capitulates, and when he seems reluctant to pursue the matter further, it is she who insists on announcing their engagement. *You Never Can Tell*

CLANDON, MRS. LANFREY: A 'celebrated authoress of great repute in Madeira', where she has lived for eighteen years after separating from her husband, Fergus Crampton. A great believer in women's rights, she has educated her daughter Gloria according to her own 'advanced ideas', but has been less successful with the twins Dolly and Philip.

53

Bringing them to England to meet their father, she encounters him unexpectedly at a luncheon party, and it is evident that no reconciliation is possible. *You Never Can Tell*

CLANDON, PHILIP: The seventeen-year-old son of Mrs. Clandon and her estranged husband Fergus Crampton. Like his twin sister Dolly, he is high-spirited, impertinent, and unconventional, but 'with perfect manners and a finished personal style which might be envied by a man twice his age'. He is fond of referring to his 'knowledge of human nature', and when he eventually meets his father he is the only member of the family to treat him light-heartedly and with a certain compassion. *You Never Can Tell*

CLARA: *see* Eynsford-Hill, Clara

CLEMENTINA (CLEMMY): *see* Buoyant, Clementina

CLEOPATRA: The sixteen-year-old ruler of Egypt, under Roman occupation, jointly with her brother Ptolemy. Driven by him into exile in Syria, she takes refuge from the advancing Romans in the arms of a small sphinx, where she is found by Julius Caesar. He exhorts her to behave like a queen, and takes her to Alexandria, leaving her virtually a prisoner in the palace while he prepares to capture the citadel and the lighthouse. She escapes and joins him at the lighthouse, however, by hiding in a carpet which Apollodorus is taking as a present to Caesar, and when the party is cut off by a band of Egyptian soldiers she is thrown into the sea by Rufio and borne on Caesar's back to the nearest ship. Back in the palace, she is visited by her brother's general Pothinus, who hopes to involve her in a plot against Caesar, but fails, and so accuses her of treachery to Caesar. In revenge she causes him to be murdered by her head nurse, Ftatateeta. When Caesar announces his return to Rome, Cleopatra comes to the quayside in mourning for Ftatateeta, who has been killed by Rufio, now governor of Egypt, and demands justice. Caesar replies that Rufio was justified in what he did, and Cleopatra is consoled by his promise to send Mark Anthony to her as soon as possible. She knows quite well that he does not love her, and never has, but he has made a queen and a woman of her, and she is now ready for Anthony, whom she saw and fell in love with when she was a child of twelve. *Caesar and Cleopatra*

CLEOPATRA-SEMIRAMIS: A synthetic human being, modelled by the sculptor Martellus from material made by Pygmalion in his laboratory. Like her companion Ozymandias, she works only by reflex action. Music makes her dance, a question provokes an answer, a threat of violence from Ozymandias causes her to pick up a stone with which to kill him. When Pygmalion tries to restrain her, she bites him, and he falls dead. When the Ancients accuse her, she lies and says it was the man who did it; and when they touch her she dies of discouragement and is taken away and incinerated. *Back to Methuselah, Part V: As Far as Thought Can Reach*

CLERGYMAN: *see* Hammingtap, Phosphor

CLERICAL GENTLEMAN: *see* Barnabas, Franklyn

CLERK: *see* Beamish, Horatio Floyd; Wilks

CLEVELAND, DUCHESS OF: Barbara, a mistress of Charles II. When she hears that Nell Gwynn has gone to fetch him from Isaac Newton's house, she follows and forces her way in, making such a scene that the King threatens to throw her downstairs. She also tears up a drawing of her done by the Dutch painter Kneller because it makes her look old, and insists, as the senior duchess present, on being taken in to dinner by Charles. *In Good King Charles's Golden Days*.

COCKY, COCKYOLLY BIRD: *see* Raphael

COKANE, WILLIAM DE BURGH: 'an ill-nourished, scanty-haired gentleman, with affected manners, fidgety, touchy, and constitutionally ridiculous in uncompassionate eyes'.

Aged between forty and fifty, he is a friend of Dr. Harry Trench, helping him over his engagement to Blanche Sartorius. He also persuades Trench to accept the offer of an allowance from his father-in-law, and to agree to the nefarious scheme put forward by Lickcheese for obtaining compensation for the slum property from which Trench's income is derived. He also stands to gain from the scheme. Trench usually addresses him as Billy. *Widowers' Houses*

COLLINS, BILL (WILLIAM): An elderly greengrocer, friend of Alice Bridgenorth, the wife of the Bishop of Chelsea. He has helped her arrange the wedding receptions of five daughters, and is now busy with the preparations for the wedding of the sixth, Edith. Having just been named an alderman, he arrives in his robes, at the request of General Bridgenorth, in time to join in the argument over the wedding. Both bride and bridegroom wish to call it off, having discovered some of the disadvantages of the married state. Collins points out that marriage doesn't bear thinking of; you must do it first and think (and argue) about it afterwards. He then agrees to help in the drawing up of a civil contract which will satisfy both parties and replace the religious ceremony, but insists that they must ask the advice of his remarkable sister-in-law, Mrs. George Collins, which they are very ready to do, as they always thought she did not really exist, but was a figment of his imagination. Even with her help, however, it proves impossible to evolve anything satisfactory, so Edith and her fiancé Cecil Sykes slip away to the empty church and get married in the normal way, while Collins rounds up the bridesmaids and the dispersed guests and brings them in taxis to the belated wedding reception. *Getting Married*

COLLINS, MRS. GEORGE (ZENOBIA ALEXANDRINA): The sister-in-law of Bill Collins, 'a fine figure of a woman but so susceptible that she constantly left her husband for other men, only to find they did not want her, and so came back home'. Her brother-in-law finds that her experiences have made her 'wonderful interesting' and he often asks her advice. She is also a clairvoyant. When Edith Bridgenorth decides on her wedding morning not to get married after all, and there is question of drawing up a civil contract to take the place of the ceremony, the Bridgenorth family, who have always regarded the fabulous Mrs. George as a figment of Bill Collins's imagination, agree to call her in and ask her advice. As she is Mayoress of the borough, she arrives in state, preceded by the Beadle. She indulges in a number of antics, which include going into a trance, and though she is unable to do anything for Edith, who goes off with her fiancé and gets married in the usual way, she does succeed in detaching Hotchkiss, whom she allows to call her Polly, from the divorced wife of Reginald Bridgenorth by making him fall in love with her. She also reveals that she is the Incognita Appassionata who has been writing love-letters to the Bishop of Chelsea, Alfred Bridgenorth, arranging to meet him in heaven, then goes off to the belated wedding reception, again preceded by the Beadle. *Getting Married*

COLENSO (COLLY): *see* Ridgeon, Sir Colenso

COMMANDER-IN-CHIEF: *see* Ulsterbridge, Lord

COMMISSAR: *see* Posky

COMMISSIONER: On the staff of the Institute of Diet Commissioners on the Isle of Wight. He is dictating a chapter for a new edition of his book on human diet, which deals with 'living on air'. It is to be printed in an edition of two hundred million copies for use in infant schools. *Far-Fetched Fables 4*

CONFUCIUS: Chief Secretary of the British Islands, which in A.D. 2170 are governed by a permanent Civil Service composed of Chinese, with an elected House of Commons of English lunatics holding nominal authority under their President, Burge-Lubin. Confucius despises the British, who in his opinion are barbarians, capable of nothing but sport, and also dislikes the educated negresses who have been imported to hold such posts as Minister of Health. 'For me a woman who is not yellow does not exist, save as an official.' He is not surprised when Haslam and Mrs. Lutestring turn out to be products of Creative Evolution capable of living to 300 years, and when Barnabas calls Haslam a thief for having continued to draw public money long after he ought to be dead, Confucius points out that, on the contrary, the country is in his debt, having had 260 years' work from him for the cost of one education and no superannuation. When Barnabas tries to prevent the marriage of the two long-livers, and even suggests killing them, Confucius says it would be useless, as there may be many more of them about, even, he suggests, in the present company—a supposition which infuriates Barnabas, and impresses Burge-Lubin, who thinks he may be one of them, and so declines to take risks. *Back to Methuselah, Part III: The Thing Happens*

CONRAD: *see* Barnabas, Conrad

CONSTABLES AND OTHERS: Inhabitants of Wiltstoken, who follow Cashel Byron to the castle of Lydia Carew when he is escaping from the police after his prizefight with William Paradise. *The Admirable Bashville*

COOK: At the Marine Hotel, Torbay. In white cap and apron, he helps to bring in the dishes for the luncheon at which Mrs. Clandon unexpectedly meets her husband again after a separation of eighteen years. He carves, but does not serve, and has nothing to say. *You Never Can Tell*

CORINTHIA: *see* Fanshawe, Lady Corinthia

CORNELIUS (CORNEY): *see* Doyle, Cornelius

COSSACK SERGEANT: A soldier on duty outside the bureau of Prince Patiomkin in the Winter Palace at St. Petersburg. He cautiously introduces Captain Edstaston into the room, and is kicked downstairs for his pains. He also comes in when Varinka calls for help after her uncle has been knocked down by the Captain, and is sent to fetch a gold goblet full of jewels with which Patiomkin hopes to bribe the Englishman. After Edstaston has escaped from the palace the Cossack Sergeant takes a squad of soldiers to arrest him, and receives the prisoner's knee in his epigastrium, thus, he says, wrecking his sweetbread for ever. He also receives two roubles from Edstaston's fianceé, Claire, for helping her to get into the palace. *Great Catherine*

COUNT: *see* Ferruccio, Count

COURCELLES, DE: Canon of Paris at the time of the trial of Joan of Arc, where he acts as one of the leaders of the assessors. He is angry because the sixty-four accusations of heresy which he has drawn up against Joan have been reduced to twelve, and particularly annoyed that the stealing of the Bishop of Senlis's horse has been omitted. In fact, he refers to it again during the trial, and calls down on his head the wrath of the Bishop of Beauvais, who points out that they are trying a case of heresy, not petty theft. With the other assessors he rushes out into the courtyard to see Joan burnt, but unlike his fellow-Dominican, de Stogumber, he feels no remorse afterwards. *Saint Joan*

COURT LADY: Attendant on the English Queen, Philippa of Hainault, when she joins her husband Edward III outside the walls of Calais. She announces the imminent arrival of the Queen to her husband and sons and then withdraws and is not heard of again. *The Six of Calais*

COURTIERS: Attendants on the Roman emperor when he goes to the Colosseum to watch the gladiatorial games and see the Christians thrown to the lions. When Androcles has tamed his lion, who is an old friend, Caesar calls the terrified courtiers to witness his bravery, standing with his foot on the body of the recumbent beast. *Androcles and the Lion*

Attendants on Ptolemy, Pharaoh of Egypt, when Julius Caesar comes to the palace in Alexandria. The bolder of them attempt to riot when they think they have Caesar in their power, but they are ignominiously hustled out of the throne-room by the Roman soldiers who have in the meantime captured the palace. *Caesar and Cleopatra*

Attendants on Catherine II of Russia. They are attending her *petit lever* when Patiomkin carries Captain Edstaston, kicking and swearing, into her bedroom. *Great Catherine*

Attendants on the Dauphin (later Charles VII) when Joan of Arc first comes to see him at Chinon. They are amused when Gilles de Rais pretends to be the Dauphin, in order to test Joan, and roar with laughter when she discovers the true king skulking in the background. They are also immensely diverted by Joan's odd appearance, the ladies-in-waiting laughing heartily at her rough soldier suit and short bobbed hair. *Saint Joan*

CRAMPTON, FERGUS: 'a man of about sixty, with an atrociously obstinate ill-tempered grasping mouth, and a dogmatic voice'. He is the husband of Mrs. Clandon, who obtained a deed of separation from him after three years of marriage on the grounds of cruelty, and his three children, Gloria, Dolly, and Philip, have been brought up by her in Madeira in ignorance of his identity. He meets them unexpectedly at a luncheon party to which he has been taken by a young dentist, Valentine, who has rooms in his house. Furious at what he thinks is a plot hatched by Mrs. Clandon, Valentine, and the solicitor Finch M'Comas, he quarrels with them all, but is secretly captivated by his daughter Dolly, and wishes to obtain custody of her and her brother. He is dissuaded by the Q.C. Walter Bohun, who points out that they will both be of age before the matter can be decided, and that in any case the girl will soon be married. *You Never Can Tell*

CRAMPTON, MARGARET: *see* Clandon, Mrs. Lanfrey

CRASSUS: Colonial Secretary, and a member of Proteus's Cabinet. Elderly and anxious, he is annoyed because his brother-in-law Mike, Chairman of Breakages Ltd., has been kept out of the Cabinet by King Magnus, and very angry when accused of being a jobber because one of his relatives has received a government contract. When King Magnus says he intends to resign, he points out that a king cannot do so, thus provoking Magnus to say he will abdicate. After the decisive meeting he takes all the Cabinet, except Lysistrata, who refuses his invitation, to lunch at the Ritz, on Breakages Ltd.'s expense account. He says he will not mind leaving politics. Breakages Ltd. put him in, and if he goes out will find him another job. *The Apple Cart*

CRAVEN, COLONEL DANIEL, V.C.: The father of Julia and Sylvia Craven. He has been told by his physician, Dr. Paramore, who is in love with Julia, that he is dying from the new 'Paramore's Disease', a fatal infection of the liver, and is naturally overjoyed when an article in *The British Medical Journal* proves that no such disease exists. A 'bluff simple veteran', who won his V.C. in the Sudan, and whose face is lined 'with weather, with age, with eating and smiling, and with the cumulative effect of many petty vexations, but not with thought', he tries hard to sympathise with the modern ideas of his daughters, but is shocked by Julia's free association with the philanderer Leonard Charteris, and delighted when she gets engaged to Paramore. *The Philanderer*

CRAVEN, JULIA: The elder daughter of Colonel Craven. 'A beautiful, dark tragic-looking young woman,' she is selfish and spoilt, and constantly dramatising herself. With her sister Sylvia she is a member of the newly-formed Ibsen Club in London, and prides herself on being a 'New Woman'. But in spite of her advanced views, which have led her into a free association with the philanderer Leonard Charteris, she refuses to give him up when he wants to

61

marry Grace Tranfield, and harasses him with letters and scenes of violent jealousy. Her father's physician, Dr. Paramore, is also in love with her, but she takes no interest in him until her possessive instinct is aroused by seeing him apparently flirting with Grace. In a fit of jealousy, realising that Charteris will never marry her, and that Grace has refused to marry Charteris, she agrees to become engaged to Paramore. *The Philanderer*

CRAVEN, SYLVIA: The younger sister of Julia Craven, who usually calls her Silly, and with her a member of the Ibsen Club in London, founded for 'unwomanly women and unmanly men'. 'A pretty girl of eighteen, small and trim', she is first seen at the club, where she insists on being addressed as Craven, in a 'mountaineering suit of Norfolk jacket and breeches with neat town stockings and shoes'. Beside her is a 'detachable cloth skirt' which she buttons on before going to lunch. Intensely conscious of her pioneer role as a 'New Woman', she despises her sister, and helps the philanderer Leonard Charteris to escape from her clutches by furthering Julia's engagement to Dr. Paramore. *The Philanderer*

CROFTS, SIR GEORGE: Owner, with Kitty Warren, of a chain of brothels in Europe, which bring him in a good income. 'A tall powerfully-built man of about fifty,' he is a 'gentlemanly combination of the most brutal types of city man, sporting man, and man about town'. He comes with Mrs. Warren to the cottage where her 22-year-old daughter Vivie is staying after leaving Cambridge, and is attracted by her, in spite of her obvious distaste for his presence. When she contemptuously turns down his offer of marriage, he revenges himself by telling her that her mother's business is not, as she thought, a thing of the past, but still flourishing, and also that she herself is the putative daughter of the Rev. Samuel Gardner, whose son Frank Gardner is in love with her. *Mrs. Warren's Profession*

CULLEN, SIR PATRICK: A famous doctor, about seventy, conscious of being at the end of his tether, and resigned to it. Although of Irish extraction (and therefore known as Paddy), as is shown in his plain, downright common sense, his large build, and the absence of any servility in his manner, he has spent all his life in England and is thoroughly acclimatised. He comes to congratulate his former pupil Sir Colenso Ridgeon on his knighthood, and is invited to the celebration dinner at which the promising young artist Louis Dubedat is present. He fails to respond to the young man's charm, and agrees with Dr. Schutzmaker that he is a 'young blackguard'. Dubedat is suffering from tuberculosis, for which Ridgeon has found a cure, and it is Cullen who points out to Ridgeon the dilemma in which he is placed in having to decide whether to accept Dubedat for treatment, or the poor and not very important Dr. Blenkinsop. When Sir Ralph Bloomfield Bonington takes over Dubedat and kills him, Cullen is present at his death-bed, and remarks that it is not how a man dies, but how he lives, that matters. *The Doctor's Dilemma*

CUSINS, ADOLPHUS: A young Australian, a professor of Greek, who is engaged to Barbara Undershaft. For love of her he has joined the Salvation Army, in which he finds 'the worship of Dionysus and the ecstasy of the dithyramb', beating the big drum at open-air meetings. Although outwardly gentle and considerate, he is fiercely implacable, tenacious and intolerant, capable of murder though not of cruelty or coarseness. Known to his friends as Dolly, he is delighted to change his name to that of his prospective father-in-law, Andrew Undershaft, when the latter proposes to adopt him and make him heir to his vast armaments factory. He fulfils the requirement necessary for this in being a foundling, as his parents' marriage, valid in Australia, is not recognised in England, his mother being his father's deceased wife's sister. Andrew, who has a high opinion of him, calls him Euripides in deference to his classical education, while he, sincerely appreciative of his benefactor's rascality, calls him the Prince of Darkness or Machiavelli. *Major Barbara*

CUTHBERTSON, JOSEPH: A dramatic critic, father of Grace Tranfield, a young widow who is in love with the philanderer Leonard Charteris. Like his old friend Colonel Craven, who usually refers to him affectionately as Jo, he tries to keep up with modern ideas, but is shocked by the emancipation of the New Woman, and particularly by Charteris's behaviour in regard to Julia Craven. A man of 'fervent idealistic sentiment', he is 'so frequently outraged by the facts of life that he has acquired an habitually indignant manner ... His vigilant, irascible eye, piled-up hair, and the honorable seriousness with which he takes himself, give him an air of considerable consequence.' *The Philanderer*

D

DADDY: *see* Barlow, Joseph Popham Bolge Bluebin

DANBY, MR.: The secretary of one of the smaller Bond Street picture galleries, where a one-man show of pictures by Louis Dubedat is held after his death. He knows and welcomes Sir Colenso Ridgeon, gives Jennifer Dubedat the early copies of her biography of her late husband, and goes off to fetch the catalogues for the private view, which have been delayed at the printers. *The Doctor's Dilemma*

DANDY ANDY: *see* Undershaft, Andrew

DANIEL (DAN): *see* Craven, Colonel

DANIELS, ELDER: A sanctimonious prig and hypocrite,

brother to Blanco Posnet, formerly known as 'Boozy' Posnet. He has given up drinking after a bad fit of delirium tremens, and now makes a living by selling liquor to others. As the Elder of the town, he is given the task of bringing Blanco to repentance after he has been accused of stealing a horse belonging to the Sheriff George Kemp. Actually Blanco thought it belonged to his brother, and stole it to punish Daniels for cheating him out of his share of their parents' money, and more especially for having refused to give Blanco his mother's necklace. After Blanco has been acquitted, Daniels stays to hear him preach his burlesque sermon, and then goes ahead to prepare the saloon for a bout of heavy drinking, at Blanco's expense. *The Shewing-Up of Blanco Posnet*

DARK GIRL: *see* Vashti

DARK LADY OF THE SONNETS: *see* Fitton, Mary

DARKIE: *see* Buoyant, Eudoxia Emily

DARLING DORA: *see* Delaney, Dora

DARNLEY, MARCUS: *see* Hushabye, Hector

DASHKOFF, PRINCESS: Lady-in-waiting to the Empress of Russia, Catherine II. She is present at the *petit lever* when Patiomkin carries Captain Edstaston into the Empress's bedroom, and is later faced with the unenviable task of telling Catherine that the Captain is not to be found when summoned to her presence. *Great Catherine*

DAUGHTER: *see* Eynsford-Hill, Clara

DAUPHIN: *see* Charles VII

DAVID: *see* Chavender, David

DAWKINS, DR.: A young doctor, called in by the Duchess of Dunmow to treat her son Lord Reginald Fitzambey, who is suffering from a nervous breakdown. He gives him valerian and opium pills, neither of which do him any good. *The Music Cure*

DEACONESS: An attractive and very voluble middle-aged English lady, who comes uninvited to the Court of International Justice at The Hague with a handbag full of tracts and tries to convert the three dictators. She fails, because they cannot obey the commandment to 'love one another'. When news of the destruction of the world by another ice-age is announced by the Judge, she is upset because 'in heaven I shall lose my Jesus ... I must die when I have only just learnt to live.' *Geneva*

DECK STEWARD: On the *Empress of Patagonia*, a cruise ship. He brings mid-morning beef-tea to Author A and Passenger Z. The former refuses it, but the latter accepts it with pleasure. *Village Wooing*

DELANEY, DORA: A young prostitute 'of hilarious disposition, very tolerable good looks, and killing clothes'. Affable and loquacious, she bursts in on the respectable middle-class home of Maria and Robin Gilbey to tell them that their son Bobby is in prison for being drunk and disorderly and assaulting a policeman. She has herself just been released after serving fourteen days for the same offence, and cannot afford to pay the £4 fine which would procure his liberty. 'Darling Dora', as she is called, is very kind and sympathetic towards the harassed father, but surprised because he cannot understand what she and Bobby have in common. Juggins, the Gilbeys' footman, whom Dora nicknames Rudolph because of his highly superior air, knows very well what it is, and is instrumental in persuading the parents to let the boy marry Dora after he has broken off his engagement to Margaret Knox. *Fanny's First Play*

DEMPSEY, FATHER: Parish priest in Rosscullen, a priest neither by vocation nor ambition, but 'because the life suits him'. On the whole he is an easy-going, amiable, even modest man as long as his dues are paid and his authority admitted, though he angrily rebukes the young farm lad Patsy Farrell for calling the ex-priest Peter Keegan 'Father', since in that parish the title belongs to him alone. He is one of the deputation which comes to the Doyles' house to ask Larry Doyle to stand for Parliament, but, with the others, he transfers his offer to Broadbent, being intelligent enough to see that Broadbent will be easier to manage than the self-willed Larry. *John Bull's Other Island*

DENNIS: *see* O'Flaherty, Private Dennis

DENTIST: *see* Valentine, Mr.

DERBY, LORD: A nobleman in attendance on Edward III when he accepts the surrender of Calais after a year-long siege. He has nothing to say. *The Six of Calais*

DEVIL: When John Tanner goes to sleep after being captured by brigands in the mountains of Spain and dreams that he is Don Juan in Hell, the Devil looks very like the brigand chief Mendoza, though he is older, going bald, and 'does not inspire much confidence in his powers of hard work or endurance, and is, on the whole a disagreeable self-indulgent-looking person; but he is clever and plausible', and a great talker. He is delighted when Don Gonzales decides to come and live in Hell, Don Juan taking his place in Heaven, and goes off happily after a long argument with the men, and with Doña Ana, on the subject of Nietsche and the Superman. He would like to be called Lucifer, but is always referred to as the Devil. *Man and Superman (Don Juan in Hell)*

DEVIL'S DISCIPLE: *see* Dudgeon, Richard

DEXTER, DEXY: *see* Rightside, Sir Dexter

DICK: *see* Buoyant, Richard; Dudgeon, Richard

DICKENSON, PRESIDENT: *see* Haslam, Rev. William

DINNY: *see* O'Flaherty, Private Dennis

DISSATISFIED GENTLEMAN: *see* Battler, Ernest

DOCTOR: An Egyptian, in frock coat and tarboosh, practising in the East End of London. He is at the Pig and Whistle when Eplifania Fitzfassen throws Adrian Blenderbland downstairs, and comes to see what is happening. Epifania at once falls in love with him, and as she has fulfilled the condition laid down by his mother, of earning her own living for six months, is determined to marry him. He finally agrees because he so admires her pulse, 'like a slow sledge hammer', and wants to be able to feel it every day. *The Millionairess*

A medical man fetched by the maid Phyllis after Adolphus Bastable has been poisoned. After trying three times to treat the wrong person, he is struck dead by lightning. *Passion, Poison, and Petrifaction*

Called in to treat Miss Mopply for German measles, he finds himself talking to the Monster, a 'sick bacillus', and decides, before leaving in a hurry, that his exasperating patient has driven him mad. *Too True to be Good*

DOLLY: *see* Clandon, Dolly; Cusins, Adolphus

DOLORES: A Creole lady of about forty, with the remains of a gorgeous and opulent southern beauty. She visits the office of the International Committee for Intellectual Co-operation in Geneva to demand justice against the President of the Republic of the Earthly Paradise, who has assassinated her husband, the former President. Otherwise her son will be forced to shoot the murderer, his best friend, himself. She carries a gun in her handbag, with which she threatens to shoot the Jew, who has also come to Geneva with a demand for justice, but the British Foreign Secretary, Sir Orpheus Midlander, disarms her, and the Jew flatters her so outrageously that she finally agrees to dine with him. Next day she attends the trial of the three dictators at the Court of

68

International Justice at The Hague, and insists at pistol-point that her case shall be heard. Otherwise there will be no end to private vendettas. She herself is a murderess. She killed the woman for whom her husband deserted her, although that woman was her best friend. So she too must be sentenced, and then she will kill herself. However, the Judge pacifies her by promising to sentence the slayer of her husband when his offence is proved, and forbids her to commit suicide. When the end of the world is announced, she throws her pistol into the waste-paper basket, saying: 'God will execute his own judgement on us all.' *Geneva*

DOMESDAY, DUKE OF: An elderly, delicately-built aristo-crat, well-preserved, but nearer seventy than sixty. He comes to congratulate the Prime Minister, Sir Arthur Chavender, on his programme of reform, which includes abolishing death duties, but finds himself tangling with the Labour deputation from the Isle of Cats. The Mayor tells him that there will be no compensation for nationalised land, and Aloysia Brollikins attacks him about the Domes-day Clearances, which happened before he was born. When the Foreign Secretary, Sir Dexter Rightside, refuses to support the Prime Minister, the Duke says regretfully that it was a pity Chavender spent his holiday thinking instead of playing golf, and refuses to consider becoming a dictator because he does not feel he is the man for it, though he will support a dictator when he comes. He then stops the loquacious Mr. Hipney from making any more speeches by taking him out to lunch. *On the Rocks*

DOMINICANS: *see* Assessors

DON GONZALES: *see* Gonzales, Don

DON JUAN: *see* Juan Tenorio, Don

DOÑA ANA: *see* Ana de Ulloa, Doña

DONKIN, ARCHDEACON DAFFODIL: The father of Ermyn-trude Roosenhonkers-Pipstein, whom he compelled to marry a millionaire instead of the curate with whom she was in love. Her husband died penniless, and she has returned unwillingly to the penury of her father's house. When she complains, her father advises her to become lady's maid to a princess until she can find another millionaire to marry her. *The Inca of Perusalem*

DOOLITTLE, ALFRED: An elderly but vigorous member of the 'undeserving poor', a dustman by profession, but by inclination a layabout and a heavy drinker. The father of the flower-girl Eliza Doolittle, whom he has not seen for a couple of years, he turns up at Higgins's house when he learns that she is living there, and by a combination of bare-faced impudence and Welsh oratory—his mother having been Welsh—he persuades Higgins to pay him £5 to leave Eliza with him so that he can experiment on her, by teaching her to speak so well that she can pass as a lady anywhere. Some time later he turns up resplendent in morning dress, with a flower in his buttonhole, a silk hat, and patent leather shoes, complaining that he has been sold into slavery because an American millionaire, impressed by Higgins's joking reference to him as England's most original moralist, has left him £3,000 a year on condition that he lectures six times annually for the Wannafeller Moral Reform World League. He is on his way to church, driven by middle-class morality to marry the woman he is living with, and very cleverly he cajoles everyone into supporting him through the ceremony. Although his new wife is Eliza's sixth stepmother, it is obviously the first time he has been married, though out of delicacy he has concealed from Eliza the fact that she is illegitimate. *Pygmalion*

DOOLITTLE, ELIZA: A young Cockney flower-girl, with an appalling accent and shoddy clothes. Sheltering under the portico of St. Paul's, Covent Garden, during a sudden shower, she overhears the famous phonetician Henry Higgins boasting that in six months he could turn a girl like her into a passable imitation of a duchess, merely by teaching her to speak properly. Fired by ambition to become a sales-lady in a florist's, she goes to his house and asks for lessons. Egged on by his friend, Colonel Pickering, who agrees to pay Eliza's expenses if the experiment succeeds, Higgins takes her into his house and for several months she works hard, becoming very fond of both Higgins and Pickering in the process. Helped by an unusually sensitive ear, she enables Higgins to make good his boast and attends an ambassador's garden party without difficulty. But she is then mortified to discover that both men are bored with the whole thing, and quite indifferent to what will become of her now that she can no longer return to her old life. In her dilemma she runs away and takes refuge with Higgins's mother, who has been kind to her. Confronted by an irate Higgins and a repentant Pickering, she realises that neither of them will be any use to her in the future, and is prepared to marry the kind, but brainless, Freddy Eynsford-Hill and earn a living for them both in a flower-shop subsidised by Pickering. *Pygmalion*

DORA: *see* Delaney, Dora

DORAN, BARNEY: 'a short-armed, stout-bodied, round-headed, red-haired man on the verge of middle age ... with an enormous capacity for derisive, obscene, blasphemous, or merely cruel and senseless fun.' A miller in Rosscullen, he is a typical example of 'energy and capacity wasted and demoralised by want of sufficient training and social pressure to force it into beneficent activity'. Dressed in a suit of unbrushed clothes, made of fashionable tailor's sackcloth, powdery with flour and mill dust, he joins with other Rosscullen men in suggesting that Larry Doyle, who has just returned to Ireland after an absence of eighteen years, should stand as the local candidate for Parliament, but is so shocked by Larry's outrageous opinions that in agreement with Cornelius Doyle and Father Dempsey he transfers the offer to Larry's English partner Tom Broadbent. With half a dozen friends, he later returns to the

Doyles' house to gloat over Broadbent's misadventure with Matthew Haffigan's pig, which ended in the death of the pig and the wrecking of the car in which it was being driven. *John Bull's Other Island*

DORAN'S FRIENDS: Some half-dozen men of Rosscullen, who come with Barney Doran to the house of Cornelius Doyle to gloat over the misfortunes of Tom Broadbent. Having offered to drive a pig belonging to Matthew Haffigan to the old man's farm, he has been unable to control it, and ended up by running over the pig and wrecking the car, not without some danger to himself and several spectators. They tell the story again and again, laughing heartily each time. As Peter Keegan ironically remarks: 'There is danger, destruction, torment! What more do we need to make us merry?' They finally leave, being unable to control their mirth when Broadbent returns, solemn and rather complacent about the whole affair, which, he says, 'has brought out the kindness and sympathy of the Irish character to an extent I had no conception of'. *John Bull's Other Island*

DOROTHEA, DOROTHY: *see* Clandon, Dolly

DOYLE, CORNELIUS (CORNEY): A former Irish land agent, and now a small-town businessman, 'wearing an oldish shooting-suit with elastic-sided boots quite unconnected with shooting'. Small, wiry, rather worried-looking, with sandy whiskers, he is the father of Larry Doyle, who left home eighteen years ago because he disagreed with his father on every possible point. He has returned reluctantly on business with his English partner Tom Broadbent, and his father, knowing him to be rich, and believing him to have changed his ideas, suggests that he should stand for Parliament in the local interest. But Larry's unorthodox opinions on all Irish problems so shock Corney and his friends that they transfer their offer to Broadbent, who though 'not quite right in the head', has plenty of money, and agrees with them about everything. *John Bull's Other Island*

DOYLE, JUDY: The aunt of Larry Doyle, and housekeeper to his father Corney in Rosscullen. She meets her nephew's English partner, Tom Broadbent, on his arrival in the village, and in the absence of an inn, offers to put him up. But first she gives him a magnificent 'tea', consisting of more mutton-chops than it seems possible to eat at one sitting, potato cakes, and two large glasses of illicitly distilled whisky, or 'potcheen'. This potent beverage gives him the courage to propose that evening to Larry's former sweetheart, Nora Reilly. Aunt Judy, as everyone calls her, is a placid woman, 'kindly but without concern for others; the placid product of a narrow life', and although she is sympathetic with Broadbent and Peter Keegan when they are in trouble, it is evident that nothing goes very deep with her. *John Bull's Other Island*

DOYLE, LAURENCE (LARRY): The son of Corney Doyle, and business partner of Tom Broadbent, thirty-six years old, with cold grey eyes. Clever and good-looking, he is nevertheless restless and dissatisfied, scornful of his partner's admiration for everything Irish, and loath to return to Ireland after an absence of eighteen years, partly because he knows his childhood sweetheart Nora Reilly is waiting for him. Once back in Rosscullen he is asked to stand for Parliament, but makes it clear that his opinions are not what his backers expect, and they transfer their offer to Tom Broadbent, whom they consider 'soft in the head' and easily led to adopt their point of view on Irish problems. Larry is delighted when Nora also succumbs to the blandishments of Broadbent and agrees to marry him. *John Bull's Other Island*

DRINKWATER, FELIX: One of the crew of the *Thanksgiving*, the privateer commanded by Captain Brassbound. He calls himself 'a humble British seaman', but is usually known as Brandyfaced Jack. A typical product of the London slums, 'aged about forty, a fluent talker, with a strong cockney accent, a coward, a sniveller, always with an eye to the main chance'. He arranges for Brassbound to provide an escort when Sir Howard Hallam and Lady Cicely Waynflete decide to explore the Atlas Mountains. When Marzo is wounded by an Arab bullet, Drinkwater is detailed by Lady Cicely to help nurse him, but first, to his unbounded horror, he is given a bath by his delighted fellow-seamen, from which he emerges with his hair, previously mud-coloured, a bright and flaming red. He is taken back to Mogador with the rest of the party by Muley Othman, and constantly tries to interrupt during Brassbound's trial. After the acquittal, when the crew decide that Brassbound is going to marry Lady Cicely, he proposes that he shall take the captain's place, but is howled down by his companions, and is sent off with them to prepare the *Thanksgiving* for sea. *Captain Brassbound's Conversion*

DRISCOLL, TERESA: A parlourmaid in the Irish country house of General Sir Pearce Madigan, and the sweetheart of Dennis O'Flaherty, who has been fighting with the British army under Madigan in the First World War and returns home in glory after winning the Victoria Cross. When they meet after Dennis has been taking part in a recruiting campaign he is upset to discover that all she cares about is his pension, and the possibility of his increasing it by returning to France and being wounded. Nevertheless he gives her a gold chain which he has taken from a German prisoner. She accepts it dubiously, not being sure that it is genuine; but she refuses to part with it when Dennis's mother vociferously demands it as her right, and goes off into the house, shouting and screaming, leaving Dennis disillusioned and longing for the comparative quiet of the trenches. *O'Flaherty, V.C.*

DUBEDAT, JENNIFER: A beautiful young woman, an only child, brought up in a remote part of Cornwall—'tall, slender, strong, with dark hair, and narrow, subtle, dark-fringed eyes, softly impetuous in speech and swift in her movements'. She has married the young artist Louis Dubedat who calls her Jinny-Gwinny, with the intention of protecting him from mundane matters while he perfects his art, but he is found to be suffering from tuberculosis. Hearing that Sir Colenso Ridgeon has discovered a cure for this disease, she finds her way to his consulting-room and charms him into accepting her husband as a patient. She is completely blind to his faults, accepting his cruelty and amoral way of life as the small blemishes of a genius, and she cannot understand why Ridgeon, who wants to spare her the knowledge of Dubedat's character which she must come to if he lives, hands the case over to Sir Ralph Bloomfield Bonington. When the latter's 'cure' kills her husband in three days, Jennifer blames Ridgeon. Meeting him a year later at a retrospective exhibition of Dubedat's pictures, she is horrified to learn that this elderly man, as she thinks of him, is in love with her, and refuses to believe him when he tries to tell her what Dubedat was really like, putting it all down to jealousy. She also tells him that in accordance with Dubedat's last expressed wish, she has married again. *The Doctor's Dilemma*

DUBEDAT, LOUIS: A young and very promising artist, who subordinates everything to his art, and in the ordinary transactions of daily life is a waster, sponger, liar and infernal young blackguard. He has allowed himself to be married to a charming young woman, Jennifer Dubedat, who has enough money to cushion him against the miseries of everyday life, but has deceived even her by going through a mock marriage with a chambermaid, Minnie Tinwell, whom he deserts after three weeks. Dubedat is dying of tuberculosis, but hopes to be cured by Sir Colenso Ridgeon, who has agreed after a visit from Jennifer, with whom he has fallen in love, to accept him as a patient. However, when Ridgeon finds out the truth about Dubedat's character, he hands him over to Sir Ralph Bloomfield Bonington, who very quickly kills him. Dubedat insists on being wheeled into his studio to die, and stages a most edifying and dramatic death-bed scene in the presence of his wife, a reporter, and no less than four doctors. He is 'an artist who is so entirely satisfied with his artistic conscience, even to the point of dying like a saint with its support, that he is utterly selfish and unscrupulous in every other relation without feeling at the smallest disadvantage.' *The Doctor's Dilemma*

DUDGEON, CHRISTOPHER: The younger son of Mrs. Timothy Dudgeon, usually known as Christy. 'A fattish, stupid, fair-haired, roundfaced man of about twenty-two', he has been to watch the hanging of his uncle Peter by the British troops in Springtown, and returns to tell his mother that his father also has died, of shock. He inherits £100 from his father, on condition 'he marries Sarah Wilkins', and it is he who is called on to identify his brother Richard Dudgeon when the latter is arrested in mistake for the Rev. Anderson. *The Devil's Disciple*

DUDGEON, RICHARD: The elder son of Mrs. Timothy Dudgeon, usually known as Dick, and self-christened 'the Devil's Disciple'. In reaction against his mother's harsh, unloving piety, he has become sardonic and defiant, 'a smuggler who lives with gipsies, and wrestles and plays games on Sunday instead of going to church'. But 'his forehead and mouth betray an extraordinary steadfastness; and his eyes are the eyes of a fanatic'. He is the only member of the family to show any kindness to the waif Essie, and when he is arrested by the British in mistake for the Rev. Anthony Anderson, he refuses to allow Judith Anderson, the minister's wife, to reveal his identity. When Judith later asks if he has saved her husband's life at the cost of his own because he admires him, or because he loves her, he says he has no particular interest in either of them, and acted purely on principle. He is extremely embarrassed by Judith's confession that she loves him, and after his reprieve assures her that he will never tell her husband what passed between them. *The Devil's Disciple*

DUDGEON, MRS. TIMOTHY: The mother of Richard and Christopher Dudgeon, 'an elderly matron who has worked hard and got nothing by it except domination and detestation in her sordid home and an unquestioned reputation for piety and respectability among her neighbours . . Being extremely disagreeable [she] is held to be exceeding good.' As Annie Primrose she had been in love with a wastrel, Peter Dudgeon, but married his brother because the latter was 'respectable'. After her husband's sudden death she expects to inherit the farm, but is shocked to find that it has been left to her detested elder son, 'the Devil's Disciple', and dies of heart failure soon after. *The Devil's Disciple*

DUDGEON, TITUS: The youngest of the Dudgeon brothers, 'a wiry little terrier of a man'. He is uncle to Richard Dudgeon, who calls him 'an upright horse dealer', and like the rest of the family is shocked when the will reveals that his late brother Timothy has left his farm to the profligate Richard. *The Devil's Disciple*

DUDGEON, MRS. TITUS: The wife of Titus Dudgeon, who comes with her husband to the reading of his brother Timothy's will, 'immense and visibly purse-proud'. She has nothing to say. *The Devil's Disciple*

DUDGEON, WILLIAM: The eldest of the Dudgeon brothers, uncle to Richard Dudgeon, who calls him 'a reformed drunkard'. A 'large shapeless man, bottle-nosed and evidently no ascetic at table', he attends the reading of his late brother Timothy's will, but only speaks once. *The Devil's Disciple*

DUDGEON, MRS. WILLIAM: The wife of William Dudgeon, 'an anxious little woman, left derelict near the door' when she comes with her husband to the reading of Timothy Dudgeon's will. She is rescued by her brother-in-law Titus, who places her on the sofa between himself and his wife. She has nothing to say. *The Devil's Disciple*

DUNN, BILLY: A burglar caught stealing Lady Utterwood's diamonds. The family cannot decide whether to prosecute him or not, and after some argument they give him a pound and let him go. But in the doorway he meets Captain Shotover, who recognises him as a rascally pirate who once served under him as bosun and robbed him shamefully. In addition he is the absconding husband of Nurse Guinness, a servant in Shotover's house. She takes him to the kitchen for a meal, but when the air-raid begins and he is sent to the cellar, he thinks it not safe enough and with 'Boss' Mangan decides to shelter in the cave where Shotover stores his dynamite. It receives a direct hit and both men are killed. *Heartbreak House*

DUNN, ELLIE: The daughter of Mazzini Dunn, engaged to 'Boss' Mangan, who, under pretext of helping her father, has ruined him. Invited by Hesione Hushabye to the house of her father, Captain Shotover, she confesses to her that she has fallen in love with the handsome and romantic 'Marcus Darnley'. She is heart-broken when she discovers that he is Hesione's philandering and untruthful husband. In despair she tells Mangan that she will marry him immediately, but he has fallen in love with Hesione, and tries to make her change her mind by confessing that he deliberately forced her father into bankruptcy. Disillusioned, she turns to the 88-year-old Shotover, with whom she has discovered a remarkable affinity, for consolation. But he can give her none. He can only expound his own philosophy of life, and tell her to stand firm in adversity. She says she would like to marry him, but this is not possible, as he has a black wife in Jamaica. So 'in the sight of Heaven' she becomes his 'white' wife, saying: 'I give my broken heart and my strong soul to its natural captain, my spiritual husband and second father.' When a bomb falls on the garden, killing Mangan and Billy Dunn, she is quite unmoved, agreeing with Hesione that it was 'a glorious experience', and hoping the raiders will return again the next night. *Heartbreak House*

When Shav wants to prove to Shakes that he is the better dramatist, he calls up Ellie Dunn from *Heartbreak House*, which he considers a better play than *King Lear*, to recite some of her lines with Shotover. *Shakes versus Shav*

DUNN, MAZZINI: The father of Ellie Dunn, a little elderly man with credulous bulging eyes and earnest manners. He has been ruined by the machinations of 'Boss' Mangan, whom he now works for, and is anxious that Ellie should marry Mangan and so be well provided for. He is invited to the house of Captain Shotover, who mistakes him for a rascally bosun who once served under him, and will not believe Mazzini's denials until the real Billy Dunn turns up disguised as a burglar. Mazzini catches him, almost shooting his ear off with a duelling pistol belonging to Hector Hushabye. *Heartbreak House*

DUNOIS, JACK: The Bastard of Orleans, fighting for Charles VII against Henry VI of England. He is encamped on the bank of the Loire when Joan of Arc comes to tell him that he must cross the river and attack Orleans. He points out that he is waiting for a west wind to blow his landing rafts over, as the English hold the bridge, and he cannot move while the east wind continues to blow. Joan is just taking him off to the local church to pray for a west wind when it comes, and they dash off to fight. Dunois attends Charles's coronation in Rheims cathedral, and afterwards tries to explain to Joan why the courtiers are jealous of her, why the Church is only waiting to catch her out in some indictable offence, and why the English have set a price of £16,000 on her head. He also tells her that when she tries to fight a battle with too few men, she will be captured and put to death, and no one will lift a finger to save her. He plays no part in her trial, but twenty-five years later, in the Epilogue, he is able to tell Joan that he has kept his word and that there are no longer any English soldiers on French soil. *Saint Joan*

DUVAL, CAPTAIN: *see* Inca of Perusalem

DUVALLET, LIEUTENANT: A young French officer in the merchant navy, who picks up Margaret Knox in a music-hall, takes her dancing, and gets involved in a boat-race night rag which ends in their both being sent to prison for assaulting a policeman. As soon as he is released he pays Margaret's fine and takes her home, where her father, Joseph Knox, is extremely rude to him, even going so far as to ask him his intentions. He has none, he says; he is married, with two daughters, and he invited Margaret to go out with him because 'only an Englishwoman could spend an evening with a strange man without ulterior motives'. *Fanny's First Play*

E

ECRASIA: A handsome young woman with marked features, dark hair, and an authoritative bearing. She comes, in A.D. 31,920, to the Festival of Arts, and quarrels bitterly with the sculptor Arjillax because he will not admit her right to criticise his work. He has modelled busts of the Ancients instead of the beautiful youths she expected. She also scorns Pygmalion because he is a scientist and not an artist, and has a very poor opinion of his synthetic automata, saying they are noisome and poison the air. When they have killed Pygmalion and been killed themselves, and the Ancients take advantage of the incident to try and explain to the young people the future that awaits them, Ecrasia argues with them, maintaining that 'without art, the crudeness of reality would make the world unbearable', and refusing to believe that she will ever grow beyond the need for love and beauty. When the Ancients have gone away in despair, she looks round for someone to spend the night with, but both Arjillax and Strephon turn away from her, and she goes off alone, remarking: 'After all, I can imagine a lover nobler than any of you.' *Back to Methuselah, Part V: As Far as Thought Can Reach*

EDITH: *see* Bridgenorth, Edith; Haldenstedt, Edith

EDITOR: The man in charge of the gladiators at the Colosseum in Rome. He tries to make Androcles renounce Christianity so that he can employ him in the menagerie, as he is so good with animals, and he hates having to use his gladiators to fight Christians, wishing they could all be thrown to the lions instead. *Androcles and the Lion*

EDSTASTON, CAPTAIN CHARLES: A young Englishman who has fought at the battle of Bunker's Hill, and is therefore sent to St. Petersburg to give the Empress Catherine a first-hand account of the American Revolution. He is ushered into her presence somewhat unceremoniously, being carried to her *petit lever* by Prince Patiomkin pretending to be drunk. To his horror she is amused and attracted by him, and he finds himself being treated by everyone with the deference due to the Empress's favourite. He manages to escape, and has rejoined his fiancée Claire when he is captured by the police and returned to the palace, trussed up and helpless, in which condition he is tickled so unmercifully by Catherine that he screams aloud. Claire rushes to his rescue, is angry when she finds he is, as she thinks, flirting, but finally forgives him. Edstaston is then allowed to go, but not before he has advised Catherine to 'marry some good man who will be a strength and support' to her old age. *Great Catherine*

EDWARD III: Plantagenet King of England from 1327 to 1377. Having laid siege to Calais for a year, he demands the surrender of the keys of the city by six prosperous burghers, clad only in their shirts, with ropes round their necks by which to hang them afterwards. When they arrive he gives orders for their death, but is persuaded by his wife, Philippa of Hainault, to spare the lives of five of them. The sixth, Piers de Rosty, is so rude to the Queen that she urges the King to hang him. But Edward discovers that he is 'a dog of Champagne'—the province from which his own grandmother came—and sends him off with a lewd jest. *The Six of Calais*

EE PEE (EARTHLY PROVIDENCE): *see* Buoyant, Bastable

EGG: *see* Amaryllis

EGYPTIAN DOCTOR: *see* Doctor

ELDER: *see* Bagot, Mr.; Daniels, Elder

ELDER YOUTH: *see* Janga

ELDERLY GENTLEMAN: *see* Barlow, Joseph Popham Bolge Bluebin

ELDERLY LADY: *see* Mopply, Mrs.

ELIZA: *see* Doolittle, Eliza

ELIZABETH I: Queen of England, 1558–1603. She is sleepwalking on the terrace of the Palace at Westminster, dreaming of Mary Queen of Scots, when William Shakespear [*sic*], who has come to a rendezvous with Mary Fitton, overhears her mutterings and jots some of them down for use in Lady Macbeth's sleep-walking scene. He then wakes her up, but still does not know who she is, and is about to kiss her when Mary Fitton cuffs them both. Elizabeth then reveals herself as the Queen; Mary is terrified of her anger, but Shakespear argues with her freely, and when Mary has been sent away he tries to interest her in his plans for a National Theatre in London, devoted to the performance of his plays. She says she will leave that to posterity, and prophesies truly that every other Christian country will have a 'playhouse at the public charge' before England will venture on one. *The Dark Lady of the Sonnets*

ELLIE: *see* Dunn, Ellie

EMIGRATION OFFICER: *see* Hyering, Hugo

EMMA: *see* Women in the Barn

EMMY: Housekeeper to Sir Colenso Ridgeon, 'an old woman who has never known the cares, preoccupations, responsibilities, jealousies, and anxieties of personal beauty'. With the complexion of a never-washed gipsy and a face covered in hairy moles, she is a warm-hearted, bustling, motherly creature, very popular with Ridgeon's patients, treating everyone as a good nanny treats a child who can just toddle. It is she who persuades Ridgeon to see Jennifer Dubedat when she comes to consult him about her husband's illness. *The Doctor's Dilemma*

EMPEROR: *see* Caesar; Napoleon, Cain Adamson Charles

EMPRESS: *see* Catherine II

ENGLISH SERGEANT: *see* Sergeant

ENGLISH SOLDIER: He comes in during the Epilogue to say that he is allowed one day out of Hell every year in honour of Joan of Arc, in recognition of the fact that when she was being burnt to death he gave her a little cross made of two sticks of wood bound together. *Saint Joan*

ENGLISH SOLDIERS: *see* Soldiers

ENRY: *see* Straker, Henry

ENSIGN: In the army of Julius Caesar in Egypt. He carries the eagle at the head of the victorious troops who burst into the throne-room of Cleopatra in the Syrian palace where she has taken refuge. *Caesar and Cleopatra*

ENVOY: *see* Bluebin, Ambrose Badger

ENVOY'S DAUGHTER: *see* Bluebin, Ethel Badger

ENVOY'S WIFE: *see* Bluebin, Molly Badger

EPIFANIA (EPPY): *see* Fitzfassen, Epifania

ERMYNTRUDE: *see* Roosenhonkers-Pipstein, Ermyntrude

ERNEST: *see* Battler, Ernest; Fessler, Dr. Ernest

ESSIE: The illegitimate daughter of Peter Dudgeon, first referred to merely as the Girl, 'cowed and wretched, a wild, timid-looking creature with black hair and tanned skin, in a dirty ragged dress and bare feet'. After her father has been hanged by the British as a rebel, she is sent to Mrs. Timothy Dudgeon, who takes her in reluctantly, and treats her with great severity. The only person who is kind to her is the Devil's Disciple, Richard Dudgeon, who has been left in charge of her by his father's will. Filled with gratitude and adoration for him, she goes with him to the foot of the gallows, and is the first to rejoice when he is reprieved. *The Devil's Disciple*

ESTIVET, BROTHER JOHN D': Canon of Bayeux at the time of the trial of Joan of Arc, where he acts as promoter, or prosecutor. He is young and well-manned, but vulpine beneath his veneer, and, like the other judges and assessors, a Dominican monk. He is careful to explain that although he has been ordered to present the case against the accused, he would hasten to her defence if he did not know that better men than he have been sent to reason with her, but that she utters blasphemies every time she opens her mouth. He is, however, very quick to point out anything she says which can help to lead to her condemnation, and finally heads the clamour for her execution, going out with the other monks to see her sentence carried out. *Saint Joan*

ETHEL: *see* Bluebin, Ethel Badger

EUDOXIA: *see* Buoyant, Eudoxia Emily

EUGENE: *see* Marchbanks, Eugene

EURIPIDES: *see* Cusins, Adolphus

EUSTACHE: *see* St. Pierre, Eustache de

EVANS, FEEMY (EUPHEMIA): A prostitute in a small
American town, a bold creature 'in her early twenties, with
impudent manners, battered good looks, and a dirty-fine
dress'. When Blanco Posnet is on trial for stealing a horse,
she swears that she saw him on it, knowing that this will
lead to his conviction and death. But when an unknown
woman turns up to tell the court that Blanco gave her the
horse to take her dying child to the doctor, and that she has
brought it back safely, Feemy retracts her evidence, saying
it was given out of spite because Blanco had repulsed her.
After his release Blanco points out that they are both
failures at being wicked—he nearly died in a vain attempt
to save a child's life, and she has told a lie to save his—so
they might as well marry. But she refuses, though she agrees
to shake hands with him, and they part good friends. *The
Shewing-Up of Blanco Posnet*

EVE: In the Garden of Eden, Adam calls her to see a fawn
that has broken its neck. She invents the name 'death' for
its condition, and realises that she and Adam may also die;
and then there will be no more people, only birds and
beasts and snakes. But a voice within her tells her this must
not be: and the Serpent, who has learned human speech,
explains how she can prevent it, by conceiving and giving
birth, with the help of Adam. Centuries later, exiled to
Mesopotamia, she sits and spins while Adam digs. She is
angry with Cain for having killed his brother Abel, and for
wanting her to produce more and more men so that he can
have the pleasure of fighting them. She dreams of descendants who will be neither farmers, like Adam, nor
killers, like Cain, but musicians, artists, poets, telling
'beautiful lies in beautiful words'. Man, she says, 'need not
always live by bread alone. There is something else', and

when it has been discovered 'there shall be no more digging nor spinning, nor fighting nor killing.' *Back to Methuselah, Part I: In the Beginning*

In the summer of A.D. 31,920 the ghost of Eve returns to see what her descendants have made of the world, and is pleased with what she finds. 'The diggers and the fighters have dug themselves in with the worms. My clever ones have inherited the earth. All's well.' *Back to Methuselah, Part V: As Far as Thought Can Reach*

EXECUTIONER: A 'stalwart British soldier in his shirt-sleeves', detailed to hang Richard Dudgeon. He has nothing to say, but is kept busy pinioning Richard's hands, putting the noose round his neck, and helping him into and, after his reprieve, out of the cart. *The Devil's Disciple*

With his attendants he brings Joan of Arc to her trial in Rouen, and complains during the proceedings that the English have built the pyre too high for him to get near her and make her death easier. When sentence has been passed he goes out to light the fire. In the Epilogue he says that though he was a master of his craft, he could not kill Joan. Her heart would not burn and it would not drown, and now she is alive everywhere. But, like the others, he begs her not to return from the dead. *Saint Joan*

EYNSFORD-HILL, CLARA: The sulky, dissatisfied daughter of a well-bred but impoverished gentlewoman, who when in society acts with the gay 'bravado of genteel poverty'. She is contemptuous of the flower-girl Eliza Doolittle when they shelter together under the portico of St. Paul's, Covent Garden, but admires her so much in her later role as a 'young lady', educated by Henry Higgins and Colonel Pickering in furtherance of a bet, that she foolishly tries, without success, to emulate her 'new small talk' and use of bad language. *Pygmalion*

EYNSFORD-HILL, FREDDY: A silly, brainless, but kind young man, who falls desperately in love with Eliza

Doolittle after she has been turned from a flower-girl into a lady by the efforts of Henry Higgins and Colonel Pickering. Ignored by her two mentors after the success of their experiment, Eliza turns to Freddy for comfort, but it is evident that if she marries him, she will be forced to earn a living for them both. *Pygmalion*

EYNSFORD-HILL, MRS.: A conventional lady of good family, striving to bring up a son and daughter on an inadequate income, and foolish enough to think that the flower-girl Eliza Doolittle is intimate with her boy Freddy merely because she addresses him carelessly by his rightful name. When she meets Eliza again after her metamorphosis into a 'lady' by Henry Higgins, she confesses that she cannot get used to the 'new small talk' which includes such terms as 'bloody', and deprecates the use of such words by her somewhat downtrodden daughter Clara. We are not told what her reaction is to the eventual marriage of Freddy and Eliza. *Pygmalion*

F

FAIR GIRL: *see* Maya

FANNY: *see* O'Dowda, Fanny

FANSHAWE, LADY CORINTHIA: The beautiful and romantic president of the anti-suffragette league. With a Mrs. Banger, she calls on General Mitchener to offer her help against the militant suffragettes, but her high-flown notions, combined with Mrs. Banger's ferocity, convert him to the suffragette cause. Lady Corinthia considers the suffragettes a pack of dowdies, and, being already known as 'the Park Lane Nightingale', says she intends to rule through beauty, charm, and the Arts. 'When a woman is on the throne the country is ruled by men, and therefore ruled badly; whereas when a man is on the throne the country is ruled by women, and therefore ruled well.' But Mitchener tells her that if he has to choose between pitching all the dowdies into the Thames, or pitching all the lovely and accomplished ladies there, the latter would have to go every time, as the dowdies do all the work. Lady Corinthia then offers her hand to the Prime Minister, Balsquith, but he says he wants an Egeria rather than a wife. She thinks this will suit her very well, and leaves after inviting him to her next musical at-home. *Press Cuttings*

FARRELL, MRS.: A highly respectable Irish widow with eight children, employed at the War Office. When General Mitchener hears that Mrs. Banger is to marry General Sandstone, he proposes to Mrs. Farrell, as being the only woman he knows capable of supporting him against Mrs. Banger. After phoning her daughter, a very successful Variety star who is about to marry a duke, Mrs. Farrell consents to marry him, mainly because she thinks the duke might prefer his mother-in-law to be a general's wife rather than a charwoman. *Press Cuttings*

FARRELL, PATSY: A young Irish farm labourer employed by Cornelius Doyle. A callow, flaxen-polled, downy-chinned lad, clad in corduroy trousers, unbuttoned waist-coat, and coarse blue striped shirt, he looks helpless and silly; but this is partly due to his cunning, since by pretending to be a bigger fool than he is, he makes life easier for himself. Credulous, superstitious, and completely illiterate, he is despised by the older men in the village, and it is a remark by Larry Doyle to the effect that if returned to Parliament he would bring in an Act to give Patsy and his like at least £1 a week that makes them realise his unfitness to represent them at Westminster. Patsy was in the car in which Tom Broadbent was driving a pig to the farm of Matthew Haffigan when it escaped and was run over. The car, after demolishing a market stall and the corner of a building, was totally wrecked, and Patsy had two fingers put out of joint. The blacksmith put them back for him, and Broadbent compensated him so handsomely that he said he would be willing to break all his fingers and toes on the same terms. *John Bull's Other Island*

FARWATERS, SIR CHARLES: With his wife he visits the Unexpected Isles, and is very attracted to the local priestess Prola. Twenty years later he is in residence, as Governor, and has taken part in a eugenic experiment which has resulted in four perfect children entirely without a moral conscience. He persuades the young clergyman, Phosphor Hammingtap, to become the island's bishop and marry both the girls, Maya and Vashti. When the Angel announces the Day of Judgement, and the children, being of no use on earth, vanish, Sir Charles survives, and goes back to work, advising his wife to get on with some gardening to justify her continued existence. *The Simpleton of the Unexpected Isles*

FARWATERS, LADY: As a Lady Tourist, she visits the Unexpected Isles with her husband, Sir Charles, and tries to convert the priest Pra, whom she finds extremely seductive. Twenty years later, as the wife of the Governor, she is a bland and attractive matron, very unlike the gaunt and affected tourist who once distributed tracts to the heathen. She is also one of the parents of the four perfect but amoral children, Janga, Kanchin, Maya, and Vashti, and is very pleased when the young clergyman, Phosphor Hammingtap, is marooned by pirates on the island, as he will provide the solution to the problem of the next generation. After the Day of Judgement she is advised by her husband to get on with her gardening to justify her continued existence, and does so, since, as she says, 'I shall feel safer with my gardening basket.' *The Simpleton of the Unexpected Isles*

FATHER: *see* Smith, Mr.

FATHER ANTHONY: *see* Soames, Rev. Oliver Cromwell

FEATHERED ONE: *see* Raphael

FEEMY: *see* Evans, Feemy

FEMALE FIGURE: *see* Cleopatra-Semiramis

FEMALE PADEREWSKI: *see* Thundridge, Strega

FERDINAND: *see* Flopper, Sir Ferdinand

FERROVIUS: A man with 'the strength of an elephant and the temper of a wild bull', who has become a Christian and converted a great many people by his mere presence. He is condemned to death and sent to the Colosseum in Rome, where Caesar is so struck by his fine physique that he offers him a place in the Praetorian Guard. When he refuses, he is sent with the other Christian prisoners into the arena to fight the gladiators. Although he has said he will not fight, he is given a sword, and the mere sight of him causes the gladiators to hang back. But when the official Whip is sent into the arena to urge them on, Ferrovius goes berserk, kills him, and then kills five more men. Caesar is so delighted that he pardons the prisoners, orders the remaining gladiators to become Christians, and again offers Ferrovius a place in his guard, which, heartbroken at his betrayal of the faith, he finally decides to accept. *Androcles and the Lion*

FERRUCCIO, COUNT: Son of the ruler of Padua. He has been banished from his father's court for having seduced Madonna Brigita, whose brother, Cardinal Poldi, is determined to avenge his sister's honour. He therefore arranges for an innkeeper, Squarcio, who needs money for his daughter's dowry, to assassinate the Count after he has been lured to the inn by the daughter, Giulia. She seeks absolution for her sin, before committing it, from a very old blind friar, who then reveals himself as the Count in disguise. He rushes to the inn to kill Squarcio, but is told it is no use fighting, as Squarcio is a professional assassin and is bound to win. After a good meal, at which they are joined by Giulia's fiancé, Sandro, Ferruccio offers to buy

Giulia, or even to marry her, if they will let him go. But they refuse, and face to face with death—his first 'glimpse of reality'—he finds his manhood and rushes at Squarcio with a dagger. This glances harmlessly off the coat of mail worn by the innkeeper, and he and Sandro entangle the Count in a fishing net. Believing him to be mad, and knowing it is bad luck to kill madmen, who are under the special protection of Heaven, they offer to escort him to a safe place if he will pay the money needed for Giulia's dowry. *The Glimpse of Reality*

FESSLER, DR. ERNEST: A young Viennese doctor, engaged to Edith Haldenstedt, the daughter of a leading psychiatrist. When her father is found dead in a flat where he has been meeting his mistress, Fessler endeavours to console her, but only succeeds in irritating her to such an extent that she breaks off the engagement. Later, through the intervention of Jitta Lenkheim, who has revealed herself to Edith as her father's mistress, the couple are reunited and Fessler agrees to help Jitta's husband in the sorting and editing of Haldenstedt's papers. *Jitta's Atonement*

FIELDING, SERGEANT: One of the soldiers in an expeditionary force commanded by Colonel Tallboys. He attracts the attention of Susan Simpkins, who is masquerading as the Countess Valbrioni, but at first he refuses to take any notice of her, thinking she is a lady. When he discovers that she was once shut up in a prison cell for nine months with nothing to read but the Bible, he is interested, as he is struggling with the difficulties raised by his own reading of the Bible and *The Pilgrim's Progress* in the light of his army experiences. From interest he proceeds to affection, and finally takes advantage of the long sermon preached by Aubrey Bagot to steal away with Susan to get married. *Too True to be Good*

FIFFY: *see* Buoyant, Frederick

FIRSTBORN: *see* Buoyant, Tom

FITTON, MARY: Maid-of-honour to Queen Elizabeth I. She has made an assignation to meet William Shakespear on the ramparts of the Palace of Westminster, and finds him there with another woman. In a fury she boxes both their ears, only to find that the woman is the Queen. She confounds herself in excuses, in the course of which she reveals that she is Shakespear's Dark Lady of the Sonnets, and is sent away, protesting that she is 'of all ladies most deject and wretched'. *The Dark Lady of the Sonnets*

FITZAMBEY, LORD REGINALD: A young under-secretary in the War Office who has had a nervous breakdown after being severely censured for gambling on the Stock Exchange. Hearing, in his official capacity, that the British Army is to become vegetarian, he had bought up a vast quantity of shares in the British Macaroni Trust. He is too brainless to understand what he has done wrong, and is consequently shattered by the storm raging round him. His mother, who knows he is fond of music, has engaged a famous pianist, Strega Thundridge, to play to him for two hours. At first she drives him distracted, but soon, under the influence of classical music, he confesses that he longs to marry a strong passionate woman for whom he can create a peaceful home, while she desires a meek, clinging, affectionate husband to return to after her exhausting concerts. Triumphantly they play the Wedding March together to cement their union. *The Music Cure*

FITZFASSEN, ALASTAIR: A splendid athlete, with whom the millionairess Epifania Ognisanti di Parerga falls in love. He agrees to marry her, but first, in fulfilment of a promise made to her father, she gives him £150 and says she can only become his wife if he makes it into £50,000 in six months. By a combination of luck, and frauds which ought to have landed him in jail, he does so. But Epifania soon tires of him, all his brains being in his muscles, and he of her, since she is a typical *monstre sacré*, overbearing, egotistical and hot-tempered. For relief he turns to the homely and gentle Patricia Smith, and hopes Epifania will agree to a divorce so that he can marry her. But she refuses with contumely, until she happens to fall in love with an Egyptian doctor whom she decides to marry. *The Millionairess*

FITZFASSEN, EPIFANIA: A handsome, overpowering, eccentric young woman, whose father has left her thirty millions, and made her promise to marry only a man who can take £150 and turn it into £50,000 in six months. Alastair Fitzfassen has done this, so she marries him, but soon finds she has made a mistake. 'I, Epifania Ognisanti di Parerga, saw myself as the most wonderful woman in England marrying the most wonderful man. And I was only a goose marrying a buck rabbit.' So she goes to her solicitor, Julius Sagamore, intending to make a will leaving all her money to her husband—which will inevitably lead to his ruin—and then commit suicide. But Sagamore puts her off by solemnly presenting her with a recipe for a good poison. So she decides to leave her husband but not to divorce him, as she does not wish him to marry his mistress, Patricia Smith. However, she falls in love with an Egyptian doctor. When she insists on his fulfilling her father's proviso, he tells her that because of a promise he made to his mother, she also must pass a test, and with an initial sum of thirty-five shillings in her pocket must keep herself for six months. She does this by taking over a sweat-shop in the East End, and by turning the old pub, the Pig and Whistle, into a smart riverside café called The Cardinal's Hat. As the doctor has also fulfilled the necessary condition, as it were retrospectively by giving his £150 to the widow of a man whose inventions have made millions for those who exploited them, Epifania tells Sagamore to arrange for her divorce and remarriage. *The Millionairess*

FITZTOLLEMACHE, GEORGE: The husband of Lady Magnesia Fitztollemache, a saturnine figure in evening dress partially concealed by a crimson cloak. He is about to murder his faithless wife with a dagger when she sneezes; a second attempt is thwarted by the singing of the Angels, which wakens her. When her lover Adolphus Bastable comes to show her his new clothes, George, mad with jealousy, gives him a poisoned drink, but later repents and tries to save his life by making him first eat plaster from the ceiling and then drink water in which Magnesia's plaster bust has been dissolved. This solidifies and turns Adolphus into a statue, which Magnesia and George raise up and put in their bed-sitting-room. *Passion, Poison, and Petrifaction*

FITZTOLLEMACHE, LADY MAGNESIA: The unfaithful wife of George Fitztollemache, who first tries to murder her, and then poisons her lover, Adolphus Bastable. When she realises Adolphus is dying, she promises to transfer her romantic love to her husband, but reserves the right to spend most of her time weeping on the tomb of Adolphus. To prevent this, George gives Adolphus an antidote to the poison, plaster of lime, which solidifies inside him, turning him into a plaster statue which Magnesia helps to place in their bed-sitting-room. *Passion, Poison, and Petrifaction*

FLANCO: *see* Fortinbras, General Flanco de

FLAVIA: *see* Chavender, Flavia

FLOPPER, SIR FERDINAND: A solicitor called in by Bill Buoyant, the millionaire, to explain to his numerous children their financial situation in the event of his death, which is, quite simply, that they will be penniless, but able to live on their father's reputation and company director-ships. Flopper is rather overwhelmed by the exuberance and diverse talents of the combined family, especially when the old man's daughter by his first wife joins them, and finally leaves because no one seems to be taking any notice of him. But he calls on Buoyant first, and tells him he thinks the family needs an alienist rather than a solicitor, particularly Clementina, who intends to marry a man who says he only wants her for her money. He also says that he would like to adopt Buoyant's youngest daughter Eudoxia (Darkie) as his daughter, but she refuses, as all she is interested in is housekeeping. *Buoyant Billions*

FLOWER GIRL: Employed by a florist in Vienna, she brings a large bunch of roses to the flat rented by Professor Bruno Haldenstedt for meetings with his mistress Jitta Lenkheim, and stays to help the housekeeper Mrs. Billiter arrange them. Although adequately tipped by Mrs. Billiter, she is quite ready to accept another tip from Haldenstedt, and leaves reluctantly, having been much impressed by the luxury of his little hide-out. *Jitta's Atonement*

See also Doolittle, Eliza

FOOTMAN: A servant in the house of Count O'Dowda, who shows in the guests when they come to watch his daughter's play. *Fanny's First Play*

See also Bashville; Juggins

FOREMAN: *see* Jurymen

FORTINBRAS, GENERAL FLANCO DE: One of the dictators (Franco) called for judgement before the Court of International Justice at The Hague. He arrives late, after Battler (Hitler) and Bombadone (Mussolini), just as the latter, who considers him no better than his 'valet', is saying he will not dare to appear. When all present have tried to prove that their own countrymen are best fitted to rule the world, he says merely: 'Let these gentlemen manage their own countries and leave us to manage ours.' He also reminds Battler, who is boasting that he has never failed to win a battle, that he has not yet fought one. When the end of the world through a new ice-age is announced by the Judge, Flanco hurries off to consult the Pope. *Geneva*

FOX, GEORGE: The founder of the Society of Friends, or Quakers; known also as the man in leather breeches. He calls on Isaac Newton, hoping to discuss with him the scriptural problems raised by his new philosophy, but arrives at the same time as 'Mr. Rowley'—Charles II—who wishes to see Newton's new telescope. He and Fox have an interesting discussion, which is interrupted by the arrival of Nell Gwynn, the Duchess of Cleveland, and the Duchess of Portsmouth, followed by the Duke of York and the Dutch painter Kneller. Fox argues with them all, and manages to get in some shrewd blows, but also learns some home truths, particularly from Nelly, who makes him take her down to dinner, saying he must dine with publicans and sinners, and say grace for them, to which he replies 'You remind me that where my Master went I must follow.' *In Good King Charles's Golden Days*

FRANK: *see* Gardner, Frank

FRANKLYN: *see* Barnabas, Franklyn

FREDERICK: *see* Buoyant, Frederick

FREDDY: *see* Eynsford-Hill, Freddy

FRIAR: *see* Ferruccio, Count

FTATATEETA: Head nurse to Cleopatra, 'a huge, grim woman, her face covered with a network of tiny wrinkles, and her eyes old, large, and wise; sinewy handed, very tall, very strong; with the mouth of a bloodhound and the jaws of a bulldog.' She is ruthless in her behaviour, murdering Pothinus on Cleopatra's orders, and being herself murdered by Rufio, who cuts her throat before the altar of Ra. Julius Caesar, who cannot pronounce her name, calls her Teetatota or Totateeta indifferently, much to the amusement of Cleopatra. *Caesar and Cleopatra*

FUSIMA: An inhabitant of Ireland in A.D. 3000, who is nearing the end of her second century. She comes across Joseph Barlow, a visitor from the British capital of Baghdad, wandering alone on the island, and stays with him until his guardian, Zozim, comes to take him off her hands. *Back to Methuselah, Part IV: Tragedy of an Elderly Gentleman*

G

GARDNER, FRANK: The son of the Rev. Samuel Gardner, 'a pleasant, pretty, smartly dressed, clever good-for-nothing', with a charming voice and agreeably disrespectful manners. He is carrying on a discreet flirtation with Vivie Warren, who is staying in a cottage near his father's rectory, and there meets her mother Kitty, who turns out to be an old flame of his father's. When Sir George Crofts accuses Vivie of being the elder Gardner's daughter by Kitty, Frank does not believe it, but he realises that they have little in common, and accepts her dismissal of him philosophically. *Mrs. Warren's Profession*

GARDNER, REV. SAMUEL: 'a beneficed clergyman of the Established Church', just over fifty, and the father of Frank Gardner. 'Externally he is pretentious, booming, noisy, important. Really he is that obsolescent social phenomenon, the fool of the family, dumped on the Church by his father, the patron.' He disapproves of his son's friendship with Vivie Warren even before he discovers that her mother, Kitty, is the 'Miss Vavasour' with whom he became entangled as a young man, before entering the Church. Being something of a snob, he is however delighted to entertain her friends Sir George Crofts and Mr. Praed, and sits up till four in the morning with the former, telling dubious stories and getting drunk. He is not present when Crofts tells Vivie that Gardner is her father, but he later assures Frank it is not true, though he probably believes it. In the text he is referred to throughout as Rev. S. *Mrs. Warren's Profession*

GARNETT, PROSERPINE: Secretary to the Rev. James Morell, with whom she is in love. 'A brisk little woman of about thirty, of the lower middle class, neatly but cheaply dressed in a black merino skirt and a blouse . . . pert and

97

quick of speech ... not very civil, but sensitive and affectionate.' She is rude to Morell's father-in-law Mr. Burgess, who tries to get Morell to dismiss her. Included in Burgess's impromptu supper-party after one of her employer's lectures to a working-class club, she gets slightly tipsy on unaccustomed champagne, and is seen home rather apprehensively by Morell's curate, the Rev. Alexander Mill. She is usually known as Prossy or Pross. *Candida*

GAUNT, JOHN OF: Son of Edward III. As a child of seven, he is present at the siege of Calais, and watches the surrender of the six burghers and their departure after his mother, Philippa of Hainault, has obtained a pardon for them. *The Six of Calais*

GENTLEMAN: An official of the Anthropometric Laboratory on the Isle of Wight. He interviews the unauthorised Tourist who has landed from his own boat and thinks he is a genius, and also the Tramp who has come as a stowaway and says he is good for nothing, and decides that they will both be very useful for experimental purposes: 'a nincompoop who thinks he's a genius and a genius who thinks he's a nincompoop'. *Far-Fetched Fables 3*

An unnamed English Roman Catholic of the year 1920 who announces to the characters assembled in Charles VII's dream that the canonisation of the former Maid of Orleans as Saint Joan has now been ratified, and will be celebrated annually on 20 May, the anniversary of her death. When she proposes returning from the dead, he says the possibility was not contemplated in the recent proceedings, and he must return to Rome for further instructions. *Saint Joan*

GENTLEMANLY JOHNNY: *see* Burgoyne, General

GEORGE: *see* Crofts, Sir George; Fitztollemache, George; Fox, George; Kemp, George

GHOSTS: *see* Adam, Cain, Eve, Lilith, Serpent

GILBEY, BOBBY: A rather silly young man who has been

far too strictly brought up, and therefore gravitates naturally to Dora Delaney. When they have both been in prison for assaulting a policeman after a rather hectic night out, he comes home and wonders how he can break off his engagement to Margaret Knox. She solves the problem by coming to break it off herself, having also been in prison for the same offence. They decide that their engagement was a mistake, engineered by their fathers, who are in partnership, and Bobby is therefore free to marry Darling Dora, while Margaret pairs off with the Gilbeys' footman, Juggins, whom she has admired secretly for some time. Her parents are delighted, as they have just discovered that he is the brother of a duke. *Fanny's First Play*

GILBEY, MARIA: A placid, elderly lady, who takes very calmly the news that her son Bobby has been in prison for assaulting a policeman, and also the breaking off of his engagement to the apparently very suitable Margaret Knox in favour of marriage with the ebullient Darling Dora Delaney. She is, however, rather flustered to discover that her admirable footman, Juggins, is the brother of a duke. *Fanny's First Play*

GILBEY, ROBIN: The father of Bobby Gilbey, an irascible elderly gentleman, soft, stout, with white hair and a thin smooth skin. He is very put out when the ebullient Dora Delaney comes to tell him that his strictly-brought-up son is in prison for assaulting a policeman, and delivers himself of a few home truths to the young lady before going to pay the boy's fine and bring him home. He is with difficulty persuaded to allow Bobby to marry Dora, and does so mainly because he dare not go against the advice of his footman, Juggins, who has just revealed that he is the brother of a duke. *Fanny's First Play*

GILLES: *see* Oudebolle, Gilles d'; Rais, Gilles de

GIRL: An assistant at the Anthropometric Laboratory on the Isle of Wight. She is the first to notice both the unauthorised

Tourist, who has landed on the island from his own boat, and the Tramp, who has come over from the mainland as a stowaway, and goes to the canteen to fetch the latter some bread, because he is hungry. *Far-Fetched Fables 3*

GIRL FROM THE FLORIST'S: *see* Flower Girl

GISBOURNE, ADELAIDE: A beautiful and accomplished actress, the mother of Cashel Byron, who ran away from home ten years ago. Taken by Lord Worthington to watch an illegal prizefight, she recognises her son in one of the contenders, and pursues him to the castle of Lydia Carew, where he has taken refuge from the police. There she reveals that he is the son of Bingley Bumpkin FitzAlgernon de Courcy Cashel Byron, sieur of Park Lane and Overlord of Dorset, who committed suicide three months after their marriage. Cashel is prepared to go to prison rather than go home with her, but luckily Lord Worthington arrives in his four-in-hand, and offers her his hand in marriage, which she accepts. *The Admirable Bashville*

GIULIA: The daughter of the innkeeper Squarcio, who has been hired by Cardinal Poldi to assassinate Count Ferruccio, the seducer of the Cardinal's sister. Giulia, who needs money for her dowry before she can marry the young fisherman Sandro, is ordered to entice the Count to her father's inn, but before doing so she seeks absolution from a blind old friar, who is the Count in disguise. Learning of the plot against him, he rushes to kill Squarcio, but Giulia points out that her father is bound to win, as he is a professional fighter. She refuses to be bought by the Count, or even to become his wife, in return for sparing his life, and helps her father and her fiancé to capture him. But when they decide to escort him to a safe place, on the grounds that he is mad, and that his murder will bring them bad luck, she agrees to the Count's proposition that she shall accompany him to town, and pose to a famous artist for a portrait of Saint Barbara, thus earning the money she needs for her dowry. *The Glimpse of Reality*

GIUSEPPE: *see* Grandi, Giuseppe

GLADIATORS: At the Colosseum in Rome. They assemble behind the royal box, awaiting their turn to enter the arena; among them are a Retiarius and a Secutor. They are very amused when Spintho is eaten by the lion by mistake, but when some of them are sent into the arena to fight the Christians, they are so terrified at the sight of Ferrovius that they hesitate to attack him. After he has killed six of them the survivors return and are told by Caesar that they are to become Christians. They take to their heels again when Androcles and the lion come out of the arena, but are called back to see how their Emperor has 'tamed the beast', and finally watch Androcles and his pet walk away unmolested. *Androcles and the Lion*

GLENMORISON, SANDY: The President of the Board of Trade. He comes to ask the Prime Minister, Sir Arthur Chavender, why he has not included Home Rule for Scotland in his reckless socialist programme of reform. He is, however, pleased with the nationalisation of the banks, as it will enable the small shopkeepers to borrow on easy terms, and they will therefore vote for him and keep him in Parliament. But when the Foreign Secretary, Sir Dexter Rightside, denounces Chavender's reforms, Glenmorison decides to go in with him, as he considers him indispensable. He has not been trained to use his mind like a Scotsman, he says; but that is just what gives him such a hold on the country. *On the Rocks*

GLORIA: *see* Clandon, Gloria

GOATHERD: Look-out for Mendoza and his brigands. When first seen, he appears to be 'either a Spaniard or a Scotchman; probably a Spaniard, since he wears the dress of a Spanish goatherd and seems at home in the Sierra Nevada, but very like a Scotchman for all that'. His job is to signal the arrival of cars which the brigands then hold up, robbing the occupiers. *Man and Superman*

GONZALES, DON: The Commander of Calatrava, father of Doña Ana, killed in a duel by Don Juan Tenorio. When John Tanner falls asleep in the brigands' camp and dreams that he is Don Juan in Hell, he meets the Commander, who has assumed the shape of his own statue (which once feasted with Don Juan and then led him down into Hell) because he was so much more admired in marble than he ever was in his own person. He nevertheless looks remarkably like Roebuck Ramsden, the guardian of Tanner's future wife, Ann Whitefield. The Commander is now in Heaven, but finds it so boring that he is only too ready to change places with Juan and live permanently in Hell. *Man and Superman (Don Juan in Hell)*

GRACE: *see* Tranfield, Grace

GRAND CHAM: *see* Tarleton, John

GRAND DUCHESS OF BOETIA: *see* Annajanska

GRANDI, GIUSEPPE: The cheerful, bullet-headed, black-haired forty-year-old landlord of a small inn at Tavazzano, where General Bonaparte has quartered himself after the battle of Lodi. He is delighted at his good fortune in being under the protection of the General, as this means the victorious French soldiers will not loot his possessions. He even dares to wear 'a pair of gold earrings which would otherwise have been hidden carefully under the wine-press . . . with his little equipment of silver plate'. Although shrewd, he is credulous enough to believe that the Strange Lady who is also staying in his inn is a witch, and that he has seen her flying away on his best broomstick. *The Man of Destiny*

GRANNY: *see* Ramsden, Roebuck

GRANTHAM, LESBIA: The younger sister of Alice Bridgenorth, whose brother-in-law, General Bridgenorth, has been in love with her for many years. A handsome woman, tall, slender, sure of herself, terrifying to the young and shy, fastidious to her finger-tips, tolerant and amused rather than sympathetic, she refuses him each time he proposes on the grounds that she is not a marrying woman. She would very much like to have children, but, she says: 'If I am to be a mother, I really cannot have a man bothering me to be a wife at the same time.' When the family are trying to draw up a civil contract for her niece Edith, to take the place of the marriage ceremony, she joins in the discussion and says she would be willing to enter into an alliance with General Bridgenorth 'on honorable conditions'. When these prove impossible, she decides to remain single. As Bill Collins says: 'A pity! A fine lady wasted!' *Getting Married*

GREGORY: *see* Lunn, Gregory

GROOM: In attendance on the Black Prince just before the arrival of the six burghers of Calais with the keys of the city. He has nothing to say, and has hardly made his appearance before he is flying from the wrath of Edward III. *The Six of Calais*

GRUFF-AND-GRUM: *see* La Tremouille, Duc de

GUARDSMEN: A group of about a dozen young noblemen under Belzanor, who are on duty in the courtyard of the Syrian palace where Cleopatra has taken refuge when Bel Affris arrives to announce that Julius Caesar is coming to sack it. They are driven out with the rest of the garrison when the palace attendants flee in terror on learning that both Cleopatra and the sacred white cat are missing, but turn up on the quayside at Alexandria to watch Caesar embark for Rome. *Caesar and Cleopatra*

GUINNESS, NURSE: A woman servant in the household of Captain Shotover, who recognises the burglar, Billy Dunn, as her former husband, and on Shotover's orders takes him to the kitchen to be fed. She is, however, sorry that Mazzini Dunn, who is not related to him, did not shoot him while he had the chance. On the orders of the police, she extinguishes all the lights in the house when the air-raid begins, but Hector Hushabye turns them on again. *Heartbreak House*

GUNN, GILBERT: A dramatic critic (based on William Archer) who is invited to Florence Towers to see a play written by Fanny O'Dowda, played by a professional cast. After the play, which has been given anonymously, he says he is sure it is by Granville-Barker, and that it is a lot of pretentious nonsense. When told that Fanny is the author, he recants and says it is 'capital—charming'. *Fanny's First Play*

GUNNER, MR.: *see* Baker, Julius

GUS: *see* Highcastle, Lord Augustus

GWYNN, NELL: A former actress, and the mistress of Charles II. She comes to fetch him from Isaac Newton's house, but gets tired of waiting and goes in. She is coldly received by the housekeeper, Mrs. Basham, and by George Fox, who is visiting Newton, but charms them both. She much enjoys the tantrum indulged in by the Duchess of Cleveland, whose jealousy has led her to pursue Nelly to the house, is amused by the inopportune arrival of the Duchess of Portsmouth, and insists on being taken in to dinner by Fox, saying 'George: today you will dine with publicans and sinners.' *In Good King Charles's Golden Days*

H

HAFFIGAN, MATT (MATTHEW): An elderly peasant farmer, 'small, leathery, peat-faced, with a deep voice and a surliness which is meant to be aggressive and is only pathetic'. After being evicted from his farm for non-payment of rent, he has bought another under the new Land Purchase Act, and is now all for the landlord as against the tenant. He is one of the Rosscullen men who come to the Doyles' house to ask Larry Doyle to stand for Parliament, but he is too stupid to understand much of what is going on, taking the most general remark as a personal insult, and constantly reverting to his old grievances. Having bought a pig from Cornelius Doyle, he accepts Tom Broadbent's offer to drive it home, only to rush off in terror when he discovers that this means going in a motor car. *John Bull's Other Island*

HAFFIGAN, TIM: A seedy, stunted, short-necked, bullet-headed wastrel, with a red nose and a furtive eye. In a suit of shabby black, he looks like a tenth-rate schoolmaster ruined by drink. Born in Glasgow, of Irish parentage, he hoodwinks Tom Broadbent into believing him to be a true Irishman, who will help him with his land development scheme in Ireland. Broadbent engages him as his 'Irish' secretary, and sends him off to get ready for the journey with a £5 note in his pocket, whereupon Broadbent's partner, Larry Doyle, who knows the Haffigans well, prophesies truly that he will never be seen again, there being too many public houses on the way to Paddington. *John Bull's Other Island*

HALDENSTEDT, AGNES: The narrow-minded and conventionally correct wife of a well-known Viennese psychiatrist. She has allowed herself to be submerged by the domestic details of life, and takes no interest in his work, but when he is found dead in a flat in which he has been meeting his mistress, she is furiously angry and determined to discover the identity of the woman. At one moment she suspects the truth; it was Jitta Lenkheim, the wife of one of her husband's colleagues. But Jitta cleverly leads her to believe that it was some chance acquaintance for whom he had no real affection, and she finally accepts the situation, devoting all her energies to the furthering of her husband's reputation by the publication of his last book, *The Fetters of the Feminine Psyche*, under the aegis of Lenkheim and her daughter Edith's fiancé, Dr. Fessler. *Jitta's Atonement*

HALDENSTEDT, PROFESSOR BRUNO: A fifty-year-old

Viennese psychiatrist, married to a dull wife, with one grown-up daughter. He has fallen in love with Jitta Lenkheim, the wife of one of his colleagues, and has rented a small flat where they can meet in secret. She is there with him one night when he dies suddenly of a heart attack, and to avoid a scandal she leaves hurriedly, unseen by anyone. To make up to Lenkheim for his betrayal, Haldenstedt has arranged for his new and, as he thinks, epoch-making work on *The Fetters of the Feminine Psyche* to be published under Lenkheim's name, on the grounds that he supplied much of the material for it. But Lenkheim, who disagrees profoundly with the conclusions drawn by Haldenstedt from his work, refuses to allow it, though he does agree to edit the work as a tribute to his late colleague. *Jitta's Atonement*

HALDENSTEDT, EDITH: The daughter of a famous Viennese psychiatrist, who dies suddenly while in a rented flat with his mistress. Both her mother and her fiancé, Dr. Fessler, try to keep the details of his death from her, but she is resentful at being treated as a child, and when she learns the facts she shocks them by trying to find out the name of the unknown woman who, she is sure, brought her father much happiness. She discovers that it was Jitta Lenkheim, wife of one of her father's colleagues, and is delighted that he should have been loved by someone able to appreciate him as he deserved, which she is sure her mother could not do. While promising to keep Jitta's secret, she is sufficiently consoled by her discovery to renew her engagement, which she had broken off in a quarrel with Dr. Fessler. *Jitta's Atonement*

HALLAM, SIR HOWARD: A Judge of the High Court, on holiday with his sister-in-law, Lady Cicely Waynflete, in Morocco. They decide to make an expedition into the Atlas Mountains, and for fear of Arab attacks they are escorted by Captain Brassbound and some of his crew. Hallam, who has illegally got possession of his late brother's sugar plantations in the West Indies, does not know that Brassbound is his dispossessed nephew, filled with hatred for his uncle and a desire to avenge his own wrongs and those of his mother, who died in poverty. He therefore betrays Hallam to the sheikh Sidi el Assif, who has sworn to murder all unbelievers. Hallam, who can easily find arguments to justify his behaviour, faces the threat of death or slavery with composure, but is rescued from his predicament by the Cadi Muley Othman, acting on orders from the American naval captain, Kearney. *Captain Brassbound's Conversion*

HAMMINGTAP, PHOSPHOR: A young English clergyman, curious and apprehensive, with a baby complexion and a childish expression, credulous and disarmingly propitiatory. He is found by the priest Pra wandering about in the Farwaters' garden, where Janga, Kanchin, Maya, and Vashti are sitting in their shrines. He explains that some pirates who captured him at Weston-super-Mare, to be their chaplain, got tired of him and marooned him on the island. When he adds, by way of excusing his simple-mindedness, that he was the result of an experiment by his father, a biological chemist, who overdid the nitrogen, Pra thinks he may be useful in furthering his own eugenic experiments, and suggests that he should remain on the island as 'husband' to all the women of the party, but particularly to the two young girls Maya and Vashti. After some demur Iddy, as he is usually called—short for Idiot—agrees, being already very attracted to Maya. When the children disappear after the Day of Judgement, and their parents cannot even remember their names, Iddy says they were 'Love, Pride, Heroism, and Empire'; and Maya was Love. He then decides to return to England, to look for a village and a cottage; a garden and a church; and to be content with his little black coat and little white collar, and the words spoken by Jesus. *The Simpleton of the Unexpected Isles*

HANNAH: *see* Women in the Barn

HANWAYS, HILDA: Secretary to the Prime Minister, Sir

Arthur Chavender. She arrives late for work one morning because the unemployed are demonstrating and have held up her taxi, and then finds it very difficult to get Chavender through all the work he has to do because he is constantly interrupted by visitors and deputations. In the end she has to hurry him off to an official luncheon, after promising to pack all the works of Karl Marx, Lenin, Trotsky, etc., for him to read while he is on holiday, and then goes to lunch herself with Lady Chavender, who has asked her at the last minute because she is short of a woman. When, some months later, the Prime Minister has upset all his colleagues by making a red-hot socialist speech, she ushers them all in to remonstrate with him, and when the unemployed finally burst into Downing Street and start breaking the windows, she is so horrified by the brutality of the police that she rushes out to attack them. *On the Rocks*

HARDMOUTH: *see* Rosty, Piers de

HARRY: *see* Trench, Dr. Harry

HASLAM, REV. WILLIAM: In the 1920s he is a young clergyman engaged to Cynthia Barnabas. He listens to her father and uncle expounding their belief that Creative Evolution will soon produce men and women capable of living to 300 years, but does not believe it, and says comfortably that 'it won't be one of us, anyhow'. *Back to Methuselah, Part II: The Gospel of the Brothers Barnabas*

In A.D. 2170 Haslam is still alive, aged 283 and looking about fifty. He is now Archbishop of York, having previously been Archbishop Haslam, Archbishop Stickit, President Dickenson and General Bullyboy. These men are all presumed to have died by drowning, but this was only Haslam's device for finishing off one career and starting another. His secret is discovered when Barnabas, the Accountant General, happens to see a film showing all four dignitaries during their lifetime, and recognises them as the present Archbishop. Called to account, Haslam explains that he is obviously the first, and as far as he knows the only, example of the longevity prophesied by the Brothers Barnabas. But he discovers that Franklyn Barnabas's former parlourmaid is also a long-liver, only nine years younger than himself. She too is in office, being Domestic Minister of the British Islands. To save England from the rule of black and yellow men, they decide to marry and found a race of long-lived Englishmen. *Back to Methuselah, Part III: The Thing Happens*

HASSAN: An Arab porter in Mogador, who with two Krooboys conducts Sir Howard Hallam and Lady Cicely Waynflete to the house of the missionary Leslie Rankin, together with two camel-loads of baggage. Although he has already been heavily overpaid by Lady Cicely, he tries unsuccessfully to get some more money out of Rankin. *Captain Brassbound's Conversion*

HAWKINS, LAWYER: The family friend who comes to read the will of Timothy Dudgeon, by which he leaves his farm to his scapegrace son Richard, much to the disgust and disappointment of his widow. Hawkins is 'a brisk middle-aged man in brown riding gaiters and yellow breeches looking as much squire as solicitor'. *The Devil's Disciple*

HE: *see* American Journalist; Apjohn, Henry; Jew; Smith, Junius

HE-ANCIENT: A being, thousands of years old, who has long ago outlived the childish pleasures of eating, drinking, love-making, listening to music, and dancing. He finds himself by mistake among a group of young people, and realises that one of them, Chloe, is older than her companions because she too is tiring of these things, and is ready to give herself wholly to mathematics. When he tells her she will soon be ready for the life he lives, and a youth protests at its dullness, he replies: 'Infant! one moment of the ecstasy of life as we live it would strike you dead!' He returns to the group, with the She-Ancient, after

Pygmalion has been killed by the automatic figures he has created in the laboratory, and when they have been removed he tries to explain the future to the young people. His destiny is to be immortal, but he is still tied to a remnant of material existence by his body. Soon there will be no bodies, only pure thought. The youngsters find this too difficult to understand, and the Ancients, wearying of fruitless discussion, go sadly away. *Back to Methuselah, Part V: As Far as Thought Can Reach*

HECTOR: *see* Hushabye, Hector; Malone, Hector, jun.

HENRY: *see* Apjohn, Henry; Trench, Dr. Harry; Higgins, Henry; Straker, Henry

HER HUSBAND: *see* Bompas, Edward

HER LOVER: *see* Apjohn, Henry

HERM: A hermaphrodite working at the Genetic Institute on the Isle of Wight. He is dressed in a tunic, embroidered with a vine twining round an elm, and chequered sleeves. He is very worried because he cannot find anything about hermaphrodites in the nineteenth-century treatises on physiology which he is studying, though he is sure they must have existed, and he is also anxious to give up making human beings under laboratory conditions and to become a mind without a body. *Far-Fetched Fables 5*

HERSELF: *see* Bompas, Aurora

HIGGINS, HENRY: A dedicated phonetician, author of Higgins's Universal Alphabet, and an impassioned collector of local speech and vowel-sounds, of which he claims to recognise 130. Talking to his friend Colonel Pickering while sheltering from the rain under the portico of St. Paul's, Covent Garden, he boasts that he could take anyone—for instance, a Cockney flower-girl who is listening to their conversation—and teach her to speak so well that he could pass her off as a duchess at an Ambassador's garden-party. The girl, Eliza Doolittle, turns up at his house next morning, asking for lessons, and the two men decide to experiment with her. At first Higgins thinks good speech will be enough, but after Eliza has attended an At Home at his mother's house and half-shocked, half-amused everyone by her racy conversation, which includes the famous phrase 'Not bloody likely', he realises that education is also necessary. He puts Eliza through an intensive course of art, music, and literature, and eventually succeeds in his objective, triumphantly. He then becomes bored with the whole project, and cannot understand why Eliza turns on him in a fury, accusing him of indifference and callous behaviour. He has never been interested in anything but his work, and is completely careless about himself and other people, including their feelings. When Eliza has taken refuge with his mother, who is sorry for the havoc her son has created, he follows her and makes it quite clear that he has no sentimental interest in her, and would prefer her to stand on her own feet; which she does, by marrying Freddy Eynsford-Hill. *Pygmalion*

HIGGINS, MRS.: The mother of Henry Higgins, whose eccentricities she is willing to condone, but whose bad manners drive her to despair. She is, however, very fond of him, and reluctantly allows his protégée, Eliza Doolittle, a Cockney flower-girl whom he has taught to speak like a lady, to make her social début at one of her At Homes. She points out to Higgins that Eliza's education is far from complete; though she speaks like a lady, the subject matter of her conversation is still that of a guttersnipe. Higgins and his friend Colonel Pickering acknowledge the justice of this, and set to work to improve Eliza's mind as well as her vowels, with complete success. When Eliza realises that they have lost all interest in her once they have achieved their object of passing her off as a 'princess at an ambassador's garden party', it is with Mrs. Higgins that she takes refuge, and it is Mrs. Higgins who furthers her romance with the foolish but kind-hearted and infatuated Freddy Eynsford-Hill. Mrs. Higgins also agrees to attend the wedding of Eliza's father, the dustman Alfred Doolittle, after he has been left a large legacy by an eccentric American millionaire and is forced by middle-class morality to marry the woman he is living with. *Pygmalion*

HIGHCASTLE, LORD AUGUSTUS: A distinguished member of the ruling classes, at present disguised as a colonel; it is 1916. He has been making an unsuccessful recruiting speech in Little Pifflington, and is in the Mayor's parlour when his brother, Hungerford Highcastle, known as Blueloo, telephones to let him know that a female spy will shortly try to steal from him the secret list of anti-aircraft gun emplacements. A Lady then arrives, and says she has come to warn him against her sister-in-law, who will stop at nothing to get the list from him. He reassures her, and when his clerk, Horatio Beamish, has returned to him the list, which he left on his breakfast-table, he puts it away carefully. However, the Lady manages to extract it and then telephones Blueloo to say she has won her bet. *Augustus Does His Bit*

HILDA: *see* Hanways, Hilda

HILL, JENNY: An eighteen-year-old Salvation Army lass, pretty, pale, overwrought. She brings the unemployed Peter Shirley to the West Ham shelter for a meal, and is knocked down by the brutal Bill Walker when he comes looking for his girl, whom Jenny has converted. She forgives him, and refuses the £1 which he offers in compensation, going off happily with her tambourine to join in the meeting held to celebrate the £1,000 given to the shelter by Andrew Undershaft. *Major Barbara*

HIPNEY, MR.: A member of the deputation from the Isle of Cats which comes to see the Prime Minister, Sir Arthur Chavender, a 'sunny, comfortable old chap in his Sunday best'. He lets all the others talk their heads off, and then remains behind when they have gone. He tells Chavender a few home truths, and advises him to read Karl Marx before trying to argue with young people who have educated themselves out of the gutter. When the deputation returns some months later to protest against Chavender's proposal to abolish strikes and introduce compulsory labour, Hipney is not with it, but he comes in and tells the assembled Ministers that what England needs now is not democracy, but a dictator. *On the Rocks*

HODSON: Valet to Tom Broadbent, an elderly, respectable man, 'old enough to have lost all alacrity and acquired an air of putting up patiently with a great deal of trouble and indifferent health'. He goes to Ireland with Broadbent, and finds that much as he likes Irishmen in London, he hates them in their own country. The snivelling and moaning of Matthew Haffigan about his grievances finally drives him to protest, and in a strong Cockney accent very different from his usual refined speech he embarks on a long speech about the much worse sufferings of Englishmen, including his own grandfather. He is willing to make the Irish a present of England so that they can find out what suffering is really like, and is in favour of Home Rule because he thinks that, once Ireland is out of the way, the English may get some attention paid to them at Westminster. *John Bull's Other Island*

HORACE: *see* Brabazon, Horace

HOTCHKISS, ST. JOHN: A young gentleman, known to his family as Sonny, who talks about himself with energetic gaiety, and to other people with a sweet forbearance (implying kindly consideration for their stupidity) which infuriates those who are not amused by him. He is a born mischief-maker, always willing to add fuel to the flames of an argument, and an arrant snob—snobbism, he declares, constituting the strength of the English. He has become involved with Leo, the young wife of the elderly Reginald Bridgenorth, who has persuaded her husband to give her grounds for divorce; but when they all meet at the wedding of Edith Bridgenorth, Leo's niece, Hotchkiss recognises another guest, the indomitable Mrs. George Collins, as a coal-merchant's wife with whom he was once in love. He succumbs to her fascination once again, and persuades Leo to return to her husband so as to leave him free to cultivate his friendship with Mrs. Collins. *Getting Married*

HOTEL MANAGER: A very haughty and condescending individual who receives the Princess with an affability bordering on insolence, and fobs her off with an inferior room and poor service until routed by her new lady's maid, Ermyntrude Roosenhonkers-Pipstein. *The Inca of Perusalem*

The son of the elderly and old-fashioned owner of a dismal riverside pub called The Pig and Whistle. Epifania Fitz-fassen, having to earn her living for six months in order to qualify for marriage with her Egyptian doctor, gets a job there as scullery maid, and in a very short time has taken the place over, renamed it The Cardinal's Hat, and made it an attractive hotel, throwing out the old people, and installing the son as manager. He tells Alastair Fitzfassen and Patricia Smith the story when they lunch there, gets into trouble for allowing them into the hotel when Epifania arrives unexpectedly, and escapes from the resultant confusion as soon as he can. *The Millionairess*

HOTSPOT, ADMIRAL SIR BEMROSE: First Lord of the Admiralty. He is 'a half-witted admiral; but the half that has not been sacrificed to his profession is sound and vigorous'. After the Prime Minister, Sir Arthur Chavender, has made a speech which infuriates most of his colleagues by its socialistic content, Hotspot calls to congratulate him. He is particularly pleased with the raising of all naval pay free of income tax, and the promise of as many new aircraft-carriers as he wants. But when Sir Dexter Rightside comes out in opposition to Chavender, Hotspot supports him, because they were at school together. *On the Rocks*

HUMPHRIES, TOM: The Mayor of the Isle of Cats, and leader of a deputation which comes to see the Prime Minister on the subject of local unemployment. The meeting is inconclusive. Some months later, when the Prime Minister, under the influence of Karl Marx, whom he has just read for the first time, puts forward a red-hot socialist programme, the deputation returns to protest against compulsory labour and the outlawing of strikes. The Mayor insists that both items must be dropped from the programme, or he will see that the Prime Minister never shows his face in the Isle of Cats again. *On the Rocks*

HUSHABYE, HECTOR: The husband of Captain Shotover's elder daughter, Hesione, who keeps him like a tame cat in her father's house. Indolent and frustrated, he seeks compensation in posing as 'Marcus Darnley', a romantic figure who captures the imagination and affection of the young Ellie Dunn, leaving her heartbroken when she discovers the truth. He is attracted to Hesione's sister Ariadne when she returns home after a long absence, and makes love to her, but the only person he really loves, even when he is deceiving her, is his wife. He is only too aware of the futility of himself and his generation: 'We are wrong. We are useless, dangerous, and ought to be destroyed.' When the air-raid begins, he defies the police by turning on all the lights, and even thinks of setting fire to the house to guide the bombers to their target. But when the bomb falls, it is Mangan and Billy Dunn who are killed, while the rest of the party escape unharmed. 'Safe! And how damnably dull the world has become again.' *Heartbreak House*

HUSHABYE, HESIONE: The elder daughter of Captain Shotover, forty-six, handsome, with black hair, eyes 'like the fishpools of Heshbon', a white skin, and a statuesque figure. She has an amused, though rather contemptuous, affection for her husband, Hector, who has been masquerading as the romantic 'Marcus Darnley' and only laughs when she discovers that Ellie Dunn has fallen in love with him, not at all understanding that the girl is really broken-hearted. But she is well aware, when she stops to think, of the futility of her existence. When Ellie reproaches her, she says: 'When I am neither coaxing and kissing nor laughing, I am just wondering how much longer I can stand living in this cruel damnable world'; and when Mangan, who is engaged to Ellie, has fallen in love with her and complains of her unkindness, she says: 'Cruelty would be delicious if one could only find some sort of cruelty that didn't really hurt.' She is thrilled by the air-raid, saying that the noise in the sky is like Beethoven, and when the bombers have gone, leaving the Rectory in ruins and two of the house-party dead in the garden, she says it was a wonderful experience, and hopes the planes will come back again the next night. *Heartbreak House*

HYERING, HUGO: As Emigration Officer in a small tropical port, he is persuaded by a Young Woman named Sally, who has landed with no passport or papers, to take her on a tour of the island. On a cliff overlooking the sea, he tells her of his frustrations and unhappiness, and tries to commit suicide, but cannot nerve himself to take the fatal jump until booted from behind by the local priest, Pra. Later he rises from the sea, regenerated and clad in a white robe in place of his grubby tropical suit, and throws Sally over the cliff so that she too may be regenerated. Twenty years later, happily married to her, he is Political Secretary to the Isles. With the Farwaters, Pra, and Prola, he is one of the six parents of four biologically perfect children without any moral conscience, who, being useless, disappear on the Day of Judgement. Hyering, who realises that 'the day of judgement is not the end of the world but the beginning of real human responsibility', goes quietly back to work, and persuades his wife to do the same. *The Simpleton of the Unexpected Isles*

HYERING, SALLY: Referred to only as the Young Woman, she arrives without papers or passport in the Emigration Office of a small tropical port, and persuades the man in charge, Hugo Hyering, to take her on a tour of the island

before sending her back on the next boat. After being thrown into the sea, and rising regenerated, she marries him. Twenty years later, as Sally Hyering, she is the busy wife of the Political Secretary of the Isles, and one of the parents of the four perfect children, Janga, Kanchin, Maya, and Vashti. She welcomes the arrival on the island of the clergyman, Phosphor Hammingtap, as he can be a husband to both the girls. After the Day of Judgement, when her husband advises her to do something useful to justify her continued existence, she decides to concentrate on crossword puzzles, because they 'cultivate the mind'.
The Simpleton of the Unexpected Isles

HYPATIA: *see* Tarleton, Hypatia

I

IDDY: *see* Hammingtap, Phosphor

IDDY TOODLES: *see* Barlow, Joseph Popham Bolge Bluebin

INCA OF PERUSALEM: An impressive figure in military uniform, with fierce upstanding moustaches. He looks very like the Kaiser of the First World War, and behaves in a similar fashion. Disguised as Captain Duval, he comes to the hotel where an unnamed princess is staying, having chosen her to be the bride of one of his numerous sons, but is received by her new lady's maid, Ermyntrude Roosen-honkers-Pipstein. She realises at once who he is, and he too recognises her as the daughter of his old friend Archdeacon Daffodil Donkin. In any case she is too intelligent to be a princess, and he is so charmed by her conversation that he proposes to her, only to be refused on the grounds that he is already married and has not enough money to support her in luxury. They decide to further their acquaintance, however, 'in the strictest honour', by driving round the town together and taking tea at the Zoo. *The Inca of Perusalem*

INCOGNITA APPASSIONATA: *see* Collins, Mrs. George

INQUISITOR: *see* Lemaître, Brother John

IRAS: One of Cleopatra's slave-girls, 'a plump, good-natured creature, rather fatuous, with a profusion of red hair, and a tendency to giggle'. *Caesar and Cleopatra*

J

JACK: *see* Dunois, Jack; Tanner, John

JACQUES: *see* Wissant, Jacques de

JAFNA: *see* Pandranath, Sir Jafna

JAMES: *see* Morell, Rev. James; York, Duke of

JANGA: The elder of the two 'biologically perfect' boys of mixed Eastern and Western parentage, who, with their two equally perfect sisters, live on the Unexpected Isles. He warns the young clergyman Phosphor Hammingtap to beware of his sister Maya; brings in the newspaper which announces the dissolution of the British Empire; and proclaims the independence of the island, appointing the priestess Prola, who threatens to box his ears, its 'absolute ruler'. With the other three children he vanishes on the Day of Judgement, because, says the priest Pra, they were useless: 'we taught them everything except common sense.' *The Simpleton of the Unexpected Isles*

JEAN: *see* Aire, Jean d'

JEMIMA: Wife of King Magnus, a pleasant, homely body who knows all about his liaison with Orinthia and does not mind, as she is sure of his real affection. She is present when the American Ambassador comes to say the United States has decided to rejoin the British Commonwealth, and at first thinks it is a good idea, as all the best families have emigrated to Ireland for the Horse Show, and the American wives will be a pleasant change from the English peeresses. She also thinks Magnus would make a very good Emperor of the new empire, and civilise the Americans. She leaves him on the terrace when the Cabinet ministers arrive at five o'clock for his answer to their ultimatum, but returns afterwards to insist that Magnus, who is upset and fretful after getting his own way, shall come to dinner as usual. *The Apple Cart*

JENNIFER: *see* Dubedat, Jennifer

JENNY: *see* Hill, Jenny; Joan

JESSIE: *see* Women in the Barn

JEW: A middle-aged gentleman of distinguished appearance, with a blond beard and moustache, top-hatted, frock-coated, and gloved. He comes to ask Begonia Brown, as secretary of the International Committee for Intellectual Co-operation, to apply to the Court of International Justice at The Hague for a warrant against the dictator, Ernest Battler, who has assaulted, plundered, ruined and exiled him. Later he meets other complainants and goes with them to the Court, where Battler admits his agents are guilty of the charge, but warns the Jew to keep away from his country. 'The world is wide enough for both of us. My country is not.' When the news comes that a new ice-age is fast approaching, the Jew dashes from the Court to telephone his stockbroker. *Geneva*

JINNY-GWINNY: *see* Dubedat, Jennifer

JITTA: *see* Lenkheim, Jitta

JO: A young waiter at the Marine Hotel, Torbay, where he helps the head waiter, Walter Boon, to serve the luncheon at which Mrs. Clandon unexpectedly meets her estranged husband. He does not speak. *You Never Can Tell*

See also Cuthbertson, Joseph; Waggoner Jo

JOAN: A young girl from Domrémy, known variously as the Maid of Orleans, Joan of Arc, or, at home, as Jenny, who arrives at the castle of Vaucouleurs in the spring of 1429, saying she has been commanded by God to lead the Dauphin, at present disinherited by the Treaty of Troyes, to Rheims Cathedral to be crowned Charles VII of France. She persuades Richard de Baudricourt to send her to Charles at Chinon, under escort, and succeeds in putting enough spirit into that poor shambling creature to get him to Rheims in the wake of her victorious army. After the coronation she decides to return home, much to the King's relief, but during a sortie against the Burgundians she is captured, sold to the English, and made to stand trial for heresy. In spite of her obvious naïveté and sincerity, she is condemned to death by burning as a heretic, mainly as a sop to the English, who have threatened to wreck the town if she is acquitted. Years after her death she returns in a dream to Charles VII, and learns that he is now firmly established on the throne, and the English have been driven out of France. A messenger then appears from the year 1920 to tell her that she has been vindicated and canonised, and chapels and statues to her are being put up in France and England. She wonders wistfully what would happen if she were to return from the dead, and they all anxiously beg her not to, and she is left alone, exclaiming: 'O God that madest this beautiful earth, when will it be ready to receive Thy saints? How long, O Lord, how long?' *Saint Joan*

JOCK: *see* Menagerie Keeper

JOE: An elderly, anxious, poor, and ratlike East Ender, who with his wife employs some half-dozen girls, at starvation wages, in a basement in the Commercial Road, sewing buttons on overcoats. When Epifania Fitzfassen comes looking for work, in order to qualify for marriage with the Egyptian Doctor, he thinks she is an inspector, and gives her five shillings to go away. But when she outlines her plans for bypassing the middlemen and dealing direct with the wholesalers, he cannot resist the temptation to make some money, in spite of the pleas and lamentations of his poor-spirited wife, who would rather go on as they are. *The Millionairess*

An unseen worker in the dockyard of a small tropical port, who is told by the Station Master to collect a stretcher and two or three helpers to take away the body of the emigration clerk, Wilks, who has committed suicide. *The Simpleton of the Unexpected Isles*

See also Joseph

JOEY: *see* Percival, Joseph

JOHN: *see* Estivet, John d'; Gaunt, John of; Lemaître, Brother John; Stogumber, John de; Tanner, John; Tarleton, John

JOHNNY: *see* Gaunt, John of; Tarleton, Johnny

JOHNNY JUDGE: *see* Judge

JOHNSON: A member of the escort under Captain Brassbound which accompanies Sir Howard Hallam into the Atlas Mountains. 'A black-bearded, thickset, slow, middle-aged man, with an air of damaged respectability', he is the dissolute son of a sea captain from Hull, considers himself a gentleman, and despises both the Cockney Drinkwater and 'the ignorant and immoral foreigner' Marzo. After Brassbound's trial and acquittal, Johnson takes the crew back to the harbour to prepare his ship for going to sea. *Captain Brassbound's Conversion*

See also Balsquith

JOSEPH: *see* Barlow, Joseph Popham Bolge Bluebin; Cuthbertson, Joseph; Knox, Joseph; Percival, Joseph; Proteus, Joseph; Wallaston, Joseph

JOURNALIST: *see* American Journalist

JUAN TENORIO, DON: When John Tanner goes to sleep in the brigands' camp, he dreams that he is Don Juan in Hell. There he meets the Devil, who looks very like the brigand chief Mendoza; his former love Doña Ana, who looks like his future wife Ann Whitefield; and, on a visit from Heaven, the statue of Doña Ana's father, Don Gonzales, whom Juan killed in a duel, bearing a striking resemblance to Ann Whitefield's guardian, Roebuck Ramsden. Don Juan, who finds Hell excessively boring, and deplores the arrival of Doña Ana, is only too glad, after a long discussion, to take the place of Don Gonzales, who is equally bored with Heaven, and he leaves after persuading Doña Ana not to accompany him. *Man and Superman (Don Juan in Hell)*

JUDGE: A Dutchman, much younger than a British judge, but 'very grave and every inch a judge', even in the face of provocation from Begonia Brown's foolish sweetheart, who insists on referring to him as Johnny Judge. It is he who discovers that Begonia, who attracts him very much, has on her own initiative applied for warrants against the three dictators on a charge of crimes against humanity. He insists that the warrants must be issued; they will serve to set the Court in motion, as it had not previously been able to function for lack of material. Although he has no powers to compel the dictators to attend his court, he is sure they will come—'where the spotlight is, there will the despots be gathered'—and he is justified when they all turn up. Unfortunately nothing has been decided one way or the other before a telephone call to the Judge announces the end of the world through a new ice-age, but he has the satisfaction of knowing that he has been obeyed. 'They blustered, they defied us. But they came. They came.' *Geneva*

JUDITH: *see* Anderson, Judith

JUDY: *see* Doyle, Judy

JUGGINS: The footman of Robin Gilbey, a 'rather low-spirited man of about thirty-five, of a good appearance and address, and iron self-command'. Dora Delaney, who comes to tell the Gilbeys that their son Bobby is in prison, is convinced he is a gentleman, and calls him Rudolph, a nickname adopted by all the other young people. She is justified when it turns out that he is the younger brother of a duke. Having persuaded the Gilbeys to let their son marry Dora, he himself proposes to Bobby's former fiancée, Margaret Knox, and is accepted. *Fanny's First Play*

JULIA: *see* Craven, Julia

JULIUS CAESAR: *see* Caesar, Julius

JUNIUS: *see* Smith, Junius

JUNO, MRS.: An attractive young woman who has been holidaying on board ship without her husband and flirting with Gregory Lunn under the impression that he is unmarried. During a discussion in the hotel lounge on their return to England she discovers to her surprise that Lunn thought she was a widow. He has just embraced her when her husband, accompanied by Lunn's wife, comes into the lounge. Explanations and discussions follow, which bore Mrs. Juno, who firmly refuses to give up speaking to all the men who admire her—if she did there would be no one left to talk to. In the end the two couples decide to exchange partners whenever they feel like it and go into dinner together. *Overruled*

JUNO, SIBTHORPE: A fussily energetic little man, known to his wife as Tops. An inveterate romantic, he gives himself an air of gallantry by greasing the points of his moustaches and dressing very carefully. During a sea voyage unaccompanied by his wife he has fallen in love with Mrs. Lunn, who is so used to be being admired that she is rather bored by him. In a hotel lounge on their return to England they meet their respective spouses, who have also met on a boat and enjoyed a harmless flirtation. Mr. Juno, who is extremely conventional at heart, would like to resolve their dilemma by divorce or a duel, but as neither man can afford a scandal, and the women are merely amused by Juno's attitude, they decide to remain friends, and all go into dinner together. *Overruled*

JURYMEN: A group of townspeople from a small town in America who come to the courthouse to try Blanco Posnet for the crime of horse-stealing, which is punishable by death. They have first to clear the court of a number of women who have been shucking corn, and who attack the prisoner both verbally and with their fists until bundled outside. When order is restored, the jurymen settle down, but the prisoner objects to the foreman because he is prejudiced; to which he retorts 'We mean to hang you; but you will be hanged fair.' Nestor, a juryman with a long white beard, who is drunk, also announces that any man that is not prejudiced against a horse-thief is not fit to sit on a jury. He then goes to sleep. The jurymen do their best to convict the prisoner, Squinty going so far as to start dragging him to the gallows, but when the stolen horse is returned by the woman to whom Blanco lent it to take her dying child to the doctor, and the prostitute Feemy Evans withdraws her evidence against him, the case collapses. The jurymen are then treated to a sermon from Blanco, and adjourn to drink in the local saloon at his expense. *The Shewing-Up of Blanco Posnet*

K

KAISER: *see* Inca of Perusalem

KANCHIN: The younger brother of Janga, and like him and

his sisters Maya and Vashti the result of a eugenic experiment aimed at amalgamating the best qualities of East and West. With them he disappears on the Day of Judgement, because, says Lady Farwaters, one of his six parents, 'We have taught them everything except how to work for their daily bread instead of praying for it.' *The Simpleton of the Unexpected Isles*

KEARNEY, CAPTAIN HAMLIN, U.S.N.: The officer commanding the cruiser *Santiago*. He learns from Leslie Rankin, via the owner of a yacht in Mogador harbour, of the plot against Sir Henry Hallam, and sends the Cadi Muley Othman to rescue him. He then conducts the trial of Captain Brassbound, charged with having endangered the lives of Hallam and his sister-in-law Lady Cicely Waynflete, and releases him on hearing the evidence given by Lady Cicely. Before going back to his ship he invites her, her brother-in-law, and Mr. Rankin to lunch on board. *Captain Brassbound's Conversion*

KEEGAN, PETER: A crazy, visionary ex-priest, 'fifty, white-haired, with the face of a saint'. He lost his faith 'when the mystery of this world was revealed to him' at the bedside of a dying Hindoo, and realised that 'this earth is hell, and that we are sent here to expiate crimes committed by us in a former existence'. He has therefore been deprived of his priestly office, being succeeded by Father Dempsey, who persecutes him and insists that he must no longer be called 'Father'; he wanders about the fields and hills of Rosscullen, striking terror into the hearts of superstitious peasant lads like Patsy Farrell, who believe that he confessed and absolved a 'black man', for which he was cursed and sent mad. He is about the only man in Rosscullen who does not see cause for coarse laughter in Broadbent's misadventure with the pig, which wrecked his car and killed itself in doing so, and he is very much against Broadbent's scheme for building a hotel—or even a Garden City—on the edge of Rosscullen. *John Bull's Other Island*

KEEPER: *see* Menagerie Keeper

KEMP, GEORGE: The sheriff of a small American town on the frontier. He is particularly bitter against horse-thieves, and when called on to preside at the trial of Blanco Posnet for stealing a horse from Elder Daniels which actually belonged to the sheriff, he is obviously ready to condemn him to be hanged. He does, however, endeavour to conduct the trial with some semblance of fairness, until it is interrupted by the arrival of the woman to whom Blanco gave the horse so that she could take her dying child to the doctor. In the light of this new evidence, he allows Blanco to go free, even offering to sell him the horse 'at a reasonable sum' so that he can get out of town fast. *The Shewing-Up of Blanco Posnet*

KEMP, STRAPPER: The younger brother of Sheriff George Kemp, from whom he has borrowed a horse, lending it later to Elder Daniels. When the horse is stolen, presumably by Daniels' brother Blanco Posnet, Strapper tracks him down and brings him back to stand his trial, fully expecting that he will be lynched or hanged without more ado, in spite of the fact that the horse is missing. He is furious when it turns out that Blanco has given the horse to a woman to take her dying child to a doctor, and is therefore set free. *The Shewing-Up of Blanco Posnet*

KÉROUAILLE, LOUISE DE: *see* Portsmouth, Duchess of

KIDDY: *see* Redbrook, Kiddy

KITTY: *see* Warren, Mrs. Kitty

KNELLER, GODFREY: The Dutch painter, who comes to Isaac Newton's house in search of Charles II. He makes a drawing of the Duchess of Cleveland, which she tears up because it makes her look so old, and says he will paint Newton, though he cannot agree with him that the line of beauty is straight. Obviously, it must be curved. *In Good King Charles's Golden Days*

KNOX, AMELIA: The mother of Margaret Knox, 'a plain woman, dressed without regard to fashion, with thoughtful eyes and thoughtful ways that make an atmosphere of peace and some solemnity'. Mrs. Gilbey, wife of her husband's partner, says of her that she is 'very religious, but quite cheerful'. Although amazed and ashamed by her daughter's behaviour, and unable to understand her point of view, she finally accepts it all in a spirit of resignation, and advises her to marry Juggins, not because he is a duke's brother, but because he is a man of sterling worth. *Fanny's First Play*

KNOX, JOSEPH: The father of Margaret Knox, a small businessman, thin, hard, ugly, with coarse black hair and a blue jaw. When he finds that his daughter has been in prison for assaulting a policeman, he is horrified, as he has often dismissed a shop-girl for coming in half an hour late in the evening. He is equally horrified by her friendship with the French lieutenant, Duvallet, and by her insistence on telling everyone about her adventures. To his surprise they make her, and her parents, more popular than they were. But he still finds it hard to reconcile himself to the vagaries of the young, though he is suitably impressed when Margaret, having broken off her engagement to Bobby Gilbey, gets engaged to the footman Juggins, who turns out to be the brother of a duke. *Fanny's First Play*

KNOX, MARGARET: The heroine of the play written by Fanny O'Dowda. Strictly brought up, she has suddenly broken loose, gone to a music-hall alone, picked up a Frenchman, Lieutenant Duvallet, and become involved in a fight with the police. In the excitement she hits a policeman and knocks out two of his teeth. Refusing to give her name and address, she is sent to prison for a month, but Duvallet, who has only had to serve fourteen days, pays her fine when he is released and takes her home. She tries to explain to her pious mother and narrow-minded father the happiness and self-confidence she has found in behaving without restraint, and also the important revolution in her feelings and beliefs brought about by her prison experiences. (Fanny is here drawing on her own experience, as she was herself in prison for suffragette activities.) They cannot understand her; she meets the same lack of comprehension in her fiancé, Bobby Gilbey, who has just been in prison for the same offence. She breaks off her engagement, and is immediately proposed to by the Gilbeys' footman, Juggins, whom she has admired for a long time. Her father is too overawed by the fact that Juggins is brother to a duke to oppose the marriage, and her mother accepts it because she likes Juggins personally. *Fanny's First Play*

KROOBOYS: Two West African natives in Mogador who help Hassan with the English visitors' luggage. *Captain Brassbound's Conversion*

L

LA HIRE, CAPTAIN: A French war-dog at the Court of Charles VII, 'with no court manners and pronounced camp ones'. He is notorious for his foul language, and is taken aback when Joan of Arc tells a swearing soldier that he should not blaspheme when at the point of death; whereupon he falls into the castle well and is drowned. La Hire promptly swears never to swear again. When Charles is reluctant to see Joan, La Hire helps to persuade him into it, and after the king's coronation at Rheims he comes out strongly in favour of her plan to attack Paris at once, saying he could follow her to hell when the spirit rises in her. *Saint Joan*

LA TREMOUILLE, DUC DE: Constable of France, and Lord Chamberlain at the Court of the Dauphin, later Charles VII; 'a monstrous arrogant wineskin of a man.' He dislikes and despises his royal master, and tries to prevent him from seeing Joan of Arc when she comes to the castle at Chinon. When Charles gives her command of the army, and La Tremouille protests, saying that he is its commander, she laughs at him, calling him old Gruff-and-Grum, and sweeps the assembly out with a wave of her drawn sword, leaving him cursing impotently. *Saint Joan*

LA TREMOUILLE, DUCHESSE DE: Wife of the Constable of France. When Joan of Arc is going to be brought into the presence of Charles VII in front of the assembled Court, and tested by seeing if she can pick him out from the assembled courtiers while Gilles de Rais pretends to be the King, the Duchess sits beside him pretending to be the Queen. She is scornfully amused at the sight of Joan in her soldier's uniform, with short bobbed hair, and makes all the ladies-in-waiting laugh with her. But Joan is quite prepared to believe that she is the Queen, and stares after her as she goes, much impressed by her stately bearing and lovely clothes. *Saint Joan*

LADIES-IN-WAITING: *see* Courtiers

LADVENU, BROTHER MARTIN: A young Dominican monk who attends the trial of Joan of Arc. He thinks she is innocent, and as soon as she recants on hearing that she is to be burnt at the stake, he hurriedly prepares a document for her to sign, reading it aloud to her and then guiding her hand while she makes her mark. When she withdraws her recantation rather than face life imprisonment, he is in despair, and goes with her to the stake, fetching a crucifix from a neighbouring church to comfort her in her last moments. But she sends him away in case he is caught in the flames. This convinces him of her innocence, and twenty-five years later he is able to tell Charles VII that mainly through his efforts she has been rehabilitated. *Saint Joan*

LADY: An unnamed woman who tells Lord Augustus Highcastle that her sister-in-law has made a bet with his brother Hungerford, known as Blueloo, that she will steal from him a secret list of gun emplacements. Augustus's clerk, Beamish, comes in with the list, which Augustus had left on his breakfast table, and the Lady deftly intercepts it, replaces it with a sheet of blank paper, and leaves. She then calls from the street to tell Augustus what she has done, taking Beamish to witness that she got clean away, and returns to tell Blueloo on the phone that she has won her bet. She consoles Augustus, who knows he will be laughed at for his folly, by pointing out that he must not grudge men home from the trenches a bit of fun at his expense. *Augustus Does His Bit*

An unnamed woman doctor, engaged by Lady Chavender to induce her husband to take a holiday from being 'too busy about nothing'. She announces herself as 'a messenger of death' and 'a ghost from the future', but reverts to normality in order to tell the Prime Minister that he is suffering, not from overwork, but from lack of mental exercise, and needs to spend a few weeks in her remote Welsh sanitorium, thinking. He resists at first, but finally agrees to go, taking with him the complete works of Marx, Lenin, Trotsky and other Communist writers. *On the Rocks*

LADY TOURIST: *see* Farwaters, Lady

LANDLORD: The owner of the house in which Lady Magnesia Fitztollemache and her husband George rent a bed-sitting-room 'in a fashionable quarter of London'. Attracted by the noise made by George when hacking bits off the ceiling to act as antidote to the poison which he has given to his wife's lover, Adolphus Bastable, he comes to complain, sends for the police, is accused of murder, and struck dead by lightning. *Passion, Poison, and Petrifaction*

LARRY (LAURENCE): *see* Doyle, Laurence

LAVINIA: A good-looking, resolute young woman who has become a Christian and is on her way with a group of Christian prisoners to die in the Colosseum at Rome. Four officers of the escorting regiment offer to marry her if she will only sacrifice to the gods, but she refuses, though she is obviously attracted by the Captain. She finds him on duty at the Colosseum when she arrives there, and he secures a special pardon for her when Caesar, delighted by the splendid show given by Ferrovius, releases the prisoners. She offers to go into the arena instead of Androcles, on the grounds that the audience will prefer to see a woman torn in pieces, but he refuses. Before leaving the Colosseum she says she 'will strive for the coming of the God who is not yet', but that the 'handsome Captain' may come and argue with her if he wishes. *Androcles and the Lion*

LEMAÎTRE, BROTHER JOHN: A Dominican monk, who acts as one of the two judges at the trial of Joan of Arc, representing the Inquisition. He insists on disregarding all the minor charges brought against her, and concentrates on that of heresy. He realises from the beginning that the trial will go against her, and when she has been sentenced goes to watch her execution, but not before remarking that she was, of course, innocent, and had not understood a word of what was being said. He returns during the Epilogue, no more anxious than the others that Joan should rise from the dead, and while admitting that there was a miscarriage of justice in her case, does not see how the Inquisition could have decided otherwise, nor indeed how it could be dispensed with under existing circumstances. *Saint Joan*

LENKHEIM, PROFESSOR ALFRED: A good, solid, hard-working Viennese doctor, who has been drawn, somewhat against his inclination, into working with a colleague, Professor Bruno Haldenstedt, on a new book on feminine psychology. But although he has supplied much of the material used, he is not in favour of the conclusions drawn from it. When Haldenstedt dies suddenly in scandalous circumstances—he had been spending the evening in a rented apartment with an unknown woman—and the manuscript is found with only Lenkheim's name on the title-page, Lenkheim refuses to accept the attribution. This makes his wife Jitta angry, and she inadvertently betrays that she was Bruno's unknown mistress, and that he charged her to make Lenkheim father his work, of which he himself had a very high opinion, in compensation. This Alfred refuses to do, though once his anger with his wife has died down, he agrees to edit the book, and also to forgive her, particularly in view of the fact that he himself has been having an affair with the wife of a mutual friend. *Jitta's Atonement*

LENKHEIM, JITTA: The wife of a well-known Viennese doctor, 'one of those attractively refined women whose wistfully sensitive unsmiling mouths and tragic eyes' make 'imaginative men fancy unfathomable depths in their natures'. She has become the mistress of Bruno Halden-stedt, a psychiatrist with whom her husband has been working on a new book, and is with him in a small rented apartment when he dies suddenly of a heart attack. Before his death he makes Jitta promise that the work, which he thinks of as epoch-making, shall be published under her husband's name to make up for their betrayal of him. As Jitta has managed to escape unseen from the flat after Bruno's death, no one at first suspects her of being the 'unknown woman' in the case, but her secret is eventually discovered both by her husband, Alfred Lenkheim, and by Haldenstedt's daughter Edith. To atone for her conduct, Jitta agrees to settle down quietly with her husband and forget the past, and also persuades Alfred, who will not accept the authorship of the new work, which he dis-approves of, to see it through the press and do for it all that he would do for one of his own books. *Jitta's Atonement*

LENTULUS: A foolish, foppish young Roman, who sees the Christian prisoners at the entrance to Rome, and jeers at them. After being rebuked by Lavinia, whom he calls 'a plucky little filly', he amuses himself by striking Ferrovius to see what he will do, and is disconcerted when he turns the other cheek. Ferrovius then endeavours to convert him, and so terrifies him that he collapses and is carried away by his servants and his friend Metellus. *Androcles and the Lion*

LEO: *see* Bridgenorth, Leo

LEONARD: *see* Charteris, Leonard

LESBIA: *see* Grantham, Lesbia

LEXY: *see* Mill, Rev. Alexander

LICKCHEESE: A rent-collector employed by Sartorius to extort the meagre rents on his slum property. When first seen he is 'a shabby, needy man, with dirty face and linen, scrubby beard and whiskers, going bald'. Dismissed for spending a trifling sum on repairs to a tenement staircase, he somehow obtains money by blackmail, and uses it to buy up and improve slum property scheduled for demolition, thus becoming entitled to substantial compensation. Visiting Sartorius again 'in evening dress', with fur-lined overcoat, diamond stud, silk hat, and handsome watch-chain, he draws him into a similar nefarious scheme in respect of his own property, together with Dr. Harry Trench, Sartorius's prospective son-in-law, and Trench's friend Cokane. *Widowers' Houses*

LIEUTENANT: 'A tall chuckle-headed young man of twenty-four', with an aristocratic self-assurance that the French Revolution has failed to shake. 'He has a thick silly lip, an eager credulous eye, an obstinate nose, and a loud confident voice . . . yet is of a babbling vitality which bustles him into the thick of things.' Having been robbed of dispatches which he was carrying to General Bonaparte at Tavazzano, he thinks the Strange Lady who is at the same inn as the general is the culprit, disguised as a woman, but is easily made to believe by the lady, who stole the package while disguised as a man, that it was done by her twin brother. *The Man of Destiny*

LILITH: The mother of Adam and Eve, who lost her life in making man and woman of her own flesh, and because the burden of creation was too great, decreed that child-bearing should be shared between them, but gave the greater burden to the woman. In the year A.D. 31,920 her ghost returns to see what her descendants have made of her gift of life, and finds they have taken the agony from birth, since their children are hatched from eggs, and have solved the problem of longevity. She wonders whether to destroy them, but decides to wait until they have achieved 'redemption from the flesh . . . all life and no matter'. One day they will be equal with her, and supersede her, for 'of Life only is there no end . . . and it is enough that there is a beyond.' *Back to Methuselah, Part V: As Far as Thought Can Reach*

LINA: *see* Szczepanowska, Lina

LION: In his native jungle he meets Androcles, who earns his gratitude by extracting a thorn from his right front paw. Later he is captured and taken to Rome, where he meets Androcles again in the arena of the Colosseum. Instead of eating him up, he greets him as an old friend and plays with him, much to the amazement of Caesar, who attributes Androcles' power over animals to his Christianity. The lion then chases Caesar, but Androcles, who has nicknamed him Tommy, chastises him and points out that Caesar is his friend, whereupon the lion allows himself to be tickled and petted. Finally he and Androcles leave the Colosseum together, unmolested. *Androcles and the Lion*

LIZA: *see* Doolittle, Eliza

LIZZIE: *see* Lysistrata

LOMAX, CHARLES: A typical young man-about-town, known as Cholly; his one claim to fame is that he plays the concertina very well. He is engaged to Sarah, daughter of Lady Britomart Undershaft, and although he will be a millionaire at thirty-five, he is until then restricted to £800 a year. His future mother-in-law therefore asks her estranged husband, Andrew, owner of a large armaments factory, for a dowry for their daughter. Although Andrew is not much impressed by Cholly, he agrees to finance the marriage, and invites the young man to visit the factory with the three Undershaft children, who are going to see it for the first time. Unfortunately Cholly has no more sense than to light a cigarette in one of the explosives sheds, thus calling down on his head the wrath of the foreman, Bilton. *Major Barbara*

LOONY: *see* Schutzmacher, Dr. Leo

LORD CHANCELLOR: *see* Boshington, Sir Cardonius

LOTTIE: *see* Women in the Barn

LOUIS: *see* Dubedat, Louis

LOUISE: *see* Portsmouth, Duchess of

LOUKA: Maidservant to Raina Petkoff, a 'handsome, proud girl . . . so defiant that her servility to Raina is almost insolent'. Ambitious and unscrupulous, she is engaged to her fellow-servant Nicola, but is not averse to flirting with Raina's fiancé, Major Saranoff, who eventually marries her. *Arms and the Man*

LUBIN, HENRY HOPKINS: One of the leaders of the Liberal Party in opposition in the 1920s, who calls on the Barnabas brothers, Franklyn and Conrad, hoping for their support in the forthcoming general election. He is somewhat distracted by the presence of Franklyn's young daughter, Cynthia, with whom he endeavours to flirt. She thinks he is rather sweet, but has no opinion of his old-fashioned political ideas; he encourages her to put forward her own ideas, but when she persuades her father to explain his belief in the imminent development through Creative Evolution of persons living to a great age—even 300 years— he is politely incredulous, even though his fellow-Liberal, Burge, says he intends to adopt Cynthia's slogan of 'Back to Methuselah' and to use some of the brothers' arguments in his next speech. *Back to Methuselah, Part II: The Gospel of the Brothers Barnabas*

LUCIAN: *see* Webber, Lucian

LUCIFER: *see* Devil

LUCIUS SEPTIMIUS: A Roman officer who followed Pompey to Egypt after the battle of Pharsalia, defeated him, cut off his head, and sent it to Julius Caesar. Later, meeting Caesar in Alexandria, he is amazed to be greeted with reproaches instead of gratitude, and angrily throws in his lot with Pothinus and Achillas, Caesar's enemies. 'A clean-shaven, trim athlete of about forty, resolute mouth, and handsome, thin Roman nose', he is something of an opportunist, and when he thinks Caesar is likely to win the battle for Egypt, he goes to the palace to report that the city is in revolt, but that reinforcements are on the way under Mithridates of Pergamos. Whereupon Caesar finally accepts him as an ally and they go off to conquer the Egyptians under Achillas. *Caesar and Cleopatra*

LUNN, GREGORY: The husband of Seraphita Lunn. Handsome, and something of a dandy, he promised his mother that he would never make love to a married woman. Meeting on board ship the fascinating Mrs. Juno, he flirts with her under the mistaken impression that she is a widow. Back in England, he discovers his mistake and suffers agonies of remorse over what he thinks of as a guilty passion, but cannot refrain from embracing the object of his adoration. At that moment his wife and Mrs. Juno's husband Sibthorpe, who have also been indulging in a flirtation on another ship, come in and discover them. After a lengthy discussion on the ethical position of the two couples, which bores the women, they all decide to remain friends and to change partners when they feel like it. *Overruled*

LUNN, SERAPHITA: A tall, imposing, handsome, languid woman with flashing dark eyes and long lashes. She looks passionate, but is really very prosaic and level-headed, and rather bored with all the men who fall in love with her. She has however enjoyed a shipboard flirtation with the would-be romantic Sibthorpe Juno, who amuses her. When they return to England and meet their respective spouses, have also been indulging in a harmless flirtation on a different ship, Mrs. Lunn—who before her marriage was Sally Jenkins, and on marrying a Mr. Lunn decided to drop the Sally—persuades them all that no harm has been done, and that they might as well continue to be friends, each wife being allowed to borrow the other's husband when she feels like it. *Overruled*

LUTESTRING, MRS.: In the 1920s she is a parlourmaid in the house of Franklyn Barnabas, but is leaving to get married. She has looked into Conrad Barnabas's book on longevity, and is rather upset by the idea that she might have to stay with the same man for several hundred years. Also, cook, who looked into the book with her, has worked out that if you lived to be 200 years old you might marry your own great-great-great-great-great-great-grandson, and she wonders if it would be respectable. Conrad reassures her that as a biological necessity it will become respectable, so she need not worry. *Back to Methuselah, Part II: The Gospel of the Brothers Barnabas*

Ironically, the parlourmaid is the first woman to fulfil the prophecy of the Brothers Barnabas by living to a great age, and in A.D. 2170 she is 274 and Domestic Minister under Burge-Lubin, President of the British Isles. Her secret is revealed when the Archbishop of York, formerly the Rev. Haslam, is found to be equally old. They have both cheated the authorities by pretending to die several times. Worried by the growing power of the black and yellow races, Mrs. Lutestring and the Archbishop decide to marry and found a race of long-lived Englishmen and women. *Back to Methuselah, Part III: The Thing Happens*

LYDIA: *see* Carew, Lydia

LYSISTRATA: A former schoolmistress, usually known as Lizzie, who is Powermistress-General in the administration of the Prime Minister Proteus, during the reign of King Magnus. She agrees with the King that the present wave of prosperity cannot last, makes an impassioned attack on her *bête noire*, Breakages Ltd., the big industrial corporation which she thinks is ruining the country. When Magnus refuses to sign Proteus's ultimatum, saying he will abdicate, become a commoner, and stand for Parliament, she is delighted, as she thinks he will become the next Prime Minister and help her lead a party in the House against Breakages Ltd. She is bitterly disappointed when Proteus, realising he has been outwitted, tears up the ultimatum and restores the *status quo*, and is taken home by Amanda Postlethwaite for a nice cup of tea. *The Apple Cart*

M

MACBETH: When Shakes is trying to prove that he is a better playwright than Shav, he summons up Macbeth. But Macbeth's head is cut off by Rob Roy. *Shakes versus Shav*

MACHIAVELLI: *see* Undershaft, Andrew

M'COMAS, FINCH: Mrs. Clandon's solicitor, who has reluctantly agreed to bring together her estranged husband, Fergus Crampton, and his three children, Gloria, Dolly, and Philip, whom he has not seen since they were babies. M'Comas's plans are, however, frustrated by Mr. Crampton's unexpected appearance at the Clandons' luncheon table, and after a stormy meal everyone agrees to take the advice of an eminent Q.C., Walter Bohun (the son of their waiter, Walter Boon), who dissuades Crampton from going to law to obtain custody of his children. *You Never Can Tell*

MADIGAN, GENERAL SIR PEARCE: The British owner of an estate in Ireland, one of whose tenants, Dennis O'Flaherty, has joined the British Army during the First World War and been awarded the Victoria Cross. Madigan brings him back to the village to help in a recruiting campaign, but when his mother and his sweetheart, Teresa Driscoll, who is Madigan's parlourmaid, indulge in a slanging match over a gold chain which O'Flaherty has taken from a German prisoner, Madigan helps the young man to push the quarrelling women into the house, and agrees with him that it is better to be in the army than to live at home. *O'Flaherty, V.C.*

MAGNESIA: *see* Fitztollemache, Lady Magnesia

MAGNUS: King of England at some unspecified date in the future. He has a poor opinion of present-day democracy, and gets his own way by a mixture of quickwittedness and charm. When the Prime Minister, Proteus, annoyed by the King's public reference to the royal veto, presents him with an ultimatum, he promises to give him an answer at five o'clock and goes off to spend an hour with his mistress, Orinthia. She wants him to divorce his dull wife Jemima and marry her, but he refuses. Being a wife is not her job. While he is having tea with Jemima the American Ambassador arrives to tell him that America has decided to rejoin the British Empire, with him as Emperor. Magnus is wary of the offer, as he thinks it may mean the end of England, and promises to think it over. He then meets his Cabinet again, tells them he has decided to abdicate, become a commoner, stand for Parliament, and perhaps even become Prime Minister himself. Realising he has been outwitted, Proteus tears up the ultimatum, and leaves, forgetting to discuss the American offer of federation. *The Apple Cart*

MAGSY: *see* Knox, Margaret

MAID OF ORLEANS: *see* Joan

MAIDENS: A group of beautiful young girls of the future—A.D. 31,920. Hatched fully grown from eggs, they have four years in which to enjoy the pleasures of music, art, love-making, and dancing before turning their backs on sensual pleasures and embarking on the long process of becoming She-Ancients, pure intellects with practically no bodies. Some of them officiate at the hatching of Amaryllis, the Newly-Born, one carrying her tunic, others the implements for her ceremonial bath, others flowers and beribboned wands. They also attend the festival of art at which Pygmalion produces his loathsome automata made in the semblance of twentieth-century human beings, one of which kills its creator; and after the tragedy they try very hard to understand the explanations given by the Ancients, but are not advanced enough to grasp them. *Back to Methuselah, Part V: As Far as Thought Can Reach*

MAIDENS FOUR AND FIVE: Students at the Sixth Form School on the Isle of Wight. Four is older than Five, and is anxious to know why people do different things and think different thoughts. Five likes stories, even though she knows they are not true, and she is the only one who knows the story of the Sphinx. It is Five's desire to know where thoughts come from that seems to evoke the presence of the archangel Raphael, 'the feathered one', who describes himself as 'an embodied thought', and she is the only one to be affected by his 'magnetic field'. *Far-Fetched Fables 6*

MAJOR BARBARA: *see* Undershaft, Barbara

MAJOR DOMO: A gorgeously apparelled Court official in the royal palace at Alexandria. He superintends the banquet given on the roof of the palace by Cleopatra for Julius Caesar, and, on Cleopatra's orders, sends for a sacred image of a sphinx with attendant priest. *Caesar and Cleopatra*

MALE FIGURE: *see* Ozymandias

MALE TOURIST: *see* Farwaters, Sir Charles

MALONE, HECTOR, SEN.: A self-made rich American businessman, maker of office furniture. Of Irish peasant stock himself, he determined that his son, Hector Malone, jun., shall marry an English lady of title. Going to Spain to look into the affairs of Mendoza Ltd., which he has financed—not knowing that Mendoza is a brigand—he opens by mistake a letter addressed to his son, and learns that he has married Violet Robinson. When they all meet in a garden in Granada, Mr. Malone threatens to disinherit his son for disobedience, but is so impressed by Violet's common sense and clearheadedness that he agrees to continue his son's allowance despite the marriage, provided Violet takes charge of the money and spends it to the best advantage. *Man and Superman*

MALONE, HECTOR, JUN.: The son of a rich American businessman, Hector Malone, sen. His father, who is of Irish peasant stock, is determined that Hector shall marry an English lady of title, but he secretly marries Violet Robinson, hoping his father will eventually relent. The young couple find themselves in an awkward situation when they become fellow-guests on a trip to Spain, particularly when the brigand Mendoza, who was formerly a waiter at the Savoy Hotel in London, recognises them as two of his most frequent and generous customers. They manage to keep their secret until they reach Granada, where Hector's father has arrived to keep an appointment with Mendoza, whose banditry he has unwittingly financed. Violet writes a note to her husband, it falls into the hands of his father, and there is a scene during which Malone disinherits his son and Hector disowns his father. But the elder Malone has formed a very favourable opinion of Violet, and agrees to continue his son's allowance, on condition that Violet quietly takes charge of it, without upsetting her young husband's confidence in his ability to earn a living for them both. *Man and Superman*

MAN: *see* Joe; Zozim

MAN IN LEATHER BREECHES: *see* Fox, George

MAN OF DESTINY: *see* Bonaparte, General Napoleon

MANAGER: *see* Hotel Manager

MANDY: *see* Postlethwaite, Amanda

MANGAN, ALFRED: A self-made businessman, commonly known as 'Boss' Mangan. He comes to Captain Shotover's house in pursuit of Ellie Dunn, who is there with her father Mazzini. He intends to marry her, but falls in love with Hesione Hushabye, Shotover's elder daughter, who runs his house. When Ellie, who has discovered that the man she is in love with is already married, says she will marry him at once, he tries to put her off by confessing that he ruined her father on purpose to profit by his failure. When the air-raid starts he is terrified and takes refuge with the burglar Billy Dunn, who is also an arrant coward, in the cave where Captain Shotover stores his dynamite. It receives a direct hit, and both men are killed. *Heartbreak House*

MANNY, SIR WALTER: A nobleman in attendance on Edward III when the six burghers of Calais come to surrender the keys of the city. He has nothing to say. *The Six of Calais*

MARCHBANKS, EUGENE: An eighteen-year-old poet, of aristocratic family, 'shy, slight, effeminate, with a delicate childish voice and a haunted tormented manner . . . He is so uncommon as to be almost unearthly'. In revolt against his background, he has been befriended by the Rev. James Morell, and has fallen in love with Morell's wife, Candida, some fifteen years his senior. With youthful arrogance he challenges Morell, saying he is unfit to be the husband of such a peerless creature, and that she must choose between them. But when Candida chooses her husband, as 'the weaker of the two', he accepts her decision resolutely, finding within himself a new source of resilience and strength struggling to achieve maturity. *Candida*

MARGARET: *see* Clandon, Mrs. Lanfrey; Knox, Margaret

MARIA: *see* Gilbey, Maria

MARKET PORTERS: Four workers in the harbour at Alexandria. They carry in the carpets which the merchant

Apollodorus is bringing to show to Cleopatra, take them into the palace, and bring out the one in which she is hidden, placing it in a small boat to be taken as a present to Julius Caesar at the lighthouse. One says the boat is too small for the load and is cursed by the Boatman; another steps on the carpet, and is cursed by the queen's nurse Ftatateeta; and all four are overcome by the liberality of the tip bestowed on them by Apollodorus. *Caesar and Cleopatra*

MARTELLUS: A sculptor in A.D. 31,920, who has already got tired of admiring the beauty of women and nature, and is therefore almost ready to embark on his life as a He-Ancient, which may last for hundreds or thousands of years. Although he declares that 'art is false and life alone is true', he agrees to help his friend Pygmalion make two synthetic human beings; but he tells the assembled youngsters before the festival at which the two automata are to appear that although they contain some of his best work, they will inspire a loathing which will cure the spectators of the 'lunacy of art' for ever. His prophecy comes true when the female figure first tries to kill the male, and then kills Pygmalion, and both figures have to be destroyed by the Ancients. In the end Martellus decides that 'the body always ends by being a bore. Nothing remains beautiful and interesting except thought, because the thought is the life'. And he goes off alone to study mathematics. *Back to Methuselah, Part V: As Far as Thought Can Reach*

MARTIN: *see* Ladvenu, Brother Martin

MARY: *see* Fitton, Mary

MARZO: One of the men who escort Sir Howard Hallam into the interior of the Atlas Mountains under the command of Captain Brassbound. Born in Hatton Garden, he is 'a horse-barrow and street-barrow Italian', wearing a 'shabby blue serge suit, a dilapidated Alpine hat, and boots laced with scraps of twine'. When the party is attacked by some marauding Arabs, Marzo is slightly wounded, and is nursed back to health by Lady Cicely Waynflete, whom he afterwards refers to as 'no lady—she saint'. *Captain Brassbound's Conversion*

MASTER OF THE REVELS: The presenter of the fight at the Agricultural Hall, Islington, between Cashel Byron and William Paradise, which ends in a riot. *The Admirable Bashville*

MATRON: On the staff of the Anthropometric Laboratory on the Isle of Wight, which has become 'a colony of the Upper Ten' after losing all its population by poison gas. She interviews an unauthorised Tourist who has landed on the island, and when he claims to be a genius, sends him to work in the laboratory 'classifying men and women according to their abilities'. She then interviews a Tramp, who has come over from the mainland as a stowaway, and claims to be a nincompoop. She sends him to the canteen for a meal, and when she is congratulated by the Gentleman on 'two big catches for today: a nincompoop . . . and a genius', she says she prefers nincompoops: 'I can always depend on them to do what was done last time. But I never know what a genius will be up to next, except that it will be something upsetting.' *Far-Fetched Fables 3*

MATT (MATTHEW): *see* Haffigan, Matt

MAYA: One of the four 'biologically perfect' children of mixed East and West parentage living on the Unexpected Isles. She attracts the young clergyman, Phosphor Hammingtap, when he arrives on the island, but refuses to love him unless he will also love her sister Vashti, since the two are one. She is in his arms when, being useless, she disappears suddenly on the Day of Judgement. Her parents forget her name; but Hammingtap says it was Love. *The Simpleton of the Unexpected Isles*

MAYOR: *see* Humphries, Tom

MAYORESS: *see* Collins, Mrs. George

MAZZINI: *see* Dunn, Mazzini

MEEK, PRIVATE NAPOLEON ALEXANDER TROTSKY: An insignificant-looking little man, serving under Colonel Tallboys in an expeditionary force against some non-existent brigands who are believed to be holding Miss Mopply for ransom. Being a man of outstanding ability, he has three times resigned a commission to return to the ranks, because it gives him a freer hand. As quarter-master's clerk, interpreter, and intelligence orderly, he is the virtual leader of the expedition, and stages a mock battle for which the Colonel is awarded the K.C.B. so ardently desired by his wife. *Too True to be Good*

MEG: *see* Knox, Margaret

MEGAERA: The shrewish wife of Androcles. She is travelling with her husband through the jungle when they meet a lion. Androcles, who calls her Meggy, urges her to escape while the lion is eating him, but she faints from terror, and when she recovers she sees him waltzing off with the animal. She rushes after him, shouting 'Coward', and is not seen again. *Androcles and the Lion*

MELLISH, BOB (ROBERT): The trainer of the prizefighter Cashel Byron. He has rented a lodge on the estate of Lydia Carew so that Cashel can train secretly for his fight with William Paradise, and is furious when Cashel and Lydia fall in love. He is present at the fight between Cashel and Paradise in Wiltstoken, and is taken by the police to Lydia's house after Cashel has taken refuge there. When Cashel has been pardoned, he sends Mellish with Paradise to the Blue Anchor, a public house kept by one Bill Richardson. *The Admirable Bashville*

MEN-AT-ARMS: *see* Soldiers

MENAGERIE KEEPER: He is in charge of the animals at the Colosseum in Rome, and when he discovers how clever Androcles is with them he begs him to give up Christianity so that he can be employed in the menagerie. He is furious when Spintho gets himself eaten by the lion, which he had kept hungry on purpose for his appearance in the arena. The gladiators, who disrespectfully call him Jock, are very amused. After Androcles comes out of the arena with his friend the lion, the keeper again asks if he may have him for the menagerie. Caesar says he will be given as a slave to anyone who can lay hands on him, and the menagerie keeper rushes forward, only to retreat when the lion shows fight. *Androcles and the Lion*

MENDOZA: The leader of a band of brigands operating in the mountains of the Sierra Nevada, a 'tall, strong man, with a striking cockatoo nose, glossy black hair, pointed beard, upturned moustache, and a Mephistophelean affectation which is fairly imposing'. His eyes and mouth are by no means rascally; he has a fine voice, and a ready wit. Formerly a waiter at the Savoy Hotel in London, he has been driven to crime through unrequited love for an English cook named Louisa, and as President of the League of the Sierra, is financed unwittingly by an American businessman, Hector Malone, sen. Having captured the car in which John Tanner and Henry Straker are travelling to Granada, he discovers that Straker is the brother of his love Louisa, and is so moved that he insists on reciting poems which he has written to her, effectually sending everyone to sleep. Tanner then dreams that he is Don Juan in Hell, Mendoza figuring in his dream as the Devil. Saved from arrest by Spanish soldiers by posing as Tanner's 'escort', he accompanies him to Granada, and is present when Malone discovers his son is married to Violet Robinson and when Tanner gets engaged to Ann Whitefield. *Man and Superman*

MERCER: Clerk to the Lord Chancellor, Sir Cardonius Boshington. He tries to prevent Horace Brabazon from seeing the Lord Chancellor without an appointment, and later ushers in Anastasia Vulliamy. *The Fascinating Foundling*

METELLUS: A young Roman noble, who is rather shocked when his friend Lentulus baits the Christian prisoners, though he has no opinion of them, calling them 'awful brutes' and going with Caesar to the Colosseum to see them thrown to the lions. *Androcles and the Lion*

MIDDLE-AGED MAN: He runs into the park where the Young Man and Young Woman are talking about the inevitability of war, brandishing a newspaper which announces that the United Nations has abolished armed conflict. Although they do not believe that this is possible, he is so excited at the thought of no more war that he gives them the paper and rushes away to buy another copy. *Far-Fetched Fables 1*

MIDLANDER, SIR ORPHEUS: British Foreign Secretary. He goes to Geneva to find out from the Secretary of the League of Nations why there has been a sudden crisis in international politics, and discovers that it is due to the activities of his nephew's fiancée, Begonia Brown. As secretary of the International Committee for Intellectual Co-operation she has caused warrants to be issued by the Court of International Justice at The Hague, which has not formerly had a chance to function, against the dictators Battler, Bombadone and Flanco de Fortinbras, charging them with crimes against humanity. Sir Orpheus attends the trial, interrupting the judge occasionally to state and uphold the British point of view on various issues raised, and when news of the imminent end of the world is received, he says it must be officially contradicted until he has had time to consult the British Cabinet about the measures to be taken. *Geneva*

MILL, REV. ALEXANDER: Curate to the Rev. James Morell, whom he admires and apes in many little ways, to the annoyance of Morell's secretary, the outspoken Proserpine (Prossy) Garnett. Usually known affectionately as Lexy, he is 'a conceitedly well-intentioned, enthusiastic, immature novice'. After the impromptu supper-party given by Morell's father-in-law, Mr. Burgess, at which

Prossy drinks rather too much champagne, he kindly but apprehensively sees her home. *Candida*

MINNIE: *see* Tinwell, Minnie

MITCHENER, GENERAL: Visited at the War Office by the Prime Minister, Balsquith, disguised as a militant suffragette—the only way he can penetrate the picket lines—Mitchener advocates firm measures with the turbulent women. He is quite prepared to shoot a few to discourage the rest. But after a visit from the overpowering Mrs. Banger and the romantic Lady Corinthia Fanshawe, leaders of the anti-suffragette movement, he is so shocked that he is prepared to tolerate the suffragettes as the lesser of two evils. When he hears that Mrs. Banger is to marry the head of the army, General Sandstone, he proposes to his charwoman, Mrs. Farrell, the only woman strong enough to support him against Mrs. Banger, who reluctantly accepts him. (*Note:* Owing to the Censor's objection to the name Mitchener as being too like Kitchener, it was changed in production to Bones.) *Press Cuttings*

MITCHENS, RUMMY (ROMOLA): One of the down-and-outs in the Salvation Army shelter at West Ham where Barbara Undershaft works. 'A bundle of poverty and hard-worn humanity, she looks sixty, and is probably forty-five.' A respectable married woman, she pretends to have been worse than she was in order to please her rescuers. She is hit across the face by Bill Walker when he comes to look for his girl, but unlike Jenny Hill, she does not forgive him, and when Snobby Price steals the £1 which Walker has put on the big drum as compensation for his roughness, she lets him get away with it in order to pay Walker out for hitting her. *Major Barbara*

MOLLY: *see* Bluebin, Molly Badger

MONSTER: A microbe accused of having given Miss Mopply German measles, whereas it says it caught the disease from her. It sits by her bedside, invisible but commenting on the conversation between her mother and the doctor until the doctor is left alone, when it talks to him. When Miss Mopply jumps out of bed and floors Aubrey Bagot, who has come to steal her pearl necklace, it is cured, and bounds about joyously. Then it gets into bed beside the patient, and when she has run away with the nurse and burglar, says that the play is now over, 'but the characters will discuss it at great length for two acts more'. *Too True to be Good*

MOPPLY, MISS: A spoilt young woman, always referred to as the Patient or Mops. The only child of a fussy and very wealthy widow, she is suffering from a mild attack of German measles when her nurse, a petty criminal, admits a burglar, Bagot, into her bedroom. They have planned to steal her pearl necklace, but she wakes up and, being as strong as a horse, knocks them both down. Bagot then suggests that she should herself steal and sell the necklace, and escape with them from her mother's domination. She does so, and when they eventually run short of money she writes home to say she is being held to ransom by brigands. Disguised as a native servant to the nurse, metamorphosed into the Countess Valbrioni with Bagot as her brother, she falls in with an expeditionary force of British soldiers sent to rescue her. She is just beginning to tire of her aimless existence when her mother arrives in search of her, and so maddens Colonel Tallboys, in charge of the troops, that he hits her on the head with his umbrella. This completely changes her character, and she decides to forget all about her selfish and hypochondriacal daughter, setting off on her travels with Miss Mopply, whom she does not recognise, as her companion. Miss Mopply, however, has other ideas. She intends to found 'an unladylike sisterhood' with her mother as cook-housekeeper. *Too True to be Good*

MOPPLY, MRS.: An elderly, wealthy widow, referred to at first as the Elderly Lady, who has condemned her only child to a life of ill-health by her continual fussing. When the girl runs away and writes to say she has been captured by brigands who are holding her to ransom, Mrs. Mopply goes to rescue her, and so aggravates Colonel Tallboys, in charge of an expeditionary force sent to reduce brigandage, that he hits her over the head. This brings her to her senses for the first time, and she realises that she has sacrificed herself for others in vain. In future she will please herself, and she decides to start on her travels, offering Miss Mopply, whom she will not believe to be her daughter, a job as her companion. *Too True to be Good*

MOPS: *see* Mopply, Miss

MORELL, CANDIDA: Wife of the Rev. James Morell, 'aged thirty-three, well built, well nourished, likely to be matronly later on, but now quite at her best'. A most unlikely daughter for the obnoxious Mr. Burgess, 'she finds that she can manage people by engaging their affections, and does so without scruple'. But 'her serene brow, courageous eyes, and well-set mouth and chin signify largeness of mind and dignity of character'. Her husband loves but does not understand her, and she is appreciated at her true worth only by the young poet, Eugene Marchbanks, whom Morell has befriended. She is almost tempted to become his mistress in order that 'he may learn what love really is' and not depend for his initiation on 'a bad woman'; but when Marchbanks brings matters to a head by insisting that she must choose between Morell and himself, she chooses her husband, because he is 'the weaker of the two', and therefore needs her more than the strong and self-sufficient poetic genius. *Candida*

MORELL, REV. JAMES MAVOR: The vicar of St. Dominic's, Victoria Park, London, 'a vigorous, genial, popular man of forty, robust and goodlooking, full of energy . . . withal, a great baby, pardonably vain of his powers and unconsciously pleased with himself.' A Christian Socialist, he is an excellent preacher and much in demand as a lecturer at working-men's clubs. To his secretary and curate,

Proserpine Garnett and the Rev. Alexander Mill, he is an object of awe and affection; his coarse-grained father-in-law, Mr. Burgess, thinks he is mad; his wife, Candida, though she loves him dearly, has no illusions about him. He probably never understands why, when forced to choose between him and the young poet Eugene March-banks, who is in love with her (and she with him), she chooses her husband, because, she says, 'he is the weaker of the two'. *Candida*

MORRISON: Butler to Lady Undershaft. Having been with her since her marriage to Andrew Undershaft, whom she left shortly afterwards, he is taken aback when 'the master' appears on the doorstep one day, and asks whether he shall announce him 'or is he at home here? The occasion is in a manner of speaking new to me'. *Major Barbara*

MOTHER: *see* Eynsford-Hill, Mrs.

MOTHER HUBBARD: *see* Teacher

MULEY: An Arab boy in Mogador, servant to the missiona Leslie Rankin. *Captain Brassbound's Conversion*

MULEY OTHMAN: The Cadi of Kintali, sent by Captain Kearney to rescue Sir Howard Hallam from the Arab sheikh Sidi el Assif. 'A vigorous, fat-featured, choleric, white-haired and bearded elder', he rushes in, cudgel in hand, routs the sheikh and his followers, makes Brassbound and his crew prisoners, and takes the English hostages back safely to Mogador. He is too afraid of the power of the American navy to await Brassbound's trial, and returns hurriedly to his mountain fastness. *Captain Brassbound's Conversion*

MURDERER: *see* Fitztollemache, George

MUSICIAN: A teacher of the harp, an old man with 'a lined face, prominent brows, white beard, moustache and eye-brows twisted and horned, and a consciously keen and pretentious expression'. He brings one of his slave-girls to play before Cleopatra, who immediately wants to learn the harp. He says it will take at least four years. When she says he must teach her in a fortnight or be thrown to the crocodiles, he replies: 'True art will not be thus forced.' *Caesar and Cleopatra*

N

NAPOLEON: *see* Bonaparte, General Napoleon

NAPOLEON, CAIN ADAMSON CHARLES: The Emperor of Turania. As General Aufsteig, he has come to Ireland, in the year A.D. 3000, to ask the oracle at Galway how he can satisfy his genius for fighting, the only thing he is any good at. Clean-shaven, compact, self-centred, he looks very like his great namesake, a resemblance he encourages by dressing and standing as Napoleon did. At first he is angry because the oracle is a woman, but when she has nearly destroyed him by the force of her magnetic field, he puts his question to her. She replies that the only thing to do is to die before the tide of glory turns, and shoots him with his own pistol, unsuccessfully. 'Missed me at five yards! That's a woman all over,' he says. He leaves the temple with the intention of summoning the police, but is immobilised near the statue of Falstaff—the first preacher of cowardice, now considered a patriotic virtue—until one of the long-lived people has time to deal with him. *Back to Methuselah, Part IV: Tragedy of an Elderly Gentleman*

NARYSHKIN: Court Chamberlain to the Empress of Russia, Catherine II. He is in charge of the *petit lever* when Patiomkin carries Captain Edstaston into the Empress's bedroom, and escapes hurriedly to avoid having to tell her that the Captain is missing when she sends for him. He also supervises the arrest of Edstaston, and in the struggle is bitten on the finger by Edstaston's fiancée, Claire, whom he has tried to silence by putting what she calls his 'dirty paw' over her mouth. He takes Edstaston, trussed up on a pole, back to the palace, and is sent away by Catherine when he has the temerity to smile at Edstaston's insolence. *Great Catherine*

NATIVE: An elderly man who brings Clementina Buoyant's meals to her hut near Panama, and warns Junius Smith of her habit of calling up alligators and rattlesnakes with magic tunes on her saxophone. He also tells Junius that although he has lost his faith he must not 'throw the hatchet after the handle'. When Clementina goes to England the Native goes with her, dressed as a British valet, and warns her that Smith has followed her to her father's house in Belgrave Square. He helps the Chinese priest to purify the temple room after the conference with Flopper, and fetches his mistress for an interview with her father. He has a poor opinion of 'the pinks'. They can teach, but they cannot learn. *Buoyant Billions*

NAVAL OFFICERS: *see* American Naval Officers

NEDDY: *see* Edward III

NEGRESS: A handsome, well-educated and extremely efficient woman who in A.D. 2170 is Minister of Health for the British Islands. The President, Burge-Lubin, is strongly attracted by her, and carries on a rather heavy-handed flirtation by television-telephone, after recovering from the shock of accidentally switching her on dressed in 'corset, knickers, and silk stockings'. She is rather amused by his prudery, and by his wish to meet her and 'hold her in his arms'. She prefers 'distant flirtations; they teach self-control'. However, she relents sufficiently to invite him to join her on a steam-yacht in Fishguard Bay. He can be dropped by parachute and she will ensure that he is picked up safely. She is naturally somewhat piqued when he refuses, on the grounds that he has just discovered that he may live to be 300 years old, and is afraid of getting rheumatism. *Back to Methuselah, Part III: The Thing Happens*

NELL, NELLY: *see* Gwynn, Nell

NESTOR: *see* Jurymen

NEWCOMER: 'an obstinate-looking middle-aged man of respectable but not aristocratic appearance, speaking English like a shopkeeper from the provinces, or perhaps, by emigration, the dominions.' He has come to ask the secretary of the International Committee for Intellectual Co-operation in Geneva to issue a warrant for the arrest of the new British Prime Minister on charges of violating the constitution. She promises to apply to the Court of International Justice in The Hague for the warrant, and advises him to return in a week's time. He attends the Court, but, as he has no sense of humour, he finds most of the arguments incomprehensible or derogatory to the dignity of British democracy. When the news comes that the world is about to perish in a new ice-age, he accepts it as true because science vouches for it. *Geneva*

See also Stogumber, John de

NEWLY-BORN: *see* Amaryllis

NEWSBOY: He brings a copy of the *Star* from which Bashville reads aloud to Lydia Carew the account of Cashel Byron's prizefight with the Flying Dutchman. *The Admirable Bashville*

NEWSPAPER MAN: A cheerful, affable young man whose inability to report accurately anything he sees or hears, together with his illiteracy and lack of shorthand, render him suitable only for journalism. He interviews Louis Dubedat when he is dying, and afterwards is only prevented with some difficulty from asking Jennifer Dubedat 'How It Feels To Be A Widow'. Having overheard Dubedat beg his wife not to go into mourning for him, and to marry again as soon as possible, he remarks fatuously: 'I thought it shewed a very nice feeling, his being so particular about his wife going into proper mourning for him and making her promise never to marry again.' *The Doctor's Dilemma*

NEWTON, ISAAC: The famous philosopher is quietly at work in his house in Cambridge when he is interrupted by 'Mr. Rowley'—Charles II—who wants to see his new telescope, and the Quaker George Fox, who wants to question him on the authenticity of the scriptures. Unfortunately Nell Gwynn arrives, followed by the madly jealous Duchess of Cleveland, and by the Duchess of Portsmouth, who wants Newton to give her a prescription for a love-philtre to be used on Charles II. While they are all downstairs, the Duke of York comes in search of his brother, and insults the memory of the great Galileo, whereupon Newton knocks him down. The King then asks if he may speak to his brother in private, and Newton withdraws, to return later, lamenting that Fox's arguments have ruined the basic premises of one book he is writing, while the arguments of the Dutch painter Kneller, who has just arrived and maintains that space is curved and not straight, knocks the bottom out of another. Finally they all go into dinner, Kneller and Newton arguing hotly to the last about the perihelion of Mercury. *In Good King Charles's Golden Days*

NICOBAR (NICK): Foreign Secretary, a snaky and censorius fellow who is in Proteus's Cabinet. He is jealous of Boanerges, and takes every opportunity of sniping at him. When King Magnus announces that he intends to abdicate rather than sign Proteus's ultimatum, Nicobar exclaims: 'But you can't upset the apple cart like this', and after the ultimatum has been withdrawn he says politics are a mug's game, and he will give them up. But he doesn't mean it, and will obviously hang on in office as long as he can. *The Apple Cart*

NICOLA: Manservant to Major Petkoff, a 'middle-aged man of cool temperament and low but clear and keen intelligence, with the complacency' of the good servant who knows his value, and his place. He is engaged to the maid, Louka, and after his marriage intends to set up shop in Sofia; but he is quite willing to further her engagement to Major Saranoff, calculating that she will then become one of his best customers. *Arms and the Man*

NOBLEMAN: *see* Warwick, Earl of

NOBLEMEN: A group of gentlemen in attendance on Edward III when he accepts the surrender of Calais after a year-long siege. They include Lord Arundel, Lord Derby, Lord Northampton, and Sir Walter Manny. None of them has anything to say. *The Six of Calais*

NORA: *see* Reilly, Nora

NORTHAMPTON, LORD: One of the noblemen in attendance on Edward III when he accepts the surrender of the keys of Calais after a siege lasting a year. He has nothing to say. *The Six of Calais*

NOTE TAKER: *see* Higgins, Henry

NUBIAN SENTINEL: On guard in the Syrian palace of Cleopatra when Bel Affris comes to say that Julius Caesar is marching towards them. He deserts his post to spread the bad news among the palace attendants, and returns to produce an even greater panic when he announces that the sacred white cat has been stolen. *Caesar and Cleopatra*

NUBIAN SLAVE: Carrying a torch, he meets Cleopatra and Julius Caesar when they return to the palace from visiting the Sphinx, and guides them to the throne-room, where he lights the lamps, and is beaten by Cleopatra with a snake-skin. He runs off howling, but returns to say that the Roman soldiers have captured the palace. *Caesar and Cleopatra*

NURSE: *see* Ftatateeta; Guinness, Nurse; Simpkins, Susan

NURSES: *see* Women Servants and Nurses

O

O'DOWDA, COUNT: A handsome Irishman of about fifty, who has spent most of his life in Italy, and is a Count of the Holy Roman Empire. He dislikes modern life, and lives as far as possible in the past, dressing himself with studied elegance in the garb of the eighteenth century. He believes that his daughter, Fanny, has been shielded from all undesirable influences, but forgets that she has spent two years at Cambridge. Having, for a birthday present, hired a cast of professional players to give a private production of her first play, which he envisages as 'something like a Louis Quatorze ballet painted by Watteau', he is shocked when it turns out to be an extremely modern and provocative piece based on the experiences of two young people who have been in prison. *Fanny's First Play*

O'DOWDA, FANNY: The nineteen-year-old daughter of Count O'Dowda. Unlike her father, she is in touch with the modern world, having spent two years at Cambridge. For a birthday present she asks her father to engage a professional cast to act a play she has written, and also to invite the leading dramatic critics of the day to see it, without revealing the name of the author. She realises that the play will be a great shock to her father, who is expecting something pretty and balletic, as it is a modern problem play dealing with the experiences of two young people who get mixed up in public brawls and spend fourteen days in prison. After the performance, which is given privately at her father's rented house in the country, Florence Towers, she reveals that she is the author, and confesses also that the descriptions of prison life are based on her own experience, as she was sent to prison for a month for suffragette activities. *Fanny's First Play*

O'FLAHERTY, MRS.: A shrewish Irish peasant woman, and

an ardent patriot, who believes that her son Dennis is fighting against the British in the First World War. When he returns home after being awarded the Victoria Cross, she learns the truth and is furiously angry until her son points out that the British paid him better than anyone else would have done. She also makes a scene when she learns that he has given a gold chain which he took from a German prisoner to his sweetheart Teresa Driscoll, and continues to scream and swear until she is pushed into the house and the door slammed on her. *O'Flaherty, V.C.*

O'FLAHERTY, PRIVATE DENNIS: A young Irishman, born on the estate of General Sir Pearce Madigan, who has joined the British Army and been awarded the Victoria Cross for bravery in the field. Madigan has brought him back to his native village to help in a recruiting campaign, which he finds much more exhausting than the trenches; also he is faced with the task of explaining to his shrewish mother that he has been fighting for, and not against, the British. In addition, he meets at Madigan's house his former sweetheart, Teresa Driscoll, and is upset to find that she thinks more of his pension than of himself. The two women quarrel over a gold chain which O'Flaherty has taken from a German prisoner and given to Teresa, and when they have been finally pushed indoors by the two men, the latter agree that fighting is infinitely preferable to home life. *O'Flaherty, V.C.*

OCTAVIUS: *see* Robinson, Octavius

OFFICER: *see* Plechanoff, Major

OFFICERS: Some half-dozen English and German officers under the command of Major Swindon who attend the trial of Richard Dudgeon, one of them acting as clerk of the court. They have nothing to say. *The Devil's Disciple*

See also Soldiers

OFFICIALS: Two attendants at the palace of Alexandria who, carrying wands of office, usher in Rufio and Julius Caesar when they attend a banquet given by Cleopatra. *Caesar and Cleopatra*

OLD BILL: *see* Buoyant, Bastable

OLD HIPNEY: *see* Hipney, Mr.

OLD WOMAN: *see* Ana de Ulloa, Doña

OLDHAND, LORD: A diplomat at the Foreign Office in London, who comes to the War Office to discuss with the commander-in-chief, Lord Ulsterbridge, what should be done following the death from poison gas of the entire population of the Isle of Wight. The gas has been made from a formula which Ulsterbridge refused to buy, and was therefore sold to at least one other power, if not more. While the men are arguing, the gas comes in through the open window and kills them both. *Far-Fetched Fables 2*

ORACLE: A pythoness in the temple of Galway, whom people come to consult as they once consulted the oracle at Delphi. A party from Baghdad, the capital of the British Commonwealth, come to the temple in the year A.D. 3000. One of them, the Emperor of Turania, wants to know how he can satisfy his genius by fighting till he dies, as there is nothing else he is good at. The oracle tells him he must die in the moment of glory, and tries to shoot him with his own pistol, unsuccessfully. When the Prime Minister, Ambrose Badger Bluebin, asks her about the outcome of the next election, she gives him the reply she gave his predecessor, Sir Fuller Eastwind, fifteen years ago: 'Go home, poor fool!' As Eastwind had returned with an inspiring message, written by himself, and given out as being the oracle's reply, which won him the election, Bluebin decides that he will merely say he has received the same answer, which is true, but yet, says his father-in-law, Joseph Barlow, 'a blasphemous lie'. Barlow begs the oracle to let him stay on the island, and reluctantly she consents. But when she looks at him, he dies of discouragement, and she says sadly: 'Poor short-lived thing! What else could I do for you?' *Back to Methuselah, Part IV: Tragedy of an Elderly Gentleman*

ORDERLY: A young Stepney barber's assistant who has been conscripted into the army. Unsoldierly, slovenly, and discontented, he is particularly upset by the way General Mitchener orders him about, and objects to being thrown downstairs by Mrs. Banger. When Mitchener gets engaged to the charwoman Mrs. Farrell, the Orderly asks him to celebrate the engagement by promoting him. Mitchener agrees, but as the young man is too utterly incompetent to discharge the duties of a sergeant, he will be recommended for a commission. *Press Cuttings*

ORINTHIA: The mistress of King Magnus, romantically beautiful, but quite impractical. She is angry with him because in an old book she has found the name which he said he had invented for her alone, and calls him a liar and a humbug. She also wants him to divorce his wife Jemima and marry her—'Heaven is offering you a rose and you cling to a cabbage,' she tells him. But he says cabbages are better for every day, and she is too exhausting to live with. Being a wife is not her job. She must be content with being his respite from royalty. When he says he must leave her to have tea with his wife, she tries to prevent him by force, and they are rolling on the floor together when Sempronius, Magnus's private secretary, comes in to remind him that tea is waiting. *The Apple Cart*

ORPHEUS: *see* Midlander, Sir Orpheus

OSMAN ALI: A tall, skinny, white-clad elderly Moor, sent by Captain Brassbound to fetch Sidi el Assif. *Captain Brassbound's Conversion*

OUDEBOLLE, GILLES D': One of the six burghers of Calais who are to be hanged after they have delivered up the keys of the city to Edward III. He has nothing to say, and is set free after the queen, Philippa of Hainault, has persuaded her husband to spare the lives of five of the six hostages. *The Six of Calais*

OX DRIVER: The man in charge of a team of oxen who are dragging a caged lion to the Colosseum in Rome. He tries to take precedence over a group of Christian prisoners who are going the same way, but is ordered to come behind them by the Centurion, who argues that the lion's dinner should be there before him. *Androcles and the Lion*

OXFORD YOUTH: *see* Barking, Viscount

OZYMANDIAS: An automaton, modelled by the sculptor Martellus from synthetic material produced in his laboratory by Pygmalion. He can read, talk, boast, lie, love, hate, entirely by reflex action. When brought before the youths and maidens at the festival of art in A.D. 31,920 he tells them his name is Ozymandias, King of Kings, and his consort is Cleopatra-Semiramis. His conceit provokes the woman into throwing a stone at him. Eventually he dies of discouragement after the young people have called upon the Ancients to help them dispose of what they regard as two loathsome and corrupt horrors, and he and Cleopatra-Semiramis are incinerated. *Back to Methuselah, Part V: As Far as Thought Can Reach*

P

PADDY: *see* Cullen, Sir Patrick

PADDY PATKINS: *see* Utterwood, Lady

PAGE: A young boy employed at the Ibsen Club in London. He is scolded by Sylvia Craven, one of the members, for taking *The British Medical Journal* to Dr. Paramore instead of leaving it in the library. *The Philanderer*

At the Court of Charles VII in Chinon a page ushers in Gilles de Rais and then announces the arrival of the King.

When Joan of Arc is about to arrive with the Duc de Vendôme, the page cannot make himself heard for the chattering of the courtiers, so he borrows a halberd from one of the soldiers and bangs on the floor with it. Later, when Charles says to him 'Call for silence, you little beast, will you?' he adopts the same expedient. Both Dunois and Warwick have pages. Dunois's is watching for a kingfisher when Joan of Arc arrives, and he is the first to notice that the pennon, which was streaming westward, is now standing eastward, denoting a favourable wind for the attack on Orleans. When Dunois and Joan have gone off shouting 'For God and Saint Dennis', the page capers along behind with Dunois's shield and lance, crying: 'The Maid! The Maid! God and the Maid!' Warwick's page brings Peter Cauchon, Bishop of Beauvais, to his master's tent, and is later present briefly in Rouen before the trial of Joan of Arc, being sent to fetch Cauchon to Warwick. *Saint Joan*

PAMPHILIUS: One of King Magnus's private secretaries, whose duty it is to read all the newspapers every morning and call the King's attention to anything of importance. He leaves the room during the Cabinet meeting, but when the Prime Minister accuses him of having overheard it all, he retorts that it would be rather inconvenient if he had to be told everything that passed, and in his position it is essential that he should know what is happening. Later on he introduces the American Ambassador into the presence of the King and Queen, and returns to show him out. *The Apple Cart*

PANDRANATH, SIR JAFNA: An elderly Cingalese plutocrat, too much occupied and worried by making money to get any fun out of spending it, though he has a great deal, probably about twenty millions. He comes to congratulate the Prime Minister, Sir Arthur Chavender, on his new programme of reform, saying the City will be solidly behind him. The nationalisation of land will mean that he can go through with such schemes as the Blayport Docks reconstruction without having to compensate the landowners, and can also pay his workers less because they will not have any rents to pay to their landlords. Unfortunately the Foreign Secretary, Sir Dexter Rightside, is so enraged by Chavender's proposals, and the way in which his supporters are rallying to him, that he loses his temper and calls Pandranath 'a silly nigger pretending to be an English gentleman'; whereupon Pandranath says he will leave England, sever the connection between England and India, and allow 'the needy British imbeciles' to perish in their ignorance, vain conceit, and abominable manners. *On the Rocks*

PARADISE, WILLIAM: A prizefighter who meets Cashel Byron at the Agricultural Hall, Islington, in the presence of Cetewayo, Lydia Carew, Lord Worthington, and other Spectators and Persons of Fashion. When he attacks Cashel with bare fists, Cetewayo joins in the fight and a riot ensues. Paradise fights Cashel again at Wiltstoken, is arrested and taken to Lydia's house, and sent by Cashel with Mellish to the Blue Anchor to 'assuage his hurts'. *The Admirable Bashville*

PARAMORE, DR. PERCY: A medical gentleman, 'young as age is counted in the professions—barely forty'. Already going bald, with 'dark arched eyebrows' which give him a conscientiously sinister appearance, he wears the frock coat and cultivates the bedside manner of the fashionable physician. He has discovered a fatal infection of the liver, which he names 'Paramore's Disease', and is naturally shocked to read in *The British Medical Journal* an article proving that his disease does not exist. He cannot even rejoice with his friend Colonel Craven, whom he had believed to be suffering from this new disease. He is, however, consoled by becoming engaged to Craven's daughter Julia, mainly at the instigation of her lover, Leonard Charteris, who wishes to get rid of her so that he can marry Grace Tranfield. *The Philanderer*

PARERGA, EPIFANIA OGNISANTI DI: *see* Fitzfassen, Epifania

PARIS, CANON OF: *see* Courcelles, de

PARK ATTENDANT: He takes twopence each from the Young Man and Young Woman when they sit down on the park chairs, and says nothing more than 'Kew'—short for 'Thank you'—each time. *Far-Fetched Fables 1*

PARK LANE NIGHTINGALE: *see* Fanshawe, Lady Corinthia

PARLOURMAID: At the house of Roebuck Ramsden. She announces Mr. Ramsden's visitors, and also the arrival of the cab ordered by Violet Robinson. *Man and Superman*

Employed by Henry Higgins's mother. She shows in Alfred Doolittle when he arrives in all his wedding finery, and also fetches Eliza from her room when Mrs. Higgins sends for her. *Pygmalion*

At the lodgings of the dentist, Mr. Valentine. She shows in his visitors and patients, gives him a message from his landlord, and brings him some hot water. *You Never Can Tell*

See also Annie; Mrs. Lutestring, Mrs.

PASSENGER: Known as Z, she is a young woman, presentable but not aristocratic; in fact, a village shop assistant, who has won enough money in a newspaper competition to pay for a cruise round the world in the *Empress of Patagonia*. She is attracted by the Author, A, a widower who is busily writing a guide-book and thoroughly unsociable. She makes a bet that she will get him to talk, and with great difficulty wins it. Some months later he appears in her shop while on a walking tour. She recognises him, and having reminded him of their former meeting, suggests that he shall buy the shop, settle down, and marry her. This he is unwilling to do, but he does in fact buy the shop, keeping Z on as his assistant, and she finally wears him down by her constant harping on the subject of matrimony, until he agrees to the putting up of the banns. *Village Wooing*

See also Szczepanowska, Lina

PASTOR: *see* Fox, George

PATIENT: *see* Mopply, Miss

PATIOMKIN, PRINCE: The lover and very able first minister of Catherine II, Empress of Russia, his real name being Gregory Alexandrovich Potyomkin, sometimes transliterated Potemkin. 'Gigantic in stature and build, his face marred by the loss of one eye', he is a mixture of brutal barbarism and cool intelligence, a heavy drinker, an outrageous ruffian, and a man to be reckoned with. When Captain Edstaston comes to ask for an interview with the Empress, he is so irritated by the young man's insistence that he is not properly dressed that he picks him up and carries him off into Catherine's bedroom, pretending to be drunk so as to avoid being scolded. *Great Catherine*

PATRICIA: *see* Smith, Patricia

PATRICK: *see* Cullen, Sir Patrick

PATSY: *see* Farrell, Patsy; Tarleton, Hypatia

PAUL: *see* Petkoff, Major

PEARCE: *see* Madigan, General Sir Pearce

PEARCE, MRS.: Housekeeper to Henry Higgins. She begins by disapproving of Eliza Doolittle when she turns up to demand lessons in how to 'speak genteel', and is shocked when Higgins decides to keep the girl in his house and teach her to behave like a lady. But she gradually becomes genuinely fond of Eliza, and is always warning her not to become too fond of her teacher, knowing Higgins is unlikely to want her once she has served her purpose. *Pygmalion*

PERCIVAL, JOSEPH: A friend of Bentley Summerhays, who attributes his superior intelligence to the fact that he had three fathers—a natural one, a tame philosopher who lived in his parents' house, and his Italian mother's confessor. When Joey, or the Aviator, as he is called, crashes in his plane on the sun-parlour of the Tarletons' house, Hypatia Tarleton, who is engaged to Bentley, falls in love with his unique combination of brains and brawn. She chases him indefatigably, and he eventually succumbs, but refuses to marry her unless her father will provide them with an income of £1,500 a year, which he does. *Misalliance*

PERCY: *see* Paramore, Dr. Percy

PERSIAN: A young soldier in the service of Cleopatra, who is gambling in the courtyard of her Syrian palace with Belzanor when Bel Affris comes with news of the imminent arrival of Julius Caesar and his troops. He is swept away in the rush of palace attendants, who stampede when they hear that Cleopatra is missing and the sacred white cat has been stolen, but reappears on the quayside at Alexandria to watch Caesar embark for Rome. *Caesar and Cleopatra*

PETER: *see* Rosty, Piers de; Shirley, Peter

PETER PIPER: *see* Strammfest, General

PETKOFF, CATHERINE: The wife of Major Petkoff, an imperiously energetic woman in her early forties 'with magnificent black hair and eyes, looking astonishingly handsome and stately under all circumstances'. She helps her daughter Raina to save Major Bluntschli from his pursuers after the battle of Slivnitza, and lends him her husband's old overcoat to escape in. When he comes, after the war, to return it, she does her best to keep the truth about the episode from her husband and Raina's fiancé, Major Saranoff. But when all is discovered she is delighted to welcome the wealthy Bluntschli as her daughter's future husband. *Arms and the Man*

PETKOFF, MAJOR PAUL: 'a cheerful, excitable, insignificant, unpolished man of about fifty, naturally unambitious, but greatly pleased with the military rank which the war [of 1885–6] has thrust upon him', since, as his daughter Raina says: 'He holds the highest command of any Bulgarian in the army.' He hears the story of a young woman saving the life of Captain Bluntschli, whom he meets after the war over an exchange of prisoners, but does not realise that she is his own daughter. When Bluntschli comes to return the overcoat lent him by Raina and her mother to escape in, he is delighted to see him again, and even more delighted when the efficient and wealthy Swiss asks for his daughter's hand in marriage. *Arms and the Man*

PETKOFF, RAINA: The 23-year-old daughter of Major Petkoff, fundamentally sensible, but with a head stuffed with romantic ideas. She is engaged to Major Saranoff, hero of a recent cavalry charge in the battle of Slivnitza, but when a Swiss mercenary bursts into her bedroom pursued by a Russian officer, she hides him and helps him to escape. This she does in spite of her disgust at his unromantic views on war and women, and the fact that he carries chocolate into battle instead of ammunition. When he comes back after the war to return the overcoat she lent him, she is already more than half in love with him, and is very ready to relinquish her former hero Saranoff, who has been flirting with her maid Louka, and engage herself to Bluntschli. *Arms and the Man*

PHILANDERER: *see* Charteris, Leonard

PHILIP (PHIL): *see* Clandon, Philip

PHILIPPA OF HAINAULT: The wife of Edward III of England. She comes from her tent outside Calais just as the six burghers who have delivered up the keys of the city are going to be hanged. Filled with pity for the elderly men in nothing but shirts, with ropes round their necks, she pleads for them so eloquently that the King pardons five of them. Piers de Rosty, who has been bound and gagged for insolence, is forgotten until the young John of Gaunt draws attention to him. When freed from his bonds, he upbraids the King for yielding to a few womanish tears, and Philippa angrily demands his death. But the King, amused by his coarse jokes, and by his revelation that he is 'a dog of Champagne', indulges in a snarling match with him, and sends him back to Calais with the others. *The Six of Calais*

PHYLLIS: Lady's maid to Lady Magnesia Fitztollemache. When Lady Magnesia's lover, Adolphus Bastable, has been poisoned by her husband, Phyllis dissolves a plaster bust of her ladyship in a jug of boiling water, in the hope that it will act as an antidote; but it solidifies inside him, and Phyllis is sent to fetch a doctor. When he, the policeman, and the landlord have been struck dead by lightning, Phyllis tidies them away until the morning. *Passion, Poison, and Petrifaction*

PICKERING, COLONEL: A retired army man who is an authority on Indian dialects and the author of *Spoken Sanscrit*. Having come to England on purpose to consult the famous phonetician Henry Higgins, he is delighted to meet him while sheltering from the rain under the portico of St. Paul's, Covent Garden, but somewhat amused when Higgins boasts that he can turn anyone—for instance, the grubby Cockney flower-girl Eliza Doolittle, who is sheltering with them—into a perfect lady by teaching them to speak correctly. He is working with Higgins when Eliza turns up demanding lessons so that she can get a job in a flower-shop, and challenges Higgins to make good his boast, offering to pay Eliza's expenses if the experiment is a success. He works hard helping Higgins to win his bet, but once success has crowned their efforts he becomes bored and is glad the affair is over. However, unlike Higgins, he is conscience-stricken when Eliza runs away, and realises that they have treated the girl badly. Since neither he nor Higgins are marrying men, he is quite happy that she should marry Freddy Eynsford-Hill, and it is evident that he will be willing after their marriage to subsidise the flower-shop opened by Eliza as a means of earning a living for them both. *Pygmalion*

PIERS: *see* Rosty, Piers de; Wissant, Piers de

PIOUS PETER: *see* Cauchon, Peter

PLAIN JOHN: *see* Tarleton, John

PLECHANOFF, MAJOR: A Russian (referred to only as the Officer) who searches the bedroom of Raina Petkoff for Captain Bluntschli, but fails to find him. *Arms and the Man*

PLINY: Chancellor of the Exchequer, serving in the Cabinet under Proteus. A good-humoured and conciliatory creature, he says little, and is amused by the antics of his colleagues. When Magnus says he will abdicate, he is quite unmoved, merely remarking that 'one king is no worse than another', and he also prophesies that if Magnus becomes a commoner and stands for Parliament, he will come top of the poll. When the ultimatum has been withdrawn he tells the king that he is glad nothing has happened, and that he must not worry about the tantrums of his Ministers. 'They'll feed out of your hand tomorrow.' *The Apple Cart*

POLICEMAN: Fetched by Phyllis after George Fitztolle-mache has poisoned his wife's lover, he arrests the landlord by mistake. He is still trying to get everyone to the police station when he, the landlord, and the doctor are struck dead by lightning and rolled up against the wall by Phyllis, to be taken away the next morning. *Passion, Poison, and Petrifaction*

See also Smith, P.C.

POLLY: *see* Collins, Mrs. George; Poulengey, Bertrand de

POLLY SEEDYSTOCKINGS: *see* Smith, Patricia

POPPA: *see* Barlow, Joseph Popham Bolge Bluebin

POPSY: *see* Bagot, The Hon. Aubrey

PORTER: He carries the purchases made by Blanche

Sartorius into her hotel at Remagen on the Rhine, and speaks once, in German. *Widowers' Houses*

See also Hassan; Market Porters

PORTSMOUTH, DUCHESS OF: Louise de Kérouaille, one of the mistresses of Charles II. She comes to see Isaac Newton, believing him to be an alchemist, and is surprised to find Charles, Nell Gwynn, and the Duchess of Cleveland there. Left alone with Newton, she asks him for a prescription for a love philtre, and to satisfy her he gives her something harmless. While waiting for the meal which Mrs. Basham, Newton's housekeeper, is preparing, Louise suggests that Nelly shall recite to them, and when the 'nice piece of cod' is ready, Louise, whom Mrs. Basham calls Madam Carwell, goes down on the arm of the Duke of York, who has come in search of his brother. *In Good King Charles's Golden Days*

POSKY: A Soviet Commissar who complains to Begonia Brown, secretary of the International Committee for Intellectual Co-operation, that the Society for the Propagation of the Gospel, a subversive organisation subsidised by the British Isles, is maintaining a network of spies throughout Russia, and has caused his housekeeper, Feodorovna Ballyboushka, to defect from her duties. In the office at the same time is an English bishop who has come to complain that his footman has become a Communist. He is so shocked by Posky's revelation that there are no poor in Russia, and therefore they do not need religion to console them, that he dies of heart failure. Posky's complaint is laid before the Court of International Justice at The Hague, and he attends the trial of the three dictators, which has not reached its conclusion before the end of the world through another ice-age is announced. Posky receives the news calmly, and says he must go and consult Moscow before commenting on it. *Geneva*

POSNET, BLANCO: A drunkard and ne'er-do-well, who is

being tried by a makeshift jury in a small American town on suspicion of having stolen a horse. He denies it, but a local prostitute, Feemy Evans, swears she saw him on it, and finally he admits that he did take it, thinking it belonged to his brother, Elder Daniels, who had cheated him out of his share of their parents' money. But he does not know where it is, and will not say what he did with it. He is about to be hanged when a woman arrives and says he gave her the horse so that she could take her dying child to the doctor. Feemy, overcome by remorse, retracts her evidence and Blanco is allowed to go free. Before leaving, he preaches an impromptu sermon on God's cleverness in taking a person unawares and making them do a good deed in spite of themselves—witness his giving away a horse which would have taken him to safety, and Feemy's telling a lie to save his life. Since they have both failed as villains, he says, they should marry. But Feemy refuses, and everyone adjourns to drink at Blanco's expense in Daniels' saloon bar. *The Shewing-Up of Blanco Posnet*

POSNET, BOOZY: *see* Daniels, Elder

POSTLETHWAITE, AMANDA: Postmistress-General, a merry lady, usually referred to as Amanda or Mandy, who is always laughing at her Cabinet colleagues and the Prime Minister Proteus because they are so pompous and long-winded. She says she is the real ruler of England, because she can make people laugh, and it was by ridicule that she drove her opponent, the brother-in-law of Balbus, the Home Secretary, out of her constituency at the last general election. She sympathises with King Magnus in his stand against Proteus's ultimatum, and realises that he has something up his sleeve when he seems to be agreeing to it. So she is not surprised when he says he will abdicate, become a commoner, and stand for Parliament, and says she doesn't see why he shouldn't. When everything has returned to normal she is very sorry for Lysistrata, who has taken it all very much to heart, and says: 'Come home with

me, dear. I will sing to you until you can't help laughing.'
The Apple Cart

POTHINUS: The guardian of the young Ptolemy, and so the
virtual ruler of Egypt. 'A eunuch, passionate, energetic, and
quick-witted, but of common mind and character, im-
patient and unable to control his temper.' He tries to out-
face Julius Caesar when he comes with Cleopatra to
Ptolemy's palace in Alexandria, but is taken prisoner by
the Roman troops. Set at liberty, he first tries to involve
Cleopatra in a plot against Caesar, and then tries to dis-
credit Cleopatra by telling Caesar that she is plotting against
him. For this treacherous behaviour he is murdered by
Ftatateeta on Cleopatra's orders, and his death causes a
riot in the city. *Caesar and Cleopatra*

POULENGEY, BERTRAND DE: A French soldier, rather
unsuitably nicknamed Polly, who is quartered in the castle
of Vaucouleurs when Joan of Arc comes there. From the
first he believes in her divine mission, and helps to persuade
his superior officer, Robert de Baudricourt, to give her a
horse and an escort, which he himself commands, so that
she can go and see the Dauphin. *Saint Joan*

PRA: A priest on the Unexpected Isles, who kicks Hugo
Hyering into the sea so that he may arise regenerated. He
takes part in the eugenic experiment which produces four
perfect but amoral children, and explains to Phosphor
Hammingtap that he cannot marry either Maya or Vashti,
but must be shared in common between all the ladies of the
island family. When this creates a split in the British Empire
between those who believe in polygamy and those who do
not, and gunboats are sent on a punitive expedition, Pra
gets rid of them by telling the officers in charge that small-
pox has broken out in the harbour district. After the Angel
has announced the Day of Judgement, and the disappearance of all those who are not worth their salt, Pra discusses
their past life with Prola, and speculates about the future,

ending with 'All hail, the life to come!' *The Simpleton of the Unexpected Isles*

PRAED (PRADDY), MR.: A well-known architect, and a friend of Mrs. Warren, who calls him Praddy. Barely past middle-age, 'with something of the artist about him ... with an eager susceptible face and very amiable and considerate manners', he is delighted to meet Kitty Warren's daughter Vivie, but soon realises her strength of character and foresees the clash between her and her mother. He tries to arouse in Vivie some of his own admiration for 'the beauty and romance of life', but to his disappointment she is interested only in her work, and refuses his invitation to accompany him to Italy. *Mrs. Warren's Profession*

PRICE, SNOBBY (BRONTERRE O'BRIEN): One of the derelicts in the Salvation Army West Ham shelter, 'young, agile, an unemployed workman, a talker, a poser, sharp enough to be capable of anything except honesty or altruistic considerations of any kind'. He confesses to many sins he has not committed in order to curry favour with the Salvation Army lasses, including beating his mother, who actually beats him. When Bill Walker throws down a £1 note in compensation for having knocked down Jenny Hill, Snobby quietly pockets it and slips away when he hears his mother has come to look for him. *Major Barbara*

PRIEST: At the banquet which Cleopatra gives to Julius Caesar in the palace at Alexandria, he brings in a miniature idol of the Sphinx with a tripod and incense, so that Cleopatra can ask the Nile god to choose the name of the new city they intend to build at the source of the river; but they are interrupted by the murder of Pothinus, and the priest goes away without saying anything. *Caesar and Cleopatra*

See also Chinese Priest; Pra

PRIESTESS: *see* Prola

PRIME MINISTER: *see* Bluebin, Ambrose Badger; Chavender, Sir Arthur; Proteus, Joseph

PRIMROSE, ANNIE: *see* Dudgeon, Mrs. Timothy

PRINCE OF DARKNESS: *see* Undershaft, Andrew

PRINCESS: An unnamed spinster of royal birth who has been chosen by the Inca of Perusalem as the bride of one of his numerous sons. Reduced to poverty by the First World War, she comes diffidently to a hotel, where the manager condescendingly offers her a poor room and worse service. She is rescued by Ermyntrude Roosenhonkers-Pipstein, who becomes her lady's maid and dragoons manager and waiters into treating her properly. When the Inca arrives, the Princess is terrified, and leaves Ermyntrude to deal with him. *The Inca of Perusalem*

PRINCESS ROYAL: *see* Alice

PROLA: A priestess on the Unexpected Isles. She attracts Hyering, the Emigration Officer, and suggests to his future wife, Sally, that they should share him. Twenty years later the results of a 'eugenic experiment' destined to fuse together the best elements of East and West are four children, biologically perfect but without moral sense. They disappear at the Day of Judgement, and Prola is left discussing the future with the priest Pra, her first love. She concludes that 'the fountain of life' is within her, but that life needs both her and Pra. 'Let every day be a day of wonder for me and I shall not fear the Day of Judgement.' *The Simpleton of the Unexpected Isles*

PROMOTOR: *see* Estivet, John d'

PROSERPINE (PROSS, PROSSY): *see* Garnett, Proserpine

PROTEUS, JOSEPH: Prime Minister during the reign of King Magnus. The country is in the throes of yet another crisis, and he tells his Cabinet that he intends to present the King with an ultimatum. Either he must act constitutionally, which he seems incapable of doing, or they will all resign. Magnus promises to give them his answer that evening, but Proteus is uneasy. He knows that the King has an uncommon knack of getting his own way, either through charm or through his quick wit, and he is also adept at evading the question and throwing a meeting into confusion by getting the Cabinet Ministers to quarrel among themselves. But this time Proteus thinks he has won. Even when Magnus tries to dodge the issue by raising the question of America's offer to rejoin the British Empire with himself as Emperor, Proteus sticks to his guns. But when Magnus says he will not sign the ultimatum, but will abdicate, become a commoner and stand for Parliament with a good chance of becoming the next Prime Minister, he realises he has been outwitted once again, and tears up the ultimatum. *The Apple Cart*

PTOLEMY DIONYSUS XIV: The ten-year-old ruler of Egypt, brother of Cleopatra. Attended by his governor Pothinus, his general Achillas, and his tutor Theodotus, he receives Julius Caesar in his palace at Alexandria; 'he looks older than ten, but has the childish air, the habit of being in leading strings, the mixture of impotence and petulance, the appearance of being excessively washed, combed, and dressed by other hands, which is exhibited by court-bred princes of all ages'. An obviously frightened and unhappy boy, he is kindly treated by Caesar, which arouses the jealousy of Cleopatra. Taken prisoner with the rest of the court, but released soon after, he remains with the Egyptian army, and is drowned when his barge capsizes during the battle for the harbour. *Caesar and Cleopatra*

PYGMALION: A young scientist in A.D. 31,920, who has discovered how to make in his laboratory the material of which human beings were made. He persuades the sculptor Martellus to model from this material two figures, one male, one female, and brings them to the festival of art, where they announce themselves as Ozymandias and Cleopatra-Semiramis. Like the old-fashioned human beings, they can read and talk, boast and tell lies. They are also quarrelsome and quick to take offence. The woman tries to brain the man with a stone, and when Pygmalion intervenes, she gives him a bite on the thumb from which he dies. *Back to Methuselah, Part V: As Far as Thought Can Reach*

R

RA: The hawk-headed Egyptian god who appears in the doorway of his temple at Memphis in the alternative prologue to the play, and explains the plot and historical background to the modern audience. *Caesar and Cleopatra*

RAINA: *see* Petkoff, Raina

RAIS, GILLES DE: A young man, very smart and self-possessed, who in a clean-shaven Court wears a small curled beard, dyed blue; whence his nickname of Blue-beard. Though he tries to be pleasant, he lacks joyousness, and is not really a very nice person. In fact, when he defies the Church eleven years later, he is accused of trying to extract pleasure from horrible cruelties, and hanged. He is at Chinon with the Dauphin when Joan of Arc comes to try and persuade the King to fight against the English, and impersonates him in a childish test to see whether she can recognise the true king by instinct. Gilles attends the King's coronation at Rheims, and afterwards objects to the pride and obstinacy which he thinks are at the base of all Joan's actions. When she has gone he says: 'The woman is quite impossible. I don't dislike her, really: but what are you to do with such a character.' *Saint Joan*

RALPH: *see* Bonington, Sir Ralph Bloomfield

RAMSDEN, ROEBUCK: 'a highly respectable man of about sixty' who prides himself on being 'an advanced thinker and a fearlessly outspoken reformer'. He is, however, just as shocked as his spinster sister Susan when he hears that Violet Robinson is going to have an illegitimate baby, and profuse in his apologies when she reveals that she is married, to Hector Malone, jun. Under her father's will Ramsden has been appointed guardian of Ann Whitefield—who calls him Granny—jointly with John Tanner, whom he fears and distrusts as a red-hot revolutionary. He does all he can to break up the friendship between Ann and Tanner, and to persuade Ann to marry Octavius Robinson, not realising that Ann is determined to marry Tanner. When Tanner dreams that he is Don Juan in Hell, where he meets Don Gonzales, father of one of his many conquests, the Don bears a distinct resemblance to Ramsden. *Man and Superman*

RAMSDEN, SUSAN: 'a hardheaded old maiden lady in a plain brown silk gown, with enough rings, chains, and brooches, to shew that her plainness of dress is a matter of principle, not of poverty'. She is so severe in her judgement of Violet Robinson when she thinks that Violet is having an illegitimate baby that even her brother Roebuck is moved to protest, and she is well and truly snubbed by Violet when the truth about her marriage is revealed. *Man and Superman*

RANDALL: *see* Utterwood, Randall

RANKIN, LESLIE: A missionary in Mogador, Morocco, 'an elderly Scotsman, spiritually a little weather-beaten . . . but still a convinced son of the Free Church and the North African Mission', though in thirty years he has made only one 'convert', the disreputable Felix Drinkwater. Sir Howard Hallam and Lady Cicely Waynflete stay with Rankin before venturing into the Atlas Mountains, and he reminds Sir Howard that he was in his youth the great friend of Sir Howard's younger brother Miles. When Captain Brassbound arrives to escort the English visitors into the mountains, Rankin is struck by his likeness to Miles, and is not surprised to learn later that he is Miles's son. It is Rankin who first hears of Brassbound's plot to betray his uncle to the Arabs, and he is instrumental in sending someone to rescue the besieged party. The trial and acquittal of Brassbound take place in Rankin's house, and he is invited to lunch afterwards on board the cruiser *Santiago* by Captain Kearney. *Captain Brassbound's Conversion*

RAPHAEL: The 'feathered one' who appears to the pupils of the Sixth Form School on the Isle of Wight, and tells them that evolution can go backwards as well as forwards. He also says that he is restraining his magnetic field so as not to kill them, and that he does not fly, he levitates. He has none of the human being's physical passions, but all his intellectual ones, particularly his passion for discovery and exploration. Unfortunately he disappears before they can ask him any questions. *Far-Fetched Fables 6*

REDBROOK, KIDDY: One of the escort provided by Captain Brassbound to accompany Sir Howard Hallam into the Atlas Mountains. A pleasurably worthless young English gentleman, brought to his present plight by 'cards and drink', he is the son of the Rev. Dean Redbrook of Dunham, who is well known to Lady Cicely Waynflete, one of the party. After Brassbound's trial, at which he has appeared in a fashionable outfit belonging to Lady Cicely's ambassador brother, Redbrook is given the job of folding and packing the clothes and returning them to the lender, being the only member of the crew considered fit for such a delicate task. *Captain Brassbound's Conversion*

REDPENNY: A medical student, 'a wide-open-eyed, ready, credulous, friendly, hasty youth . . . in reluctant transition from the untidy boy to the tidy doctor'. He works for Sir Colenso Ridgeon, and is the first to congratulate him on his knighthood before being turned out of the room by old Sir Patrick Cullen, who has come on the same errand. *The Doctor's Dilemma*

REGINALD: *see* Bridgenorth, Reginald; Fitzambey, Lord Reginald

REILLY, NORA: A slight, weak woman, commonplace to Irish eyes, but to Englishmen like Tom Broadbent an attractive, ethereal creature. Since her father's death she has lived in the household of Cornelius Doyle, and considers herself engaged to his son Larry, in spite of his absence in England for eighteen years. When he finally returns with Broadbent, Nora realises that he has practically forgotten her, but is still hopeful, until, almost swept off her feet by the whirlwind courtship of Broadbent, who hears 'all the harps of Ireland' in the plaintive melody of her voice, she agrees to marry him instead. *John Bull's Other Island*

RETIARIUS: A conceited gladiator at the Colosseum in Rome, a nearly naked man with a net and trident who fights Secutor, who is armed and in armour. Retiarius wins the fight by dragging his net in the dust and so blinding his adversary, who is then easily entangled in the net; but the audience is not at all pleased at this. Retiarius defends his action before Caesar, who warns him to be careful in future. When Ferrovius has killed six gladiators in single combat, and Caesar orders all the surviving gladiators to become Christians, Retiarius answers for them, 'It is all one to us, Caesar', but also adds boastfully: 'Had I been there with my net, the story would have been different.' *Androcles and the Lion*

REV. S.: *see* Gardner, Rev. Samuel

RHEIMS, ARCHBISHOP OF: He is at Chinon with the Dauphin when Joan of Arc comes to try and persuade the French to fight. She asks for his blessing, which rather discomposes him, as there is nothing of the ecclesiastic about him except his robes and his imposing bearing; but he cannot help being impressed by her obvious sincerity and common sense, and says she comes with God's blessing and must be obeyed. He is, however, rather disconcerted when at the coronation of Charles VII in Rheims cathedral she takes the crown from him and puts it on the King's head herself, and afterwards he warns her that the Church will do nothing to save her if she falls into the hands of her enemies. When she leaves, after an impassioned speech in defence of her conduct, he says: 'She disturbs my judgement; there is a dangerous power in her outbursts. But the pit is open at her feet; and for good or evil we cannot turn her from it.' In the Epilogue he kneels to her after news of her canonisation has been received, but, like the others, deprecates her suggestion that she should return to life. *Saint Joan*

RICHARD: *see* Buoyant, Richard; Dudgeon, Richard; Warwick, Earl of

RICKY-TICKY-TAVY: *see* Robinson, Octavius

RIDGEON, SIR COLENSO (COLLY): A fashionable physician who has found a cure for tuberculosis. He is approached by Jennifer Dubedat with the request that he will undertake the cure of her husband, Louis Dubedat, a more than promising young artist who is dying of the disease. At the same time Ridgeon meets an old fellow-student, Dr. Blenkinsop, who is also tubercular. He can only take one more patient into his experimental group, and at first is inclined to favour Dubedat, particularly as he has fallen in love with the artist's wife. But when he discovers what a young blackguard Dubedat is, and how heartbreaking it will be for his wife when she discovers the truth about him —as she will, if he is cured—he hands Dubedat over to Sir Ralph Bloomfield Bonington and takes on Blenkinsop, who is completely cured. Meanwhile B.B., as Bonington is called, has killed Dubedat with incredible rapidity. A year later Ridgeon meets Jennifer, who has refused to shake hands with him at their last meeting because of his callous behaviour to her adored husband. She has written Dubedat's life, and arranged a show of his pictures. Ridgeon first tells her that he did indeed condemn Dubedat to death for love of her, and then tries to open her eyes to her late husband's real character; but in vain. She also tells him that, in fulfilment of Dubedat's last wish, she has married again, and he cries despairingly: 'Then I have committed a purely disinterested murder!' *The Doctor's Dilemma*

RIGHTSIDE, SIR DEXTER: Foreign Secretary, an explosive elderly gentleman, who considers himself a person of consequence. He is at first the only person to be affronted by the red-hot socialist speech made by the Prime Minister, Sir Arthur Chavender, after his return from the sanitorium where he has been reading the works of Karl Marx and other Communist writers, but gradually he wins his colleagues over, and when he threatens to resign they are solidly behind him. *On the Rocks*

ROB: *see* Gilbey, Robin

ROB ROY: When Shakes summons up Macbeth to prove his pre-eminence as a playwright, his adversary Shav calls on Rob Roy, who cuts off Macbeth's head, saying: 'Whaur's your Wullie Shaxper noo?' *Shakes versus Shav*

ROBERT: *see* Baudricourt, Robert de

ROBINSON, OCTAVIUS: 'a good-looking, elegant young fellow', but rather weak and effeminate, who is hopelessly in love with Ann Whitefield. He is shattered to learn that his young sister Violet is going to have an illegitimate baby, and delighted when it turns out that she is secretly married. He goes with the young couple to Granada, where he plucks up the courage to propose to Ann, but is turned down in favour of his revolutionary friend John Tanner, being, as Ann says, the sort of man who 'never marries, but lives in comfortable bachelor lodgings with broken hearts, and are adored by their landladies'. *Man and Superman*

ROBINSON, VIOLET: The young sister of Octavius Robinson. Everyone is appalled when it is said that this elegant and self-possessed young lady, 'whose personality is as formidable as it is exquisitely pretty', is going to have an illegitimate baby, and she is equally infuriated with her friends for assuming that she is 'a bad woman', particularly when the revolutionary and free-thinking John Tanner congratulates her on her courage and freedom from conventionality. This leads her to reveal that she is married to a young American, Hector Malone. The marriage has been kept secret because Hector's father wants him to marry an Englishwoman with a title. But when he meets Violet and finds how sensible and level-headed she is—she has already told her husband: 'You can be as romantic as you please about love. But you mustn't be romantic about money'— he withdraws his threat to disinherit his son, and promises Violet a handsome allowance. *Man and Superman*

ROEBUCK: *see* Ramsden, Roebuck

ROOSENHONKERS-PIPSTEIN, ERMYNTRUDE: The daughter of Archdeacon Daffodil Donkin, who forced her to marry an American millionaire. Ruined by the outbreak of the First World War, he has died, leaving her penniless, and she has returned to her father's house. When she complains of the genteel poverty of their existence, he advises her to look for another millionaire and in the meantime to take a post as lady's maid to a princess. She does so, and in that capacity interviews the Inca of Perusalem, who has chosen her mistress, an unnamed princess, to be the bride of one of his sons. Charmed by her intelligent conversation and quick wit, he proposes to her, but she refuses him on the grounds that he is already married and is too poor to offer her a life of luxury. As a compromise, they decide to spend an enjoyable afternoon together driving round the town and taking tea at the Zoo. *The Inca of Perusalem*

RORY: *see* Bompas, Aurora

ROSE: A woman student at the Genetic Institute on the Isle of Wight, wearing a tunic with green sleeves and a rose embroidered on the front. Her hair is arranged like that of the Venus de Milo. She is studying nineteenth-century books on physiology, and is shocked by the crude methods used to perpetuate the human race, and by the absurdities of religion, muddling up Jesus and Hitler, and much preferring to old-fashioned sex the modern methods of manufacturing human beings in a laboratory. *Far-Fetched Fables 5*

ROSTY, PIERS DE: One of the six burghers of Calais, here called Peter, but also nicknamed Hardmouth, who brings the keys of the city after its surrender to Edward III. He is the only one to defy the King, whom he calls 'Neddy', and is gagged and bound by the men-at-arms. When the Queen, Philippa of Hainault, has persuaded her husband to pardon the other five burghers, Piers is so rude to her that she urges Edward to hang him. But Piers, announcing that he is 'a dog of Champagne', the province from which Edward's grandmother came, indulges in a snarling match with him, and amuses the King so much by his rude jokes that he is allowed to go free. *The Six of Calais*

ROSY: *see* Hotspot, Admiral Sir Bemrose

ROWDY SOCIAL-DEMOCRAT: *see* Social-Democrats

ROWLEY, MR.: *see* Charles II

RUDOLPH: *see* Juggins

RUFIO: A Roman officer serving under Julius Caesar, a 'burly, black-bearded man of middle age, very blunt, prompt and rough . . . in iron condition'. The son of a freedman, he is devoted to Caesar, and when he discovers that Ftatateeta, whom he calls Tota, has murdered Pothinus on the orders of Cleopatra, he is afraid that his master may be the next victim. So he cuts Ftatateeta's throat before the altar of Ra, and is commended for his prompt action by Caesar, who makes him governor of conquered Egypt. *Caesar and Cleopatra*

S

SAGAMORE, JULIUS: A young solicitor who has just succeeded to the practice of his uncle in Lincoln's Inn Fields. He is visited by Epifania Fitzfassen, who wishes to make a will before committing suicide. He offers her a recipe for an excellent poison, which, as he had expected, causes her to change her mind. She is telling him about her marriage when her husband, with his mistress Patricia Smith, comes for legal advice from Sagamore, who is an old friend of his, about a divorce; they are in the middle of a fierce argument when Adrian Blenderbland, Epifania's tame lover, also arrives. By the time Epifania has finished shouting at them all and swept out of the room, the two men have forgotten what they have come for. Some months later Sagamore goes with Blenderbland to a riverside hotel which Epifania has taken over, and is instructed to arrange a divorce so that she can marry the Egyptian doctor she has fallen in love with. *The Millionairess*

ST. PIERRE, EUSTACHE DE: The leader of the six burghers who bring the keys of Calais to Edward III after the surrender of the city through starvation. As the spokesman of the group, he pleads for their lives, but in vain, and is prepared to be hanged when the Queen, Philippa of Hainault, persuades her husband to spare them all except Piers de Rosty. *The Six of Calais*

SALLY: A maid in the house of Isaac Newton, who opens the door to 'Mr. Rowley', George Fox, and the Duke of York, and is sent by Nell Gwynn to tell Charles II that she is waiting for him below in her carriage. Sally is pretty enough for Newton to tell the housekeeper, Mrs. Basham, to keep her out of Charles's way. *In Good King Charles's Golden Days*

See also Hyering, Sally; Lunn, Seraphita; Women in the Barn

SAM: *see* Gardner, Rev. Samuel

SANDRO: A pleasant, cheerful young fisherman, engaged to Giulia, whom he cannot marry until she has a dowry. To earn it, her father Squarcio has agreed to assassinate a young nobleman, Count Ferruccio, and Sandro is to help him. But by the time they have caught him in a fishing net, they decide he is mad, and it would bring them bad luck to murder a madman. So they agree to conduct him to a safe place, where Giulia can sit for a famous artist and so earn the money needed for her dowry. *The Glimpse of Reality*

SANDY: *see* Glenmorison, Sandy

SARAH: *see* Undershaft, Sarah

SARANOFF, MAJOR SERGIUS: A handsomely Byronic young officer in the Bulgarian army, the hero of a cavalry charge at the battle of Slivnitza, engaged to Raina Petkoff. Unfortunately he cannot always live up to his high ideals, and is seen by his fiancée flirting with her maid Louka, whom he finally marries. *Arms and the Man*

SARCASTIC BYSTANDER: *see* Bystanders

SARTORIUS, BLANCHE: The only child of the wealthy slum-owner Sartorius, 'well-dressed, well-fed, good-looking, a strong-minded young woman, presentably ladylike, but still her father's daughter'. Nevertheless, though quick-tempered, even violent at times, particularly in her ill-treatment of the parlourmaid Annie, she is 'fresh and attractive and none the worse for being vital and energetic rather than delicate and refined'. On holiday in Germany she deliberately attracts, and then becomes engaged to, an aristocratic young doctor, Harry Trench, but in a fit of temper breaks off the engagement when he refuses to accept any of her father's money. She is still in love with him, however, and persuades him to renew the engagement after he has agreed to take part in a nefarious scheme devised by her father and Lickcheese for the obtaining of compensation for the hastily-renovated slum property from which his income is derived. *Widowers' Houses*

SARTORIUS, MR.: 'a self-made man, formidable to servants, not easily accessible to anyone.' Fifty years old, 'tall and well-preserved, and of upright carriage', he has amassed a fortune by the exploitation of slum property and spent it on making a lady of his daughter Blanche. With Lickcheese, his former rent-collector, and Dr. Harry Trench, his prospective son-in-law, he becomes involved in a shady speculation over slum property, buying and improving it in order to claim heavy compensation when it is required for public works. *Widowers' Houses*

SAVAGE (SAVVY): *see* Barnabas, Cynthia

SAVOYARD, CECIL: A middle-aged impresario (his real name is William Tinkler) who is employed by Count O'Dowda to assemble a professional cast for the production of a play written by the Count's daughter Fanny. He has also been instructed to invite a number of outstanding dramatic critics to watch the performance. He knows nothing about the play except that it must be modern because he has not been asked to provide any costumes. After the play, which has been given anonymously, he is upset because the critics are arguing so fiercely about the authorship of it that they have forgotten to congratulate the cast. He hurries them back to the stage, where they meet and applaud the actors. *Fanny's First Play*

SCHNEIDEKIND, LIEUTENANT: A young officer in the Boetian army who supports the revolution, and is amused by the old-fashioned loyalty of his superior officer, General Strammfest, to the deposed Panjandrum. He promises not to betray him, since his own elderly father talks in just the same way, but he assures Strammfest that the revolutionaries will win in the end and there will be no restoration of the monarchy. He is interested to hear that the Grand Duchess Annajanska has joined the revolutionaries, and would have liked to stay and assist at the interview between her and Strammfest when she is brought under guard to their office; but Annajanska insists on privacy, and drives Schneidekind and his soldiers out of the office at the point of a pistol. *Annajanska*

SCHUTZMACHER, DR. LEO: A handsome middle-aged, well-dressed Jewish doctor, 'gone a little pigeon-breasted and stale after thirty, as handsome young Jews often do, but still decidedly goodlooking'. He has made a good deal of money as a 'sixpenny doctor in a Midlands town', and has retired with his wife to Hertfordshire. He comes to congratulate his old fellow-student Sir Colenso Ridgeon, to whom he is known by his nickname of Loony, on his knighthood, and is invited to the celebration dinner at which Louis Dubedat is present. He is the only guest to refuse to lend money to Dubedat, whom he instinctively recognises as a wrong 'un. *The Doctor's Dilemma*

SCRIBES: The men who take down the evidence at the trial of Joan of Arc. They have nothing to say, but are kept busy writing, and when sentence has been pronounced, they hurry off to see it carried out. *Saint Joan*

SECONDBORN: *see* Buoyant, Richard

SECONDBORN, MRS.: *see* Buoyant, Julia

SECRETARY: She is working for Lord Ulsterbridge at the War Office when Lord Oldhand from the Foreign Office comes to tell him that the entire population of the Isle of Wight has been killed by poison gas. *Far-Fetched Fables 2*

An official of the League of Nations, who is called on to

explain to the British Foreign Secretary, Sir Orpheus Midlander, that an international crisis has been provoked by the fiancée of his nephew, who has applied to the Court of International Justice at The Hague for the trial of the three dictators Battler, Bombardone, and Flanco de Fortinbras, on the charge of 'crimes against humanity'. He does not think they will appear before the Court, but they do, mainly out of curiosity. The Secretary is present at their trial, and when, before it is finished, the end of the world is announced, he is the only person present to understand the scientific terms involved. He tells the judge that he is glad something has put a stop to what he calls 'this farce of a trial', but the judge points out that the dictators, in spite of all their bluster and defiance, obeyed his summons and therefore recognised the authority of international law. And that is something gained. *Geneva*

See also Danby, Mr.

SECUTOR: A gladiator at the Colosseum in Rome. Armed and in armour, he fights the almost naked Retiarius, and is beaten by a trick. He complains to Caesar, and threatens to trip Retiarius up and strangle him next time they meet in the arena. *Androcles and the Lion*

SEEDY: *see* Smith, Patricia

SEMPRONIUS: One of King Magnus's secretaries, it being his duty to open the King's mail, including his love-letters—except those from Orinthia. He leaves his desk during the Cabinet meeting, but, like Pamphilius, listens to it all, and when reproached with eavesdropping by the Prime Minister replies pompously that 'the king's private secretaries must hear everything, see everything, and know everything'. When sent by Queen Jemima to tell the King that tea is ready, he finds him rolling on the floor with Orinthia and, very shocked, goes out of the room and coughs and knocks vigorously before coming in again. After tea he conducts the members of the Cabinet on to the terrace for a meeting, and goes out after the Queen, carrying her knitting. *The Apple Cart*

SENTINELS: *see* Nubian Sentinel; Roman Soldiers

SENTRY: *see* Soldiers

SERAPHITA: *see* Lunn, Seraphita

SERGEANT: A British soldier under the command of Major Swindon, who arrests Richard Dudgeon as a rebel American in mistake for the Rev. Anderson, and is kept very busy with all the arrangements for his trial and execution. He accepts a bribe from Judith Anderson to let her stay by the gallows, and when Richard has been reprieved he retires in good order with his escort and military band. *The Devil's Disciple*

See also Cossack Sergeant; Fielding, Sergeant

SERGIUS: *see* Saranoff, Major

SERPENT: Lying hidden in the Garden of Eden, she has learned the speech of Adam and Eve, and after the discovery of the fawn's body has brought them face to face with the reality of death she talks to Eve, explaining to her how a new concept, birth, can take away the fear of death, and also Adam's fear of immortality. She teaches them both the meaning of love and jealousy, fear and hope, tells them that by promising to be faithful to each other for ever they have invented marriage, and finally whispers to Eve the secret of conception and birth. *Back to Methuselah, Part I: In the Beginning*

In the summer of A.D. 31,920 the ghost of the Serpent returns to see what is happening to the descendants of Adam and Eve, for whom she is so largely responsible, and finds she is justified. 'I chose wisdom and the knowledge of good and evil; and now there is no evil; and wisdom and good are one.' *Back to Methuselah, Part V: As Far as Thought Can Reach*

SERVANTS: In attendance on Lentulus and Metellus when they meet the Christian prisoners at the gate of Rome. They carry away Lentulus when Ferrovius has caused him to collapse from terror, and some of them are with Metellus when he goes to the Colosseum to see the Christians thrown to the lions. *Androcles and the Lion*

SHAKES: The playwright Shakes (William Shakespeare) comes to chastise and humiliate the presumptuous Shav (George Bernard Shaw), who claims to be Shakes reincarnated and a better dramatist than Shakes ever was. Shav enters and the two men fight. Shakes knocks down Shav, who rises on the count of nine and knocks down Shakes. He too rises, and challenges Shav to improve on his Macbeth. But Shav summons Rob Roy, who cuts off Macbeth's head. Shakes then cites King Lear, whereupon Shav calls on Captain Shotover and Ellie Dunn to recite some of their dialogue from *Heartbreak House*. *Shakes versus Shav*

SHAKESPEAR [*sic*], WILLIAM: Elizabethan playwright, who has made an assignation with Mary Fitton, the original of the Dark Lady in his sonnets. When he arrives at the trysting-place on the terrace of the Palace at Whitehall, she is not there, so he talks to the Beefeater on duty, and learns that he is not Mary's only nocturnal visitor. He is then aware of the approach of a cloaked lady whom he takes to be Mary. She is sleep-walking and talking wildly, so he wakes her up and chats with her very freely; he is just about to kiss her when Mary, who has stolen up unobserved, cuffs them both, and the woman stands revealed as the Queen. Shakespear, quite unabashed, defends himself, and becomes very angry when she casts aspersions on his parentage. But he manages by discreet flattery to ingratiate himself with the Queen, even asking her help in his plans for a National Theatre in London for the performance of his plays, which she says she will leave to the judgement of posterity. *The Dark Lady of the Sonnets*

SHAMROCK: One of the young men studying at the Genetic

Institute on the Isle of Wight, where human beings are manufactured in test tubes. He cannot understand why nineteenth-century books on physiology do not mention sex. He is also worried about what will happen when everything has been discovered, but is told by Rose that 'the pursuit of knowledge and power will never end'. *Far-Fetched Fables 5*

SHAV: The presumptuous George Bernard Shaw, disguised as Shav, challenges Shakespeare (called Shakes) to prove himself the better playwright, and they fight, knocking each other down. When Shakes proudly cites Macbeth, Shav summons up Rob Roy, who cuts off Macbeth's head. When Shakes boasts of his King Lear, Shaw brings on Captain Shotover and Ellie Dunn from his *Heartbreak House*. He asks Shakes to allow his glimmering light to shine for a moment, but Shakes blows it out, saying 'Out, out, brief candle!' *Shakes versus Shav*

SHE: *see* Bompas, Aurora; Brown, Begonia; Buoyant, Clementina

SHE-ANCIENT: One of the old people who inhabit the world in A.D. 31,920. Bald, and without sexual charm, but intensely interesting and rather terrifying, she has lived for seven centuries. Normally she wears no clothes, but when coming to preside at the birth of Amaryllis, who is hatched from an egg broken open by the Ancient, she drapes herself rather perfunctorily in a ceremonial robe. She returns to the grove where the young people are playing after Pygmalion has been killed by the female automaton he has constructed, and gives orders for it to be taken away and destroyed, and then, with the He-Ancient, tries to explain to the youths and maidens the life that awaits them after childhood. She tells them of the power of thought, that can make a human being grow four heads or eight eyes, and grieves that she is still the slave of her body, looking forward to the day when 'there will be no people, only thought' and she will end as she began, 'as a vortex'. But the young

people cannot understand her, and she goes sadly away.
Back to Methuselah, Part V: As Far as Thought Can Reach

SHEIKH: *see* Sidi el Assif

SHERIFF: *see* Kemp, George

SHIRLEY, PETER: A hard-working, honest, prematurely
white-haired man of forty-six, who has lost his job to a
younger man and is starving when Jenny Hill picks him up
and takes him to the Salvation Army shelter in West Ham
for a meal of bread and treacle and watered milk. He
bravely stands up to the brutal Bill Walker when he starts
knocking people about, and arranges a fight for him with
his son-in-law's brother, Todger Fairmile, who turns out to
be the man Walker's girl has left him for, both now being
members of the Salvation Army. When Barbara Undershaft leaves the Army in a rage because Mrs. Baines has
accepted her father's 'tainted' money—made in armaments—she persuades Shirley to take her out for a meal and
talk to her about 'Tom Paine's books and Bradlaugh's
lectures' to take her mind off her troubles. Later Undershaft gives Shirley a job in his factory as gatekeeper and
timekeeper, which he hates. 'His gate lodge is so splendid
that he's ashamed to use the rooms and skulks in the
scullery.' *Major Barbara*

SHOTOVER, CAPTAIN: An 88-year-old sea captain, who
has retired to Surrey, where his married daughter, Hesione
Hushabye, keeps house for him. He has lost interest in
everything except his inventions, for which he stores
dynamite in a cave in his garden, hoping to invent a ray
which will explode the enemy's ammunition before he can
fire his gun. In this way he will rid the world of the 'human
vermin' he despises. He has outlived human affection, cares
nothing for his family, thinks England is running on the
rocks. But he is drawn to the young and unhappy Ellie
Dunn, warning her that if she seeks consolation for her
heartbreak over a married man by marrying elsewhere for

money, she will lose her soul. He tells her happiness only comes when life is over, like the sweetness of rotten fruit, and when she calls his home Heartbreak House, he says to him it is nothing but a kennel. He is quite indifferent to the bombers passing overhead, even when they blow up his cave and kill Mangan and Billy Dunn, and falls asleep as soon as they have gone. *Heartbreak House*

When Shav wishes to prove that he is a better playwright than Shakes he summons up Shotover and Ellie Dunn to recite some of their lines from *Heartbreak House*, which he considers superior to Shakes's *King Lear. Shakes versus Shav*

SIBTHORPE: *see* Juno, Sibthorpe

SIDI EL ASSIF: A sheikh in the Atlas Mountains who has made a compact with Captain Brassbound: he will allow the captain's escorted parties to pass unmolested on condition they are all Jews or believers—no Christians. When Brassbound, thirsting for revenge on his uncle, Sir Howard Hallam, who has deprived him of his father's property, brings him into the sheikh's domain, the latter arrives to capture him, but is himself captivated by Sir Howard's sister-in-law, Lady Cicely Waynflete. Brassbound, persuaded by Lady Cicely to forego his revenge, tries to save his uncle, and Sidi el Assif agrees to give him up in exchange for the lady. He is thwarted by the arrival of the Cadi Muley Othman, sent to rescue the English visitors and so avoid an international incident, and surrenders 'after an Homeric struggle'. *Captain Brassbound's Conversion*

SILLY: *see* Craven, Sylvia

SIMPKINS, SUSAN: A small-time criminal who goes as nurse to Miss Mopply so that she and her accomplice Aubrey Bagot can steal the young woman's pearl necklace. When their plan fails, and Aubrey has persuaded Miss Mopply to steal the necklace herself and travel abroad with them on the proceeds, she becomes the Countess Valbrioni, with

Aubrey as her brother and Miss Mopply disguised as her native servant. They fall in with a detachment of British troops who have been sent to rescue Miss Mopply from brigands—an invention of Aubrey's for extorting ransom money from Mrs. Mopply—and Sweetie, as she is called, falls heavily for Sergeant Fielding. She manages to distract his attention from the Bible long enough to make her attractions evident to him, and under cover of Aubrey's last long sermon they steal away to get married. *Too True to be Good*

SIMPLE-LIFER: *see* Barnabas, Cynthia

SINJON: *see* Hotchkiss, St. John

SLAVES: In the Colosseum at Rome. Three bring arms and armour for the Christians who are to fight the gladiators; six wearing Etruscan masks bring hooks, ropes, and baskets to cart away the six men killed by Ferrovius; and others bring iron bars and tridents to attack the lion when Androcles brings him out of the arena. *Androcles and the Lion*

In the palace at Alexandria. They attend on the Major Domo, laying the tables and bringing in the dishes for the banquet attended by Julius Caesar and Cleopatra. They clear everything away when news comes of the murder of Pothinus and the subsequent revolt in the city, and then disappear hurriedly before the fighting starts. *Caesar and Cleopatra*

SMITH, JUNIUS: The seventh son of a seventh son, his only ambition is to become a 'world betterer'. In the meantime his father will finance a trip round the world for him. In a jungle clearing near Panama he meets Clementina Buoyant, and falls in love with her; but she drives him away by summoning up an alligator with her saxophone. Nevertheless he pursues her to her home in London, where he makes it clear to her father, a millionaire, that he is marrying her primarily for her money, but also because he cannot live without her. The father approves of him, and sends him to buy a special licence and a wedding ring. He returns with both and issues an ultimatum: is it yes or no? She replies: 'I suppose I must take my chance.' *Buoyant Billions*

SMITH, MR.: His son Junius has just come down from the university, and he wants him to choose a profession. But Junius says the only profession he wants is that of 'world betterer', and for that he will need money. He will insure his father's life with money borrowed from his mother; and in the meantime his father will give him £1,000 to go round the world investigating the effect of the atom bomb on the anopheles mosquito, the tsetse fly, the white ant, and the locust. *Buoyant Billions*

SMITH, PATRICIA: A pleasant, quiet little woman of the self-supporting type. She is the mistress of Alastair Fitz-fassen, who is anxious to divorce his wife Epifania so that he can marry her. But Epifania, who has found Patricia's letters to her husband, signed 'Polly Seedystockings', refuses, until the time comes when she, in her turn, wants to marry someone else. *The Millionairess*

SMITH, P.C.: A London policeman who attempts to stop the rioting at the Agricultural Hall, Islington, after the fight between Cashel Byron and William Paradise, and later goes to Wiltstoken to arrest them both for a second, illegal, fight. He chases Cashel to the castle of Lydia Carew, where he has taken refuge, and when Cashel is pardoned, Smith is promoted to Inspector. *The Admirable Bashville*

SNOBBY,: *see* Price, Snobby

SOAMES, REV. OLIVER CROMWELL: Chaplain to the Bishop of Chelsea. He was formerly a solicitor, but on the death of his Nonconformist father became an Anglican, was ordained, and now, as Father Anthony, runs the business side of the Bishop's work. He is fiercely celibate, and raises every possible objection to the civil contract of marriage which the Bishop's daughter Edith wants in place of a religious ceremony. When all the arguments are over, and Edith has got married in the old-fashioned way in church, Father Anthony is left quietly working at his desk while the rest of the party go to the wedding reception. *Getting Married*

SOCIAL-DEMOCRATS: Three of the brigands with Mendoza. One is 'unmistakeably a Frenchman', named Duval; the other two are Englishmen, one sulky, argumentative, solemn, and obstinate; the other rowdy and mischievous. They all three wear scarlet ties, and are not on speaking terms. Duval is in charge of the only gun belonging to the band; the rowdy one is a coward; and the sulky one brings news of the arrival of the two armoured cars full of Spanish soldiers sent to arrest the brigands. *Man and Superman*

SOLDIERS: Roman soldiers are in charge of the Christians who are being taken to Rome to be thrown to the lions. *Androcles and the Lion*

Two Boetian soldiers of the Revolution bring the Grand Duchess Annajanska to the office of General Strammfest, not without difficulty, as she has bitten one and knocked the other down. They are both very glad to escape when she captures the General's pistol and fires at their ankles to make them go. *Annajanska*

Roman soldiers follow Julius Caesar to Egypt and capture the palace, harbour, and lighthouse of Alexandria. One sentinel is manhandled by Apollodorus and Ftatateeta when he tries to prevent Cleopatra from leaving the palace, and with two others raises the alarm when the Egyptians counter-attack. A wounded Roman soldier goes to the palace to warn Caesar of his danger when the city rises in revolt, and is sent to order the boats to the lighthouse. They all cheer Caesar before he leaves Egypt, acclaim the appointment of Rufio as their commander-in-chief, and mount guard on the quayside as Caesar's boat sails away. *Caesar and Cleopatra*

Two British soldiers from a company under the command of Major Swindon go with the Sergeant to arrest Richard Dudgeon, and later bring on the cart from which he is to be hanged. Another party with fixed bayonets lines the route to the gallows while a military band plays the 'Dead March' in *Saul*, and form a square round it, marching off in good order after Richard's reprieve. *The Devil's Disciple*

Some Russian soldiers rush in with the Cossack Sergeant when Captain Edstaston knocks down Prince Patiomkin and his niece Varinka calls for help. They also go with the Sergeant to arrest Edstaston after he has left the palace without permission, truss him up to a pole and carry him back, dumping him in a recess next to the ballroom to await the Empress. *Great Catherine*

Two armoured-car-loads of Spanish soldiers, under an officer, drive into the Sierra Nevada, with rifles, to arrest Mendoza and his brigands. They go away empty-handed, as John Tanner claims that the brigands constitute his 'escort'. *Man and Superman*

When Joan of Arc comes to see the Dauphin at Chinon, the room is heavily guarded by French men-at-arms, and the King's page borrows a halberd from one of them to thump on the floor before he can make his introduction of Joan, and later of Charles VII, audible above the chatter of the courtiers. When Joan is brought to her trial in Rouen, she has a guard of English soldiers, who push her out into the courtyard, helped by de Stogumber, after she has been sentenced to death. *Saint Joan*

There are several English soldiers present when Edward III receives the surrender of the six burghers after the siege of Calais. They bring them in, force Piers de Rosty to his knees, tie him up and gag him, and are about to take the other five to be hanged when the Queen, Philippa of Hainault, persuades her husband to forgive them. They then untie Piers de Rosty, and when the King has spared his life too, they drag him away, braying like a donkey in derision of the English. *The Six of Calais*

See also English Soldier

SOLICITOR: *see* Flopper, Sir Ferdinand

SON: *see* Smith, Junius

SONNY: *see* Hotchkiss, St. John

SOPHRONIA: *see* Clandon, Gloria

SPECTATORS: A group of Londoners sheltering from the rain under the portico of St. Paul's, Covent Garden, when Eliza Doolittle first meets Professor Higgins. They are on the whole sympathetic towards her in her verbal exchanges with him and Colonel Pickering, but dash off as soon as the rain stops. *Pygmalion*

SPECTATORS AND PERSONS OF FASHION: They attend the fight at the Agricultural Hall, Islington, between Cashel Byron and Paradise, which ends in a free-for-all. When Paradise attacks Cashel with his bare fists they cry 'Shame', and react with horror when in the ensuing mêlée he bites a lump out of Cashel's thigh. *The Admirable Bashville*

SPINTHO: A snivelling, drunken good-for-nothing, the wreck of a good-looking man gone hopelessly to the bad. He has become a Christian, and is determined to be martyred because he thinks he will then go straight to heaven. He begs some of his fellow-Christians to ill-treat him so that he can forgive them, but at heart he is a coward, and when he is taken to the Colosseum to be thrown to the lions, he recants. In an access of terror he bolts straight into the cell of a hungry lion and is eaten up. *Androcles and the Lion*

SQUARCIO: An Italian innkeeper and professional assassin, who needs money for his daughter's dowry. To earn it, he has agreed to murder Count Ferruccio, the seducer of Cardinal Poldi's sister, and sends his daughter Giulia to entice the Count to his inn. On the way she asks for absolution for her crime from an old blind friar, who is really the Count in disguise. When the Count rushes in determined to kill him, Squarcio tells him he is wasting his time. The expert is bound to win. He offers the Count a good supper, at which Giulia's fiancé, the fisherman Sandro, joins them, and when the Count's dagger has glanced harmlessly off the coat of mail which Squarcio always wears, he and Sandro trap the young nobleman in a fishing net. By this time Squarcio has decided that the Count is mad, and it will therefore be unlucky to kill him. He offers to escort him to a safe place, and agrees that Giulia shall go with them to sit for a famous artist, thus earning the money needed for her dowry. *The Glimpse of Reality*

SQUINTY: *see* Jurymen

STATION MASTER: He works in the docks of a small tropical port, and finds the body of Wilks, the clerk in the Emigration Office, after he has committed suicide. Saying: 'What a climate! The fifth this month!', he calls to an unseen Joe to bring along a stretcher. *The Simpleton of the Unexpected Isles*

STATUE: *see* Gonzales, Don

STEPHEN: *see* Undershaft, Stephen

STEWARD: 'a trodden worm, scanty of flesh, scanty of hair, any age from eighteen to fifty-five, being the sort of man whom age cannot wither because he has never bloomed'. He is trying to explain to the Captain in charge of the Castle of Vaucouleurs why there are no eggs for the garrison, and he says the hens have stopped laying ever since the arrival of Joan of Arc, whom he cannot get rid of, though ordered to do so. When the Captain, Robert de Baudricourt, has finally been persuaded to see Joan, and given her an escort to enable her to reach Charles VII at Chinon, the Steward rushes in excitedly to say that the hens are laying like mad—five dozen eggs! *Saint Joan*

STICKIT, ARCHBISHOP: *see* Haslam, Rev. William

STOGUMBER, JOHN BOWYER SPENSER NEVILLE DE: A narrow-minded, nationalistic Dominican monk, Chaplain to the Cardinal of Westminster. He tells the Earl of Warwick that Joan of Arc must be a witch; she could not otherwise have beaten the English. He is so incensed against her that he says he would like to strangle her with his own hands, and during her trial, which he attends as one of the assessors, he is constantly in trouble with the judges, particularly the Inquisitor Brother John Lemaître, for interrupting and demanding her conviction. When she is finally taken away to be burnt, he is first out of the hall in his anxiety to see the sentence carried out; but he returns, a broken man, overcome by horror and remorse at what he has witnessed. Many years later he turns up in the Epilogue, a gentle, half-witted old man, pottering about in a little English parish, and sometimes remembering that he once did a very cruel thing because he did not know what cruelty was like: he had to see it before he could understand it. When he hears that Joan has been canonised, he kneels to her, saying: 'The foolish old men . . . praise thee, because their sins against thee are turned into blessings.'
Saint Joan

STRAKER, HENRY: Chauffeur to John Tanner, a cool, competent young man 'in a neat navy-blue serge suit, clean-shaven, with dark eyes, square fingers, and short well-brushed black hair'. The product of a good Board School and an excellent polytechnic, he is a scientific socialist, and combines 'deep contempt for a gentleman with an arrogant pride in being a skilled engineer'. Tanner refers to him as Enry, as a tribute to his Cockney independence, and says he is the New Man, who has arrived unnoticed while everyone was occupied with the emergence of the New Woman. Straker knows that Ann Whitefield is determined to marry Tanner even before Tanner knows it himself, and is merely amused when the hunted man tries to escape his fate by rushing off to Spain in his new motor-car. But he is not amused when, after being captured in the Sierra Nevada by the brigand Mendoza, he learns that the latter was once in love with his sister Louisa, and offers to punch his fat head for daring to use her Christian name. He is easily blackmailed into supporting Tanner's statement that Mendoza and his brigands are in reality their escort, thus saving them all from arrest, as he does not wish the respectable name of Straker to be dragged through the courts in connection with Mendoza's trial, and goes on with Tanner to Granada, where he is present when Ann finally announces her engagement. *Man and Superman*

STRAMMFEST, GENERAL: A Boetian soldier who has joined the revolutionaries, but secretly hankers after the restoration of the Panjandrum, who has been deposed and imprisoned with his family. Strammfest is shocked to hear that the Panjandrum's daughter, the Grand Duchess Annajanska, has escaped, eloped with a young officer, and joined the revolutionaries. When she is brought into his office, he tries to argue with her, but she assures him that her father's cause is lost, and she is glad of it. The only thing that can save the Revolution is war, and she will provide a man to lead the country to victory and an honourable peace. She then appears in hussar uniform, being in fact disguised as the young man who was supposed to have eloped with her, and Strammfest hails her as the Bolshevik Empress. *Annajanska*

STRANGE LADY: A mysterious young woman, who, according to the innkeeper Giuseppe Grandi, in conversation with General Bonaparte, has arrived at his inn in Tavazzano in a hired carriage, with no servants, only a dressing bag and a trunk, leaving behind her at Borghetto 'a charger with (French) military trappings'. When Napoleon learns that the Lieutenant who was bringing him important dispatches has had them stolen from him by a young man who is apparently the lady's twin brother, he realises that she is the culprit, and after a spirited encounter he forces her to return the package to him. She then lets him know that her only interest in the affair is the recovery of a love-letter written by his wife Josephine to Barras, and that if he does not wish to ruin his career he had better not read it. He does so, but pretends he has not, and she then persuades him to burn it. *The Man of Destiny*

STRAPPER: *see* Kemp, Strapper

STREGA: *see* Thundridge, Strega

STREPHON: One of the youths who in A.D. 31,920 are dancing in front of a small temple. He is distressed because his chosen companion, Chloe, has turned out to be older than he is, and is already tired of him, turning from his love-making to intellectual pursuits. He is present at the hatching of Amaryllis, the Newly-Born, but takes no interest in her, and is appalled by the automata made by Pygmalion. He decides that when his four years of childhood are up, he will kill himself. But the Ancients tell him he will grow out of such childish notions. *Back to Methuselah, Part V: As Far as Thought Can Reach*

STUART, CHARLES: *see* Charles II

SULKY SOCIAL-DEMOCRAT: *see* Social-Democrats

SUMMERHAYS, BENTLEY: The youngest son of Lord Summerhays, sensitive and intelligent, but spoilt, selfish, with an uncontrollable temper. When thwarted, he goes into hysterics, and is petted by all the women, including his fiancée, Hypatia Tarleton. He meets his match in the Polish acrobat Lina Szczepanowska, who crashes on the Tarletons' house in a plane piloted by Joseph Percival. When Bentley starts a tantrum, she picks him up, throws him over her shoulder, and takes him off to do exercises. Captivated by her brutality, he proposes to her, but is met with an amused refusal. However, she agrees to take him as a passenger in the salvaged plane, in spite of his obvious terror. *Misalliance*

SUMMERHAYS, LORD: The elderly father of Bentley Summerhays, former Governor of the province of Jinghiskahn. He comes to stay with the family of Bentley's fiancée, Hypatia Tarleton, and before he realises the situation, has fallen in love with and proposed to Hypatia, who dismisses him scornfully as 'an old man'. When Lina Szczepanowska crashes on the house in a plane piloted by Joseph Percival, he recognises her as the woman he had an affair with in Vienna some years ago, and begs her not to mention it; but she includes him in her general denunciation of the 'love-crazy' men of the household whom she is running away from to the purer air of the circus world. He is on the whole relieved when Hypatia gets engaged to Percival. *Misalliance*

SUSAN, SWEETIE: *see* Simpkins, Susan

SWINDON, MAJOR: The British officer in charge of the troops which have invested the town of Websterbridge, New Hampshire, during the American War of Independence. A 'pale, sandy-haired, very conscientious-looking man of about forty-five', slow-witted, doggedly loyal, proud of his men, and much resenting the sarcasms and negligent attitude of General Burgoyne. He is quite prepared to hang Richard Dudgeon, who has been arrested in error, and is furious at Burgoyne's decision to evacuate the town, even though he knows that the lack of reinforcements means they cannot hold it. *The Devil's Disciple*

SYKES, CECIL: The fiancé of Edith Bridgenorth. On his wedding morning he makes a discovery concerning the legal aspect of his marriage which worries him considerably. Edith is a militant social worker, apt to make libellous statements about her opponents from public platforms, and if she is involved in a law-suit he will be responsible for her debts. As he has a mother and several sisters dependent on him, he feels he ought not to marry. Edith has also discovered that even if her husband turns out to be a murderer or insane, she cannot divorce him. They decide not to get married, but to live together in 'an alliance' based on 'honourable conditions', and a great effort is made by the Bridgenorth family and their friends to draw up a contract which shall satisfy both parties. This proves impossible, and at the height of the argument Edith and Cecil withdraw quietly and get married in the usual way in an empty church, leaving the future to look after itself. *Getting Married*

SYLVIA: *see* Craven, Sylvia

SZCZEPANOWSKA, LINA: A remarkably handsome and attractive woman, member of an old-established Polish family of acrobats and circus performers. For hundreds of years one member of the family has risked his or her life every day, and to keep up the tradition Lina accompanies the aviator Joseph Percival as passenger on a record-breaking flight which ends with a crash into the sun-parlour of the Tarletons' house. Here she becomes the focus of attention. Her host, John Tarleton, asks her to become his mistress; Lord Summerhays begs her not to reveal that they were lovers some years ago in Vienna; his son Bentley Summerhays proposes to her, forgetting that he is engaged to Hypatia Tarleton; and Johnny Tarleton offers to marry her in order to rescue her from her present 'unsuitable' life. This she considers the ultimate insult, and after an impassioned tirade on the importance of freedom and independence, and the comparative unimportance of love and conventional marriage, she prepares to fly off in the salvaged plane, taking Bentley with her to help him overcome his cowardice. *Misalliance*

T

TALLBOYS, COLONEL, V.C., D.S.O.: The officer presumed to be in charge of an expeditionary force against brigands which is in fact most efficiently led by Private Meek, thus enabling the Colonel to pursue his hobby of painting in water colours. He is supposed to be rescuing Miss Mopply and her companions, and does not realise that they are the three strangers who have put themselves under his protection. When Mrs. Mopply arrives in search of her daughter she so maddens the hot-tempered Colonel that he hits her over the head with his umbrella. The shock causes her to shed the inhibitions of a lifetime, and she goes off happily with her daughter, leaving the Colonel to rejoice in the award of the K.C.B., which he has done nothing to deserve, but which will give so much pleasure to his wife. *Too True to be Good*

TANNER, JOHN: A professed anarchist, fluent, excitable, sensitive and earnest, but with a saving sense of humour. Physically he is a big man, with a large black beard, not bad-looking, but Jupiter rather than Apollo. With the elderly Roebuck Ramsden he has been appointed guardian of Ann Whitefield, who has made up her mind to marry Jack, as she calls him. Tanner, true to his principles, champions Ann's friend Violet Robinson when it is thought that she is going to have an illegitimate baby, and is duly crushed when Violet snubs him for having dared to think her a 'bad woman' when she is in fact secretly married. As Ann has taken the opportunity to vaunt her contempt for convention, Tanner ironically suggests that she shall drive alone with him to Spain, and is horrified when she accepts. Hoping to escape her, he starts off with his chauffeur, but she follows with Violet, her husband, and her brother Octavius, and they all find themselves in Granada. Alone with Tanner, Ann forces a proposal from him, faints in his arms, and when the rest of the party arrives, announces that they are engaged. When Tanner is a prisoner in the hands of Mendoza, a Spanish brigand, and dreams that he is Don Juan in Hell, he meets there one of the Don's former loves, Doña Ana, who looks very like Ann. *Man and Superman*

TARLETON, HYPATIA: The daughter of the wealthy businessman John Tarleton, who always addresses her boisterously as Patsy. Bored with her idle life and the inane conversation of the young men she meets, she has become engaged to Bentley Summerhays, because, though small and insignificant-looking, he has brains. But she is secretly haunted by the fear that his father, Lord Summerhays, and other members of his aristocratic family will think he is marrying beneath him. When Bentley's friend John Percival crashes his plane on the Tarleton's house, Hypatia immediately falls in love with him, since he combines strength with intelligence; and when he is reluctant to marry her on the score of poverty, she begs her father to 'buy him for her'. Matters are satisfactorily settled when Tarleton agrees to give the young couple £1,500 a year. *Misalliance*

TARLETON, JOHN: A wealthy businessman, founder of Tarleton's Underwear. Known to his associates as the Grand Cham, but calling himself Plain John, he is a man of immense vitality, bursting with ideas, and would have liked to be a writer. Instead, he spends his money on the provision of free libraries, and his energy on extra-marital affairs, which his wife ignores or condones, knowing he will always return to her. When the Polish acrobat Lina Szczepanowska crashes on his house in a plane piloted by Joseph Percival, he is immediately captivated by her, but she rejects his advances, and makes him do exercises instead. Confronted by Julius Baker with a gun, he is unafraid but interested, ready to sympathise with him until he learns that all his crackbrained notions came from reading in free libraries, whereupon he swears never to endow another. He is fond of his children, but thinks his son a fool, and is only too glad to agree to Percival's demand for £1,500 a year if he is to marry Tarleton's daughter Hypatia. *Misalliance*

TARLETON, JOHNNY: A pleasant, unintelligent, rather lazy young man, only son and heir of John Tarleton, of Tarleton's Underwear. He has a very low opinion of artists and writers, and is quite sure he could write a book himself if he wanted to. The only person who admires him is his mother, but he is completely self-satisfied, patronising to his father, contemptuous of his sister's fiancé Bentley Summerhays, and always very anxious to do the right thing. When the Polish acrobat Lina Szczepanowska crashes on the Tarletons' house in a plane piloted by Joseph Percival, Johnny, like all the other men, is captivated by her, and solemnly proposes to her in order, as he says, to rescue her from her present position as a highly-paid circus performer 'which is not suitable for a nice woman'. Nor can he understand why she refuses him. *Misalliance*

TARLETON, MRS.: A shrewd and motherly old lady, wife of John Tarleton, to whom she is known affectionately as Chickabiddy. Daughter of a rent-collector, who despised her husband as 'only a linen-draper', she has made the transition from near poverty to great wealth without too much trouble, and though easily shocked and often completely baffled by the conversation of her children and their friends, displays a bedrock of common sense and practicality in an emergency. She is contemptuous of Bentley Summerhays, who is engaged to her daughter Hypatia, thinking him over-bred and a 'poor little squit'; but she knows Hypatia will not really marry him, and is delighted when the virile and intelligent Joseph Percival succeeds in capturing her affections. *Misalliance*

TAVY: *see* Robinson, Octavius

TEACHER: A matron, in cap and gown, who comes to teach Youths One, Two, and Three, and Maidens Four and Five, in the Sixth Form School on the Isle of Wight, scheduled as an Historic Monument. She explains that she can only teach them if they ask her intelligent questions; but they find it difficult to do so, as she will not allow them to ask Why—only What, When, Where, How, Who, and Which. They have just decided that the universe is either a joke or a mistake when the Archangel Raphael appears, tells them that evolution can go backwards as well as forwards, and that he has come to learn, not to teach. But before they can ask him any questions, he disappears, and the teacher dismisses them, telling them to read the Book of Job. *Far-Fetched Fables 6*

TEDDY: *see* Bompas, Edward

TEETATOTA: *see* Ftatateeta

TEMPLE YOUTH: *see* Acis

TERESA (TESSIE): *see* Driscoll, Teresa

THEODOTUS: Tutor to the young Ptolemy, a little old man with cramped and wizened limbs but a tall, straight forehead. He is present when Julius Caesar comes to the palace in Alexandria, and gloats over the death of Pompey, much to Caesar's disgust. When the ships in the harbour catch fire during the battle for the lighthouse, he rushes in to say that the library is in flames, and is horrified at Caesar's indifference to the loss of so many priceless manuscripts. Caesar advises him to ask the Egyptian general Achillas for troops to help fight the fire. This he does, leaving the Romans free to capture their objective, as Caesar had foreseen. *Caesar and Cleopatra*

THIRDBORN, MRS.: *see* Buoyant, Clara

THISTLE: One of the two men studying at the Genetic Institute on the Isle of Wight. He wears a tunic embroidered with a thistle, and red sleeves, is clean-shaven and has close-cropped hair. He is studying the nineteenth century, and has a poor opinion of the men of that time, with their incomprehensible calendar, their habit of counting in twelves, their miserable musical scale of only twelve notes instead of the present sixty-four, and their crude methods of surgery and use of drugs. He finally decides to give up historical studies and start again with modern times. *Far-Fetched Fables 5*

THUNDRIDGE, STREGA: A famous pianist, who does *not* like being called 'the female Paderewski'. She has been engaged by the Duchess of Dunmow, at a fee of 250 guineas, to play for two hours to her son, Lord Reginald Fitzambey, who is suffering from a nervous breakdown, in the hope that music, which he enjoys, will cure him. Unfortunately he only likes ragtime, and suffers acutely when Strega plays Chopin, Brahms, Bach and Schumann. But gradually she overcomes his resistance and, vanquished by Chopin's Polonaise in A Flat, he confesses that he loathes his present job in the War Office, and asks nothing better than to be married to a strong, masterful woman for whom he can create a peaceful, happy home. She then confesses in her turn that she longs for a timid, clinging husband whom she can ill-treat and cherish alternately. After a passionate embrace they celebrate their engagement by playing the Wedding March as a duet. *The Music Cure*

TIM: An Irish labourer, who is summoned off-stage by General Sir Pearce Madigan to take his horse to the stables. *O'Flaherty, V.C.*

TINKLER, WILLIAM: *see* Savoyard, Cecil

TINWELL, MINNIE: A pretty, fair-haired woman of twenty-five, chambermaid at the Star and Garter Hotel, Richmond, where Sir Colenso Ridgeon holds a celebration dinner after being knighted. She recognises, in one of his guests, the charming but amoral young artist Louis Dubedat, the husband who left her after a three-weeks' honeymoon, having spent all her savings. Ridgeon promises to put her in touch with him, but is rather taken aback when Dubedat points out that Minnie is not really his wife, in spite of her marriage lines, as she was formerly married to a ship's steward. Not having heard from him for three years, she believed herself free to marry again. Dubedat defends his behaviour towards her by saying that 'she had three weeks of glorious happiness, which is more than most people in her position get'. *The Doctor's Dilemma*

TITUS: *see* Dudgeon, Titus

TOFF (TOFFY): *see* Barking, Viscount

TOM (THOMAS): *see* Broadbent, Tom; Humphries, Tom

TOMMY: *see* Lion

TONY: *see* Anderson, Rev. Anthony

TOPS: *see* Juno, Sibthorpe

TOTA (TOTATEETA): *see* Ftatateeta

TOURIST: He lands on the Isle of Wight, which is now 'a colony for the Upper Ten', without permission, and is stopped by the staff of the Anthropometric Laboratory who, when he claims to be an unrecognised genius, send him to be used for experimental purposes. *Far-Fetched Fables 3*

TOWNSFOLK: The citizens of Alexandria, who crowd to the quayside behind the Roman soldiers to watch Julius Caesar embark for Rome after the pacification of Egypt. *Caesar and Cleopatra*

The people of Websterbridge, New Hampshire, who 'are present in force and in high spirits' to see the hanging of Richard Dudgeon in mistake for the Rev. Anthony Anderson, since the substitution of the Devil's Disciple for the good minister means that they can 'enjoy the execution without misgivings as to its righteousness or to the cowardice of allowing it to take place without a struggle'. They occasionally shout 'Hush!', 'Here they come!' or 'Silence!'; they flinch and fall silent when the clock strikes twelve, raise a cheer when Anderson arrives, jeer at the British soldiers as they march away, and carry Dudgeon off on their shoulders when he has been reprieved, cheering him as a hero. *The Devil's Disciple*

TRAMP: He stows away to the Isle of Wight, which is 'a colony for the Upper Ten' and when interviewed by the staff of the Anthropometric Laboratory explains that he is good for nothing, that he would rather beg than work, and is, in fact, not Prospero but Autolycus. They decide that he will be useful for their experiments, as he knows what other people ought to do, even though he cannot do it himself, and he can therefore be kept busy making laws for the people. *Far-Fetched Fables 3*

TRANFIELD, GRACE: A widow in her early thirties, 'slight of build, delicate of feature, and sensitive in expression . . . Her well-closed mouth, proudly set brows, firm chin, and elegant carriage show plenty of determination and self-respect.' The daughter of Joseph Cuthbertson, with whom she resides in London, she is in love with Leonard Charteris. She refuses to marry him, however, because as a member of the Ibsen Club and a 'New Woman', she despises him for philandering, and also, as she says, 'I will never marry a man I love too much. It would give him a terrible advantage over me: I should be utterly in his power.' *The Philanderer*

TRENCH, DR. HARRY (HENRY): A 24-year-old doctor, younger son of an aristocratic family, 'stoutly built, thick in the neck, close-cropped and black in the hair, with un-dignified medical-student manners, frank, hasty, and rather boyish'. While holidaying in Germany he gets engaged to Blanche Sartorius, but the engagement is broken off when he refuses to accept an allowance from his father-in-law, whose money comes from the rents of slum property in London. Trench is then shocked to discover that his own income derives from a mortgage on the same property; but later, 'coarsened and sullen', he allows himself to be drawn into a scheme devised by Sartorius and Lickcheese to improve part of the property in question in the hope of obtaining compensation when the land is required for public works. He is then rewarded with Blanche's hand in marriage. *Widowers' Houses*

TROTTER, MR.: A well-known dramatic critic (based on A. B. Walkley) who is invited to watch the production of a play by Fanny O'Dowda, given privately at her father's house by a professional cast. Although the author's name is not announced, Trotter realises after talking to Fanny before the performance that she has written it, and he is the only member of the audience to realise also that the descriptions of prison life given by the heroine Margaret Knox are based on experience, Fanny having herself been sent to prison in Cambridge for a month for suffragette activities. He is rather sad to learn from Fanny that the young ladies of Cambridge regard him as a back number, 'innocent as a lamb in a world of wolves', and that his particular style of criticism is known as 'trottering'. *Fanny's First Play*

TUNIC BEARER: *see* Maidens

TURANIA, EMPEROR OF: *see* Napoleon, Cain Adamson Charles

TWEEDED GENTLEMAN: *see* Barnabas, Conrad

TYPIST: *see* Brown, Begonia

U

ULSTERBRIDGE, LORD: Commander-in-Chief of the British Army. He has refused to buy the formula for a new lighter-than-air poison gas for £100,000 from its inventor, a Young Man, on the grounds that money spent on anything but atomic research would be wasted. The Young Man has therefore sold his invention to Ketchewayo II, Emperor of Zululand, who has used it to kill off all the inhabitants of the Isle of Wight, including the inventor, who had retired there thinking it a safe place. While Ulsterbridge and Lord Oldhand, from the Foreign Office, are deciding what to do, the poison gas comes in through the window of Ulsterbridge's London office and kills them both. *Far-Fetched Fables 2*

UNDERSHAFT, ANDREW: A wealthy industrialist (known to his workmen as Dandy Andy). He is the head of a vast armaments factory, which since its foundation has been handed down from one adopted foundling to another in memory of its foundling founder, each being named Andrew Undershaft. The present holder of the name married Lady Britomart, but she left him when their son was born, as he refused to alter what she considered a wicked tradition. Now, needing dowries for her two daughters, she sends for their father. He is very interested in his daughter Barbara, who has joined the Salvation Army, and even more in her fiancé Adolphus, in whom he sees all the qualities needed by the future head of the firm. Fortunately Cusins turns out to be virtually a foundling, and when he has seen and admired Undershaft's model factory, he accepts his offer of adoption, and the succession is safe for another generation. *Major Barbara*

UNDERSHAFT, BARBARA: The daughter of Lady Britomart, robust, jolly, and energetic. Bored with a rich, idle life, paid for by her father Andrew, who is separated from his wife, she has joined the Salvation Army, as has her fiancé Adolphus Cusins. She takes her father to visit the West Ham shelter where she works. It is due to close down for lack of money, but when a rich distiller offers the Army £5,000 for it on condition five other rich men give £1,000 each, Undershaft immediately agrees to do so. Barbara refuses the money, because it is 'tainted', having been earned by the sale of armaments, but she is overruled by the Commissioner, Mrs. Baines, who is of the opinion that it does not matter where the money comes from as long as they can use it to help the hungry and homeless. Barbara therefore resigns, but agrees to visit her father's factory, which turns out to be a model of its kind, a garden city where everyone is prosperous, well-housed, and rather smug. When her father proposes to adopt her fiancé and make him his heir, she says she will keep her promise to marry him, as she can spend her time and energy converting 'quarrelsome, snobbish, uppish creatures' rather than bribing 'weak souls in starved bodies' with scraps of bread and treacle. *Major Barbara*

UNDERSHAFT, LADY BRITOMART: The daughter of the Earl of Stevenson, and wife of the armaments millionaire Andrew Undershaft, who to her annoyance always calls her Biddy. She left him after the birth of their son because he refused to break the tradition by which the firm had always been left to an adopted foundling, but now that her two daughters need dowries, she sends for him to discuss the matter. A handsome, imperious, well-dressed woman, she is 'a typical managing matron of the upper classes ... with plenty of practical ability and worldly experience, limited ... but intelligent and liberal'. She again tries to make Undershaft leave his factory to their son Stephen, but is defeated by Stephen's own wish to go into politics; when she has seen the model village attached to the factory for the first time, she is even more determined that the property —'all that plate and linen, all that furniture and those houses and orchards and gardens'—must remain in the family. She is therefore delighted when Adolphus Cusins, who is engaged to her daughter Barbara, turns out to be a foundling, and eligible for adoption by Undershaft with a view to inheriting everything. *Major Barbara*

UNDERSHAFT, SARAH: The daughter of Lady Britomart, engaged to a rather vacuous but amusing young man, Charles Lomax. As he will not be able to support her in luxury until he is thirty-five her mother demands a dowry for her from her father, Andrew, who has not seen her since she was a baby. He is quite prepared to give her the money, and she to take it, in spite of the fact that it comes from the sale of armaments. As she says, very sensibly: 'I daresay it is very wicked of papa to make cannons; but I don't think I shall cut him on that account.' *Major Barbara*

UNDERSHAFT, STEPHEN: The only son of Lady Britomart and her industrialist husband Andrew. He cannot inherit his father's immense armaments factory, as by tradition it must go to an adopted foundling. But he does not mind, as he despises 'trade' and has decided to go into politics. His father, who has not seen him since he was a baby, has a very poor opinion of him when they meet again, and thinks he is indeed only fit for political life: 'He knows nothing and thinks he knows everything . . . He will find his natural and proper place in the end on the Treasury Bench.' Stephen, who is a gravely correct, extremely priggish young man, is very much in awe of his masterful mother, but is gently patronising towards his father, and to Adolphus Cusins, the fiancé of his sister Barbara, who eventually qualifies to inherit the Undershaft factory. *Major Barbara*

UTTERWOOD, LADY ARIADNE: Addy, younger daughter of Captain Shotover, whose pet name for her was Paddy Patkins. But she broke his heart when at nineteen she announced that she would marry anyone simply to get away from home and went off with a husband he described as a 'numbskull'. She returns after twenty-three years to find that he has forgotten her, and her sister Hesione does not recognise her. She is followed to Surrey by her brother-in-law Randall Utterwood, an effete forty-year-old who is madly in love with her, and enrages him by flirting outrageously with her other brother-in-law, Hector Hushabye, whom she meets for the first time on her arrival. It is her diamonds that the burglar-bosun, Billy Dunn, is after when he is caught by Mazzini Dunn—no relation—and when Mazzini's daughter Ellie says Shotover's house should be called Heartbreak House, because everyone in it seems to have missed happiness, Ariadne says the only thing wrong with it is that it has no stables, and therefore no horses, which are the salvation of the English. *Heartbreak House*

UTTERWOOD, RANDALL: The brother-in-law of Lady Utterwood, with whom he is in love. He follows her to her father's house when she returns there after a long absence, and becomes madly jealous of her other brother-in-law, Hector Hushabye, whom she meets for the first time and finds very attractive. She enjoys playing on Randall's emotions, and he suffers intensely from her teasing, but cannot tear himself away. When the air-raid begins he wants to take shelter in the cellar, but she shames him into staying with her in the garden. *Heartbreak House*

V

VALBRIONI, COUNTESS: *see* Simpkins, Susan

VALENTINE, MR.: An impecunious and unconventional young man 'of thirty or thereabouts', who is trying to make a living as a 'five-shilling' dentist. His first patient is Dolly Clandon, who introduces him to her sister Gloria. Valentine falls in love with Gloria, and, piqued by her apparent indifference, makes a determined effort to break down her resistance, ending up by kissing her passionately. When, however, she shows signs of yielding to him, he admits that he is a philanderer who was only trying to upset her advanced ideas. In spite of his obvious reluctance, however, they become engaged. *You Never Can Tell*

VANHATTAN, MR.: American Ambassador to the Court of King Magnus. He arrives in a state of great excitement to tell the King that the United States has decided to rejoin the British Empire with Magnus as Emperor. He is very disappointed when Magnus says he must consider the question and consult his Cabinet, but retires in good order, assuring the Queen that he will return in due course, as High Commissioner, in Court dress. *The Apple Cart*

VARINKA: The favourite niece of Prince Patiomkin. She is with him when Captain Edstaston comes to ask for an interview with the Empress, and at first tries to make him behave himself. But when he picks Edstaston up to carry him into the Empress's bedroom, she goes with him, and mendaciously tells Catherine that Edstaston is mad with love for her and insisted on being brought into her presence. When Catherine indicates that 'the mad Englishman' meets with her approval, Varinka reminds him that he owes his advancement to her help. She is also present when his fiancée Claire comes to rescue him, and is disgusted at the cold way in which they exchange one kiss, embracing her uncle passionately to show the young couple how Russians understand love. *Great Catherine*

VASHTI: The dark-haired result of a eugenic experiment in which East and West are to be mingled, as opposed to her fair-haired sister Maya. They both make love to the young clergyman, Phosphor Hammingtap, and explain to him that as they are really one, he must marry them both, as well as belonging to all the other women on the island, most of whom are too old for him. With her sister and two brothers, she disappears on the Day of Judgement, being evidently considered 'not worth her salt'. *The Simpleton of the Unexpected Isles*

VAUGHAN, MR.: A dramatic critic (based on E. A. Baughan) invited to watch the performance of a play by Fanny O'Dowda, given at her father's country house by a professional cast. Having seen it without being told the author's name, he insists that it is by Pinero, 'intensely disagreeable . . . an attempt to expose the supposed hypocrisy of the Puritan middle class in England'. When told it is by Fanny, he congratulates her, but begs her in future to give up making silly jokes and to 'sustain the note of passion'. Then she will do great things. *Fanny's First Play*

VENDÔME, DUC DE: A young, bashful, and speechless

nobleman, to whom is allotted the task of presenting Joan of Arc to the Dauphin at Chinon. *Saint Joan*

VILLIERS, BARBARA: *see* Cleveland, Duchess of

VIVIE (VIV, VIVVUMS): *see* Warren, Vivie

VULLIAMY, ANASTASIA: A beautiful and imperious young woman, found as a baby on the doorstep of 'one of the very best houses in Park Lane'. She visits the Lord Chancellor, Sir Cardonius Boshington, in his capacity as guardian of all wards in Chancery to ask him to find her a husband 'with a smooth cheek and a slender figure' whom she can bully. When she meets another foundling, Horace Brabazon, she realises that he is her ideal, and captures him. *The Fascinating Foundling*

W

WAGGONER JO: An elderly carter who finds George Kemp's horse, which Blanco Posnet has been accused of stealing, and brings it back, together with the unknown Woman to whom Blanco lent it in order that she might take her dying child to a doctor, thus saving Blanco from hanging or lynching. *The Shewing-Up of Blanco Posnet*

WAITER: At the Star and Garter Hotel, Richmond. He brings Sir Colenso Ridgeon his bill after the celebration dinner in honour of his knighthood. *The Doctor's Dilemma*

At the hotel in which the princess awaits the arrival of the Inca of Perusalem. He brings her a tray of cold tea and stale tea-cake, and is soundly scolded for his inefficiency by her new lady's maid, Ermyntrude Roosenhonkers-Pipstein. His excuse is that he is not really a waiter, but an eminent medical man ruined by the First World War. *The Inca of Perusalem*

In the garden restaurant of a hotel at Remagen on the Rhine. He speaks English with a heavy German accent, and brings beer for Cokane and Trench, and tea for Sartorius and his daughter Blanche. *Widowers' Houses*

See also Boon, Walter

WALKER, BILL: A rough customer who comes to the West Ham Salvation Army shelter in search of his girl Mog Habbijam, who has been converted by Jenny Hill and is now walking out with her own convert, Todger Fairmile. At first Walker lays about him indiscriminately, knocking down Jenny and hitting Rummy Mitchens across the face. Barbara Undershaft then works on his feelings to such an extent that being, like most British working-class men, extremely sentimental, he is almost converted; but Adolphus Cusins comes in at the critical minute beating the big drum, and Walker escapes, leaving £1 to pay for the damage he has done. This is stolen by Snobby Price. Walker returns after being beaten in a fight with Fairmile in time to taunt Barbara, when she leaves the Army because it has accepted her father's 'tainted' money, with the collapse of her ideals. *Major Barbara*

WALLASTON, JOSEPH: A Beadle in attendance on the Mayoress, Mrs. George Collins. He comes with her to the Bishop's Palace when she is called in to help draft the marriage contract between Edith Bridgenorth and Cecil Sykes, retires with the mace to wait for her in company with her brother-in-law Bill Collins, and when Edith and Cecil slip away to get married in the empty church he gives the bride away. He then returns in time to precede the Mayoress into the main hall of the Palace for the wedding reception. *Getting Married*

WALPOLE, CUTLER: A clever surgeon, who has come to the conclusion that all the illnesses that attack mankind are caused by the malfunctioning of the nuciform sac, which he therefore removes from everybody he can lay hands on. 'Never at a loss, never in doubt; if he made a mistake, he would make it thoroughly and firmly'; smartly dressed, with the air of a well-to-do sportsman, built for strength and compactness rather than height. He attends the dinner given by his friend Sir Colenso Ridgeon at which the young artist Louis Dubedat is present. Dubedat steals his gold cigarette case, and when asked for it back produces a pawn-ticket. Walpole, who would like to operate on Dubedat, is present at his death, for which he, with his colleagues Colenso and Sir Patrick Cullen, blames the treatment of Sir Ralph Bloomfield Bonington. *The Doctor's Dilemma*

WARDEN: *see* Beefeater

WARREN, MRS. KITTY: The daughter of a widow 'who had a fried-fish shop down by the Mint'. After several hard and unremunerative jobs she became a prostitute, and now owns, with her partner and former lover Sir George Crofts, a chain of high-class brothels situated in a number of European cities. She has used some of the money these have brought her to educate her only child, Vivie, keeping her in ignorance of her mother's background. When Vivie leaves Cambridge, Kitty comes to England to see her and arrange her future, being then 'a woman between forty and fifty, formerly pretty, showily dressed . . . spoilt and domineering and decidedly vulgar, but, on the whole, a genial and fairly presentable old blackguard'. She is quite unprepared for Vivie's cool reception of her mother's plans, and her announcement that she intends to work in the City at actuarial calculations and conveyancing. Kitty tries threats, ridicule, persuasion and pathos to no avail, and is finally reduced to telling Vivie the truth. But in the end she is forced to admit defeat and returns to Europe, leaving Vivie in London to earn her own living. *Mrs. Warren's Profession*

WARREN, VIVIE: The 22-year-old illegitimate daughter of Mrs. Kitty Warren, 'an attractive specimen of the sensible, able, highly-educated young middle-class English woman, prompt, strong, confident, self-possessed'. Brought up in ignorance of her mother's background, Vivie has done well at Cambridge, and intends to work in the City, 'reading Law, with an eye on the Stock Exchange'. When she finds that her mother has planned quite a different future for her, she revolts, and resists all pleas, threats, and sentimental appeals. But when she is told the brutal facts of her mother's early years and past life, she almost relents. Unfortunately her mother's former lover and present partner in the management of a chain of European brothels, Sir George Crofts, in revenge for Vivie's refusal to marry him, reveals to her that her mother's business is not wound up, as she had supposed, but is still actively flourishing; and also that she is herself the putative daughter of the pompous and weak-kneed Rev. Samuel Gardner, with whose son Frank—the only person privileged to call her Viv and Vivvums—she has been having a fairly serious flirtation. Revolted by both these discoveries, Vivie runs away to London, refuses to accept an allowance from her mother, and resists all efforts to bring them together again. Finally Mrs. Warren accepts defeat, and Vivie is left to work happily for her living. *Mrs. Warren's Profession*

WARWICK, EARL OF: Richard Beauchamp, leader of the English troops in France beaten by the French under Joan of Arc. He realises that her presence inspires the French to fight as they would never do without her, and he is determined to break her power. When she is captured by the Burgundians, who are on the side of the English, he buys her from them and hands her over to the Church to be tried for heresy. He has no interest in the religious questions involved, and is entirely a political animal, considering the new nationalism a threat not only to the authority of the Church but to the position of the great feudal barons, of which he considers himself the chief. When there seems to be a possibility that Joan will escape condemnation by the Church, he threatens to wreck Rouen, and is delighted when she is finally sentenced to be burnt to death as a heretic. But in the Epilogue he returns to tell Joan, after her rehabilitation, that 'the burning was purely political. There was no personal feeling against you, I assure you.' Political necessities, though occasionally erroneous, are still imperative. *Saint Joan*

WAYNFLETE, LADY CICELY: A celebrated lady traveller, sister-in-law of Sir Howard Hallam, with whom she makes an expedition into the Atlas Mountains, escorted by Captain Brassbound and his men. A 'woman of great vitality and humanity . . . between thirty and forty, tall, good-looking, sympathetic, intelligent, tender and humorous', she captivates every man she meets, and has a touching faith in humanity which has so far been justified. When Marzo, one of the escort, is slightly wounded in a brush with some Arab tribesmen, she nurses him; when she learns that Brassbound is Sir Howard's nephew and intends to hand his uncle over to the Arab sheikh Sidi el Assif in revenge for his having illegally obtained possession of his nephew's property, she persuades him to forgive him; and when Sidi el Assif agrees to release Sir Howard in return for his sister-in-law, she is quite prepared to go with him, convinced he will treat her 'like a perfect gentleman'. At Brassbound's subsequent trial for conspiracy to murder, she adroitly manipulates the evidence so as to bring about his acquittal. She is just about to accept his offer of marriage when the sound of a gun, recalling Brassbound to his ship, brings them both to their senses, and she lets him go, murmuring: 'What an escape!' *Captain Brassbound's Conversion*

WEBBER, LUCIAN: A civil servant, cousin to Lydia Carew. He disapproves of her friendship with the prizefighter Cashel Byron, even before he knows what the man's profession is, and that his mother is an actress. Webber escorts Cetewayo and his Zulu chiefs to the Agricultural Hall, Islington, to see the fight between Cashel and Paradise, and when Cetewayo joins in the ensuing riot, belabours him with his umbrella. When Cashel is arrested after his second, illegal, fight with Paradise, and is revealed as the son of the late Overlord of Dorset, it is Webber who brings him the Queen's pardon, and her commands for his marriage to Lydia. *The Admirable Bashville*

WHIP: A man in a hideous Etruscan mask, carrying a whip, who is sent for by Caesar to urge on the gladiators in the arena when they are frightened of Ferrovius. He becomes Ferrovius's first victim, being cut to pieces by him in a fit of rage. *Androcles and the Lion*

WHITEFIELD, ANN: The daughter of the late Mr. Whitefield, left in his will to the joint guardianship of his old friend Roebuck Ramsden and the young revolutionary John Tanner, whom Ann is determined to marry. A charming young woman, graceful, ladylike, and self-controlled, she 'inspires confidence, as a person who will do nothing she does not mean to do', and also some fear, 'as a woman who will do everything she means to do without taking more account of other people than may be necessary. . . . In short, what the weaker of her own sex sometimes call a cat!' She cleverly manages to get her own way while seeming to submit to the will of others, and never loses sight of her ultimate objective, marriage with Jack, as she calls him. She finally goads him into proposing to her in a garden in Granada—as he says: 'She makes you will your own destruction!'—faints into his arms as the rest of the party arrives, and when she recovers announces their engagement. When Tanner, sleeping in the brigands' camp in the Sierra Nevada, dreams that he is Don Juan in hell, Ann is there, thinly disguised as his former conquest, Doña Ana. *Man and Superman*

WHITEFIELD, MRS.: The mother of Ann Whitefield, 'whose faded flaxen hair looks like straw on an egg'. She has 'an expression of muddled shrewdness, a squeak of protest in her voice, and an odd air of continually elbowing away

some larger person who is crushing her into a corner ...
One of those women who are conscious of being treated as
silly and negligible, and who ... never submit to their
fate.' She is much fonder of Violet Robinson than of her
strong-willed daughter, whom she knows to be a bully, a
coquette, and a liar, and thinks it will do Ann good to
marry Tanner, though she is sorry for him. *Man and
Superman*

WIDOW: *see* Dolores

WIDOWER: *see* Buoyant, Tom

WILKS: Clerk in the Emigration Office in a tropical port.
When his superior officer, Hyering, goes off to escort the
future Mrs. Hyering on a tour of the city, he stays behind,
because, he says, he is indispensable. But the Young
Woman's slogan: 'Let life come to you', has reminded him
that he promised his mother he would get his name in the
papers, and though madly ambitious, he has done nothing
noteworthy. His sense of failure, together with the ravages
of a tropical climate, lead him to commit suicide. *The
Simpleton of the Unexpected Isles*

WILLIAM: *see* Boon, Walter; Collins, Bill; Dudgeon,
William; Haslam, Rev. William; Shakespear, William

WILLIAM THE WAITER: *see* Boon, Walter

WISSANT, JACQUES DE: Brother of Piers de Wissant, and
with him one of the hostages sent to Edward III on the
surrender of Calais, wearing nothing but shirts, with ropes
round their necks. He has nothing to say, and is pardoned
with four of his companions after the Queen, Philippa of
Hainault, has begged her husband to spare their lives. *The
Six of Calais*

WISSANT, PIERS DE: A burgher of Calais, one of the six
hostages sent to Edward III after the surrender of the city,
together with his brother Jacques. With the exception of
Piers de Rosty, they are set free after the Queen, Philippa of

Hainault, has begged her husband to spare their lives. Piers has nothing to say. *The Six of Calais*

WOMAN: A poor, dispirited elderly creature who, with her husband Joe, runs a sweat-shop in the Commercial Road. She is terrified when Epifania Fitzfassen, looking for work, comes and threatens to report them to the Home Office, and bursts into tears when the husband allows Epifania to take over the business, which she says she can manage in half a day a week. *The Millionairess*

An unnamed mother whose child is dying of croup. She is carrying it miles to the nearest doctor when she meets Blanco Posnet on a stolen horse. He lets her have it, but is later arrested for stealing it, and is about to be hanged when Waggoner Jo brings in the woman, whom he has found sitting with the dead child in her arms while the horse grazed nearby. This disposes of the evidence, and Blanco is set free. *The Shewing-Up of Blanco Posnet*

See also Fusima

WOMAN'S VOICE: An unseen operator on the television-telephone exchange which puts the President of the British Islands, Burge-Lubin, in contact with his various ministers. *Back to Methuselah, Part III: The Thing Happens*

WOMAN SERVANT: *see* Guinness, Nurse

WOMEN IN THE BARN: A group of American small-town women who are shucking nuts in the makeshift courthouse when Blanco Posnet is brought in to be tried for horse-stealing. Led by Babsy, a bumptious young slattern, the mean-spirited Emma, and the sharp-tongued Jessie and Sally, they scream insults at him, clamouring for him to be lynched or burnt, knocking him down, and scratching his face. Two of them, Hannah, old and wise, and the gentle Lottie, run away before the shouting starts. The rest are pushed out by the men who are to form the jury, but they return to watch and comment on the trial, being particularly severe on the prostitute Feemy Evans, whose evidence almost serves to hang Blanco, and much moved by the evidence of the Woman to whom Blanco lent the stolen horse. *The Shewing-Up of Blanco Posnet*

WOMEN SERVANTS AND NURSES: Slaves attendant on Cleopatra. They gather in the courtyard when the Nubian sentinel spreads the news of Julius Caesar's approach, and are kept back by the spears of the soldiers, but escape in panic when they hear that Cleopatra and the sacred white cat are missing. They go with Cleopatra and Caesar to Alexandria, and attend on Cleopatra (*see* Charmian and Iras), one slave-girl playing the harp to amuse her. They attend the first part of the banquet which Cleopatra gives to Caesar, but are sent away before the arrival of the sacred sphinx. And finally they assemble on the quayside to watch Caesar embark for Rome. *Caesar and Cleopatra*

WORTHINGTON, LORD: A well-known sporting peer, who is present at the fight 'with bare fists' between Cashel Byron and the Flying Dutchman. He takes Cashel's mother, Adelaide Gisborne, to see Cashel's second fight against William Paradise at Wiltstoken, follows her to the castle of Lydia Carew, where Cashel has taken refuge from the police, driving his four-in-hand into the room, proposes to Adelaide, and then drives her, Cashel, and Lydia, to a double wedding at St. George's, Hanover Square. *The Admirable Bashville*

WOUNDED SOLDIER: *see* Soldiers

Y

YORK, ARCHBISHOP OF: *see* Haslam, Rev. William

YORK, DUKE OF: James, the brother of Charles II. Having

returned unexpectedly from France, he tracks Charles down to Isaac Newton's house, and insists on an interview with him. He is scornful of his brother's efforts to keep England on an even keel, but Charles warns him that if he puts his Catholic ideas into practice when he is king, he will lose his throne to Orange Billy. When Mrs. Basham, Newton's housekeeper, says she is preparing dinner for all the visitors, Jamie reminds her that it is Friday, and that he and Louise de Kérouaille, being Catholics, need only three or four kinds of fish. She tells him bluntly that all they will get is 'a nice piece of cod'. *In Good King Charles's Golden Days*

YOUNG MAN: A chemist, working on the staff of a chlorine gas factory. While sitting in the park one day, he gets into conversation with a Young Woman, who says she refuses to marry and have children who may be killed in battle. An excited Middle-Aged Man brings them a newspaper which says war has been abolished, but they refuse to believe it, and the Young Woman says bitterly that it won't be long before someone invents a new weapon, like a poison gas lighter than air. This strikes the Young Man as an excellent idea, and he sets to work to solve the problem it presents. *Far-Fetched Fables 1*

YOUNG WAITER: *see* Jo

YOUNG WOMAN: Sitting in the park one day, she talks to a Young Man about the horrors of war, and like him refuses to believe that it can be abolished, whatever the United Nations may decide. When he says that neither heavier-than-air poison gas nor atomic bombs will be used in the next war, she prophesies that someone will soon invent a lighter-than-air poison gas, and is horrified when she discovers that the Young Man works in a chlorine gas factory and is, in fact, on the point of inventing just such a gas. *Far-Fetched Fables 1*

See also Hyering, Sally; Zoo

YOUNGER YOUTH: *see* Kanchin

YOUTH: *see* Buoyant, Frederick; Strephon

YOUTHS: Young men of the future—A.D. 31,920. Dressed in vaguely Greek costumes, they dance with the Maidens in front of the temple, assist at the hatching of Amaryllis, the Newly-Born, are horrified by the busts of the Ancients sculpted by Arjillax instead of the nymphs they expected, and even more horrified by the automata created by Pygmalion. They are still young enough to enjoy eating, drinking, dancing, and love-making, and to be completely puzzled by the teaching of the Ancients, being unable to believe that after four years they too will be weary of all sensual pleasures and find happiness only in the realm of pure thought—usually mathematics. *Back to Methuselah, Part V: As Far as Thought Can Reach*

YOUTHS ONE, TWO, AND THREE: Students at the Sixth Form School in the Isle of Wight. Youth One comes to the conclusion that the universe is nothing but a joke. Youth Two thinks that if the world exists it must have a creator. Youth Three is sceptical and disrespectful. He nicknames the Teacher Mother Hubbard, and calls the archangel Raphael the Cockyolly Bird. He is entirely practical, and tells the other students that they want to know too much. *Far-Fetched Fables 6*

Z

Z: *see* Passenger

ZOO: A fifty-year-old long-liver who looks very like Cynthia Barnabas. In A.D. 3000 she is put in charge of Joseph Barlow, an Elderly Gentleman from Baghdad, capital of the British Commonwealth, who has come with the Prime Minister, Ambrose Badger Bluebin, to consult the oracle. She adopts Zozim's nickname of Daddy for him, and finds him so childishly irritating that she tells him he has converted her from Conservatism to Colonisationism, because he has aroused in her an atavistic desire to murder him. The Colonisation party are of the opinion that the long-livers should take over the lands of the short-livers and exterminate them. She then takes him to the temple, where he rejoins the rest of his party, and, dressed in a purple robe, goes with him into the presence of the oracle, giving instructions when necessary. When the audience is over, she tells the Prime Minister that he has received the answer his predecessor received, fifteen years ago, then takes off her robe and goes away. *Back to Methuselah, Part IV: Tragedy of an Elderly Gentleman*

ZOZIM: A 94-year-old inhabitant of Galway in the year A.D. 3000. He is put in charge of a short-lived visitor, Joseph Barlow—the Elderly Gentleman—from Baghdad, but finds him so childish that he is glad to hand him over to Zoo, a mere fifty-year-old, while he goes to prepare for his part in the ceremony of consulting the oracle. He reappears looking rather like a Druid, with a wreath of mistletoe on his flowing white wig, a long robe, and a false beard reaching almost to his waist. As the oracle has been delayed by her encounter with Cain Napoleon, he tries to explain to the visitors the long-livers' policy of Colonisation, which consists in eliminating all the short-lived races, but cannot make them understand what he is talking about, so he ushers them into the temple and goes off with his wig, beard, and robe under his arm. *Back to Methuselah, Part IV: Tragedy of an Elderly Gentleman*

ZULU CHIEFS: In attendance on Cetewayo, with whom they go to watch a prizefight. When he joins in, they follow him shouting 'Victory and Isandhlana', but are routed by Cashel Byron. *The Admirable Bashville*

The Characters — Play by Play

('First performance' refers to the first performance of the play in the English language and by a professional company. Translations, copyright readings and amateur productions are not included.)

The Admirable Bashville, or Constancy Unrewarded

(Being the novel of *Cashel Byron's Profession* done into a stage play in blank verse)

(No. 1 of *Trifles and Tomfooleries*)

Bashville	Newsboy
Byron, Cashel	Paradise, William
Carew, Lydia	Smith, P. C.
Cetewayo	Spectators and Persons of Fashion
Constables and Others	Webber, Lucian
Gisborne, Adelaide	Worthington, Lord
Master of the Revels	Zulu Chiefs
Mellish, Bob	

First performance, Imperial Theatre, London, 7 June 1903 (Stage Society)

Androcles and the Lion, a fable play

Androcles	Editor
Beggar	Ferrovius
Caesar	Gladiators
Call Boy	Lavinia
Captain	Lentulus
Centurion	Lion
Christian Prisoners	Megaera
Courtiers	Menagerie Keeper

Metellus	Servants
Ox Driver	Slaves
Retiarius	Soldiers
Roman Soldiers	Spintho
Secutor	Whip

First performance, St. James's Theatre, London, 1 September 1913 (Lillah McCarthy and H. Granville-Barker season)

Annajanska, the Bolshevik Empress, a revolutionary romancelet

| Annajanska | Strammfest, General |
| Schneidekind, Lieutenant | Soldiers |

First performance, Coliseum, London, 21 January 1918

The Apple Cart, a political extravaganza in two acts and an interlude

Alice	Orinthia
Balbus, Bert	Pamphilius
Boanerges, Bill	Pliny
Crassus	Postlethwaite, Amanda
Jemima	Proteus, Joseph
Lysistrata	Sempronius
Magnus	Vanhattan, Mr.
Nicobar	

First performance, Festival Theatre, Malvern, 19 August 1929 (Barry Jackson)

Arms and the Man, a romantic comedy in three acts

(No. 1 of *Plays Pleasant*)

Bluntschli, Captain	Petkoff, Major
Louka	Petkoff, Raina
Nicola	Plechanoff, Major
Petkoff, Catherine	Saranoff, Major

First performance, Avenue Theatre, London, 21 April 1894 (Florence Farr season)

232

Augustus Does His Bit, a true-to-life farce

Beamish, Horatio   Lady
Highcastle, Lord

First performance, Royal Court Theatre, London, 21 January 1917 (Stage Society)

Back to Methuselah, a metabiological pentateuch

Part I: *In the Beginning*

Adam   Eve
Cain   Serpent

Part II: *The Gospel of the Brothers Barnabas*

Barnabas, Conrad   Haslam, Rev. William
Barnabas, Cynthia   Lubin, Henry
Barnabas, Franklyn   Lutestring, Mrs.
Burge, Joyce

Part III: *The Thing Happens*

Barnabas   Haslam, Rev. William
Burge-Lubin   Lutestring, Mrs.
Chinese Voice   Negress
Confucius   Woman's Voice

Part IV: *Tragedy of an Elderly Gentleman*

Barlow, Joseph   Napoleon, Cain
Bluebin, Ambrose Badger   Oracle
Bluebin, Ethel Badger   Zoo
Bluebin, Molly Badger   Zozim
Fusima

Part V: *As Far as Thought Can Reach*

Acis   Arjillax
Adam, Ghost of   Cain, Ghost of
Amaryllis   Chloe

Cleopatra-Semiramis
Ecrasia
Eve, Ghost of
He-Ancient
Lilith, Ghost of
Maidens
Martellus

Ozymandias
Pygmalion
Serpent, Ghost of
She-Ancient
Strephon
Youths

First performances, Garrick Theatre, New York, 27 February to 13
March 1922 (Theatre Guild)

Buoyant Billions, a comedy of no manners

Buoyant, Bastable
Buoyant, Clara
Buoyant, Clementina
Buoyant, Eudoxia
Buoyant, Frederick
Buoyant, Julia
Buoyant, Richard

Buoyant, Tom
Chinese Priest
Flopper, Sir Ferdinand
Native
Smith, Junius
Smith, Mr.

First performance, Festival Theatre, Malvern, 13 August 1939 (Roy
Limbert)

Caesar and Cleopatra, a history in four acts

(No. 2 of *Three Plays for Puritans*)

Achillas
Apollodorus
Bel Affris
Belzanor
Boatman
Britannus
Bucinator
Caesar, Julius
Centurion
Charmian
Cleopatra
Courtiers
Ensign
Ftatateeta
Guardsmen

Iras
Lucius Septimius
Major Domo
Market Porters
Musician
Nubian Sentinel
Nubian Slave
Officials
Persian
Pothinus
Priest
Ptolemy
Ra
Rufio
Slaves

234

Soldiers   Townsfolk
Theodotus   Women Servants and Nurses

(In a scene given at the copyright performance on 15 March 1899, but
never printed and never again acted, there were four extra characters—
a Cretan, a Nabataean, a Rhodian, and a Syrian. These have been
omitted.)

First performance, New Amsterdam Theatre, New York, 30 October
1906 (Forbes-Robertson)

Candida, a mystery

(No. 2 of *Plays Pleasant*)

Burgess, Mr.   Mill, Rev. Alexander
Garnet, Prosperpine   Morell, Candida
Marchbanks, Eugene   Morell, Rev. James

First performance, Her Majesty's Theatre, Aberdeen, 30 July 1897
(Independent Theatre Company)

Captain Brassbound's Conversion, an adventure in three acts

(No. 3 of *Three Plays for Puritans*)

American Bluejackets   Krooboys
American Naval Officers   Marzo
Beni Siras   Muley
Brassbound, Captain   Muley Othman
Drinkwater, Felix   Osman
Hallam, Sir Howard   Rankin, Leslie
Hassan   Redbrook, Kiddy
Johnson   Sidi el Assif
Kearney, Captain, U.S.N.   Waynflete, Lady Cicely

First performance, Strand Theatre, London, 16 December 1900 (Stage
Society)

The Dark Lady of the Sonnets, an interlude

Beefeater   Fitton, Mary
Elizabeth I   Shakespear, William

First performance, Haymarket Theatre, London, 24 November 1910
(Charity Matinée for the Shakespeare National Memorial Theatre)

The Devil's Disciple, a melodrama in three acts

(No. 1 of *Three Plays for Puritans*)

Anderson, Rev. Anthony
Anderson, Judith
Beadle
Brudenell, Rev. Mr.
Burgoyne, General
Dudgeon, Christopher
Dudgeon, Richard
Dudgeon, Mrs. Timothy
Dudgeon, Titus
Dudgeon, Mrs. Titus

Dudgeon, William
Dudgeon, Mrs. William
Essie
Executioner
Hawkins, Lawyer
Officers
Sergeant
Soldiers
Swindon, Major
Townsfolk

First performance, Hermanus Bleecker Hall, Albany, New York, 1 October 1897 (Richard Mansfield)

The Doctor's Dilemma, a tragedy in five acts

Blenkinsop, Dr.
Bonington, Sir Ralph
Cullen, Sir Patrick
Danby, Mr.
Dubedat, Jennifer
Dubedat, Louis
Emmy

Newspaper Man
Redpenny
Ridgeon, Sir Colenso
Schutzmacher, Dr.
Tinwell, Minnie
Waiter
Walpole, Cutler

First performance, Royal Court Theatre, London, 20 November 1906 (Vedrenne-Barker season)

Don Juan in Hell

(Act Three of *Man and Superman*, q.v.)

Ana, Doña
Anarchist
Brigands
Devil
Goatherd

Gonzales, Don
Juan, Don
Social-Democrats
Soldiers
Straker, Henry

First performance, Royal Court Theatre, London, 4 June 1907 (Vedrenne-Barker season)

236

Fanny's First Play, an easy play for a Little Theatre

The Induction	*The Play*
Bannal, Flawner	Delaney, Dora
Footman	Duvallet, Lieutenant
Gunn, Gilbert	Gilbey, Bobby
O'Dowda, Count	Gilbey, Maria
O'Dowda, Fanny	Gilbey, Robin
Savoyard, Cecil	Juggins
Trotter, Mr.	Knox, Amelia
Vaughan, Mr.	Knox, Joseph
	Knox, Margaret

First performance, Little Theatre, London, 19 April 1911 (Lillah McCarthy)

Far-Fetched Fables 1–6

First Fable

Middle-Aged Man	Young Man
Park Attendant	Young Woman

Second Fable

Oldhand, Lord	Ulsterbridge, Lord
Secretary	

Third Fable

Gentleman	Tourist
Girl	Tramp
Matron	

Fourth Fable

Commissioner

Fifth Fable

Herm	Shamrock
Rose	Thistle

Sixth Fable

Maidens Four and Five
Raphael

Teacher
Youths One, Two, and Three

First performance, Watergate Theatre, London, 6 September 1950
(Shaw Society)

The Fascinating Foundling, a disgrace to the author

(No. 5 *Trifles and Tomfooleries*)

Boshington, Sir Cardonius
Brabazon, Horace

Mercer
Vulliamy, Anastasia

First performance, Arts Theatre Club, London, 28 January 1928
(Written in 1909)

Geneva, a fancied page of history

American Journalist
Battler, Ernest
Betrothed
Bishop
Bombadone
Brown, Begonia
Deaconess
Dolores

Fortinbras
Jew
Judge
Midlander, Sir Orpheus
Newcomer
Posky, Commissar
Secretary

First performance, Festival Theatre, Malvern, 1 August 1938 (Roy
Limbert)

Getting Married, a conversation (a disquisitory play)

Bridgenorth, Alfred
Bridgenorth, Alice
Bridgenorth, General
Bridgenorth, Edith
Bridgenorth, Leo
Bridgenorth, Reginald
Collins, Bill

Collins, Mrs.
Grantham, Lesbia
Hotchkiss, St. John
Soames, Rev. Oliver Cromwell
Sykes, Cecil
Wallaston, Joseph

First performance, Haymarket Theatre, London, 12 May 1908
(Vedrenne-Barker season)

The Glimpse of Reality, *a tragedietta*

(No. 3 of *Trifles and Tomfooleries*)

Ferruccio, Count
Giulia

Sandro
Squarcio

First performance, Arts Theatre Club, London, 20 November 1927
(Written 1909)

Great Catherine (*Whom Glory Still Adores*), *a thumbnail sketch of Russian Court life in the eighteenth century*

Catherine II
Claire
Cossack Sergeant
Courtiers
Dashkoff, Princess

Edstaston, Captain
Naryshkin
Patiomkin, Prince
Soldiers
Varinka

First performance, Vaudeville Theatre, London, 18 November 1913

Heartbreak House, *a fantasia in the Russian manner on English themes*

Dunn, Billy
Dunn, Ellie
Dunn, Mazzini
Guinness, Nurse
Hushabye, Hector

Hushabye, Hesione
Mangan, Alfred
Shotover, Captain
Utterwood, Lady
Utterwood, Randall

First performance, Garrick Theatre, New York, 10 November 1920
(Theatre Guild)

How He Lied To Her Husband

Apjohn, Henry
Bompas, Aurora

Bompas, Edward

First performance, Berkeley Lyceum, New York, 26 September 1904

In Good King Charles's Golden Days, a true history that never happened

Basham, Mrs.
Catherine of Braganza
Charles II
Cleveland, Duchess of
Fox, George
Gwynn, Nell

Kneller, Geoffrey
Newton, Isaac
Portsmouth, Duchess of
Sally
York, Duke of

First performance, Festival Theatre, Malvern, 12 August 1939 (Roy Limbert)

The Inca of Perusalem, an almost historical comedietta

Donkin, Archdeacon
Hotel Manager
Inca of Perusalem
Princess

Roosenhonkers-Pipstein,
    Ermyntrude
Waiter

First performance, Repertory Theatre, Birmingham, 7 October 1916

Jitta's Atonement, a free adaptation of Siegfried Trebitsch's Frau Gittas Sühne

Billiter, Mrs.
Fessler, Dr.
Flower Girl
Haldenstedt, Agnes

Haldenstedt, Professor
Haldenstedt, Edith
Lenkheim, Professor
Lenkheim, Jitta

First performance, Shubert-Garrick Theatre, Washington, D.C., 8 January 1923

John Bull's Other Island

Broadbent, Tom
Dempsey, Father
Doran, Barney
Doran's Friends
Doyle, Cornelius
Doyle, Judy
Doyle, Larry

Farrell, Patsy
Haffigan, Matt
Haffigan, Tim
Hodson
Keegan, Peter
Reilly, Nora

First performance, Royal Court Theatre, London, 1 November 1904 (Vedrenne-Barker season)

Major Barbara, a discussion in three acts

Baines, Mrs.
Bilton
Cusins, Adolphus
Hill, Jenny
Lomax, Charles
Mitchens, Rummy
Morrison
Price, Snobby

Shirley, Peter
Undershaft, Andrew
Undershaft, Barbara
Undershaft, Lady
Undershaft, Sarah
Undershaft, Stephen
Walker, Bill

First performance, Royal Court Theatre, London, 28 November 1905
(Vedrenne-Barker season)

Man and Superman, a comedy (and a philosophy)

(For the Third Act played separately, see *Don Juan in Hell*)

Anarchist
Brigands
Goatherd
Malone, Hector, sen.
Malone, Hector, jun.
Mendoza (and Devil)
Parlourmaid
Ramsden, R. (and Gonzales)
Ramsden, Susan

Robinson, Octavius
Robinson, Violet
Social-Democrats
Soldiers
Straker, Henry
Tanner, John (and Juan)
Whitefield, Ann (and Ana)
Whitefield, Mrs.

First performance (without the Third Act), Royal Court Theatre,
London, 21 May 1905 (Stage Society)

First performance in its entirety, Lyceum Theatre, Edinburgh, 11 June
1915 (Travelling Repertory Company)

The Man of Destiny, a trifle

(No. 3 of *Plays Pleasant*)

Bonaparte, General
Grandi, Giuseppe

Lieutenant
Strange Lady

First performance, Grand Theatre, Croydon, 1 July 1897

The Millionairess, a Jonsonian comedy in four acts

Blenderband, Adrian
Doctor
Fitzfassen, Alastair
Fitzfassen, Epifania
Hotel Manager

Joe
Sagamore, Julius
Smith, Patricia
Woman

First performance, King's Theatre, Melbourne, 7 March 1936
(McMahon Players)

Misalliance, a debate in one sitting

Baker, Julius
Percival, Joseph
Summerhays, Bentley
Summerhays, Lord
Szczepanowska, Lina

Tarleton, Hypatia
Tarleton, John
Tarleton, Johnny
Tarleton, Mrs.

First performance, Duke of York's Theatre, London, 23 February 1910
(Charles Frohman's repertory season)

Mrs. Warren's Profession, a play in four acts

(No. 3 of *Plays Unpleasant*)

Crofts, Sir George
Gardner, Frank
Gardner, Rev. Samuel

Praed, Mr.
Warren, Mrs.
Warren, Vivie

First performance, New Lyric Club, 5 January 1902 (Stage Society)

The Music Cure, a piece of utter nonsense

(No. 6 of *Trifles and Tomfooleries*)

Dawkins, Dr.
Fitzambey, Lord

Thundridge, Strega

First performance, Little Theatre, London, 28 January 1914

O'Flaherty, V.C., a reminiscence of 1915

(*A recruiting pamphlet*)

Driscoll, Teresa
Madigan, General
O'Flaherty, Mrs.

O'Flaherty, Private
Tim

First performance, 39th Street Theatre, New York, 21 June 1920

On the Rocks, a political comedy

Barking, Viscount
Basham, Sir Broadfoot
Blee, Alderman
Brollikins, Alderwoman
Chavender, Sir Arthur
Chavender, David
Chavender, Flavia
Chavender, Lady
Domesday, Duke of

Glenmorison, Sandy
Hanways, Hilda
Hipney, Mr.
Hotspot, Admiral
Humphries, Tom
Lady
Pandranath, Sir Jafna
Rightside, Sir Dexter

First performance, Winter Garden Theatre, London, 25 November 1933
(Charles Macdona)

Overruled, a demonstration

Juno, Mrs.
Juno, Sibthorpe

Lunn, Gregory
Lunn, Mrs.

First performance, Duke of York's Theatre, London, 14 October 1912
(Charles Frohman)

Passion, Poison, and Petrifaction, or the Fatal Gazogene
A brief tragedy for barns and booths

(No. 4 of *Trifles and Tomfooleries*)

Angels
Bastable, Adolphus
Doctor
Fitztollemache, George

Fitztollemache, Lady
Landlord
Phyllis
Policeman

First performance, Theatrical Garden Party, Regent's Park, London,
14 July 1905

The Philanderer, a topical comedy in four acts of the early eighteen-nineties

(No. 2 of *Plays Unpleasant*)

Charteris, Leonard	Cuthbertson, Joseph
Craven, Colonel	Page
Craven, Julia	Paramore, Dr.
Craven, Sylvia	Tranfield, Grace

First performance, Royal Court Theatre, London, 5 February 1907 (Vedrenne-Barker season)

Press Cuttings, a topical sketch compiled from the editorial and correspondence columns of the daily papers during the women's war in 1909

(No. 2 *Trifles and Tomfooleries*)

Balsquith	Farrell, Mrs.
Banger, Mrs.	Mitchener, General
Fanshawe, Lady	Orderly

First performance, Gaiety Theatre, Manchester, 27 September 1909 (Miss Horniman's company)

Pygmalion, a romance in five acts

Bystanders	Higgins, Henry
Doolittle, Alfred	Higgins, Mrs.
Doolittle, Eliza	Parlourmaid
Eynsford-Hill, Clara	Pearce, Mrs.
Eynsford-Hill, Freddy	Pickering, Colonel
Eynsford-Hill, Mrs.	Spectators

First performance, His Majesty's Theatre, London, 11 April 1914 (Beerbohm Tree)

Saint Joan, a chronicle play in six scenes and an epilogue

Assessors
Baudricourt, Robert de
Cauchon, Peter
Charles VII
Courcelles, de
Courtiers
Dunois, Jack
English Soldier
Estivet, Brother John d'
Executioner and Assistants
Gentleman
Joan
La Hire, Captain
La Tremouille, Duc de
La Tremouille, Duchesse de
Ladvenu, Brother Martin
Lemaître, Brother John
Page to Charles VII
Page to Dunois
Page to Warwick
Poulengey, Bertrand de
Rais, Gilles de
Rheims, Archbishop of
Scribes
Soldiers
Steward
Stogumber, John de
Vendôme, Duc de
Warwick, Earl of

First performance, Garrick Theatre, New York, 28 December 1923 (Theatre Guild)

Shakes versus Shav, a puppet play

Dunn, Ellie
Macbeth
Rob Roy
Shakes
Shav
Shotover, Captain

First performance, Lyttleton Hall, Malvern, 9 August 1949 (Waldo Lanchester Marionette Theatre)

The Shewing-Up of Blanco Posnet, a sermon in crude melodrama

Daniels, Elder
Evans, Feemy
Jurymen (including Foreman, Nestor and Squinty)
Kemp, George
Kemp, Strapper
Posnet, Blanco
Waggoner Jo
Woman
Women in the Barn (including Babsy, Emma, Hannah, Jessie, Lottie, and Sally)

First performance, Abbey Theatre, Dublin, 25 August 1909 (Lady Gregory and W. B. Yeats)

The Simpleton of the Unexpected Isles, a vision of judgement

Angel
Farwaters, Sir Charles
Farwaters, Lady
Hammingtap, Phosphor
Hyering, Hugo
Hyering, Sally
Janga
Joe

Kanchin
Maya
Pra
Prola
Station Master
Vashti
Wilks

First performance, Guild Theatre, New York, 18 February 1935 (Theatre Guild)

The Six of Calais, a mediaeval war story in one act

Aire, Jean d'
Arundel, Lord
Black Prince
Court Lady
Derby, Lord
Edward III
Gaunt, John of
Groom
Manny, Sir Walter

Noblemen
Northampton, Lord
Philippa of Hainault
Rosty, Piers de
St. Pierre, Eustache de
Soldiers
Wissant, Jacques de
Wissant, Piers de

First performance, Open Air Theatre, Regent's Park, London, 17 July 1934

Too True to be Good, a political extravaganza

Bagot, The Hon. Aubrey
Bagot, Mr.
Doctor
Fielding, Sergeant
Meek, Private

Monster
Mopply, Miss
Mopply, Mrs.
Simpkins, Susan
Tallboys, Colonel

First performance, National Theatre, Boston, 29 February 1932 (Theatre Guild)

Village Wooing, a comediettina for two voices in three conversations

Author: A   Passenger: Z
Deck Steward

First performance, Little Theatre, Dallas, 16 April 1934

Widowers' Houses, an original didactic realistic play

(No. 1 of *Plays Unpleasant*)

Annie   Sartorius, Blanche
Cokane, William   Sartorius, Mr.
Lickcheese   Trench, Dr.
Porter   Waiter

First performance, Royalty Theatre, London, 9 December 1892 (Independent Theatre Society)

You Never Can Tell, a pleasant play in four acts

(No. 4 of *Plays Pleasant*)

Bohun, Walter, Q.C.   Cook
Boon, Walter   Crampton, Fergus
Clandon, Dolly   Jo
Clandon, Gloria   M'Comas, Finch
Clandon, Mrs.   Parlourmaid
Clandon, Philip   Valentine, Mr.

First performance, Royalty Theatre, London, 26 November 1899 (Stage Society)